THE PAC HANDBOOK

Political Action For Business

THE PAC HANDBOOK

FRASER/ASSOCIATES

BALLINGER PUBLISHING COMPANY
Cambridge, Massachusetts
A Subsidiary of Harper & Row, Publishers, Inc.

CONTENTS

Foreword

Political action committees provide corporate America with a new weapon for affecting the political process. We are hearing more about business PACs now than ever before because they have consistently proved effective over the past ten years.

Corporate America has only recently plugged aggressively into the political action system — long the purview of labor and others. These corporate PACs have been proliferating in the past decade at a rate that virtually guarantees results. The growth also indicates the positive feedback business has received from its political action efforts.

In 1974 there were only 89 corporate PACs. That number grew to 433 in 1976, 784 in 1978, and over 1,200 in 1980. Today it's 1,600. Furthermore, there were nearly 575 trade and professional association PACs reported in 1980, almost 300 labor PACs, and over 375 independent PACs. In the last election cycle, over $73.3 million were contributed to national political candidates by political action committees — a hefty sum, even in an age of spiraling campaign costs and special interest politics. That figure is sure to expand during the 1982 election cycle and into the 1984 Presidential election.

In an era of special interest politics, corporate political action committees have been wisely termed "the sleeping giants of partisan muscle." They have grown quietly in size and scope as corporations recognize the multiple benefits of both political contributions and education of their employees. Finally, business is learning to pick up the political action/education ball and run with it, and 1982 will surely witness further increases in business' role in Washington.

What's the meaning of all this corporate political activity, short of electing favorable politicians to office? PACs serve as a convenient and powerful vehicle for political expression, which reaches more than just politicians running for office. *Corporate PACs are the political voice of business in America.* They listen, they speak, and they "vote" their convictions. Their impact will continue to grow as more and more individuals come to understand the benefits of being part of the political process.

Without both employee and management participation and contributions, however, PACs are out of business. The PAC movement has perhaps done more to increase citizen participation in the political process than any other recent development. As Edmund Burke said two centuries ago: "The only thing necessary for the triumph of evil is for good men to do nothing." The PAC movement has seized on this theme and generated positive involvement and action.

What follows is a useful guidebook for businesses organizing for political action. The rules are complex. Budgeting! Organizing and Administration! PAC Communications! Trends! Models! *The PAC Handbook* provides the useful "How to's" for business political action. The burgeoning of business PACs demonstrates that corporate America is willing to accept its new role in the political environment, and *The PAC Handbook* makes that role understandable to all.

Edie Fraser
September 1981

INTRODUCTION

Introduction

Kevin Phillips
President, American Political Research Corporation

Political action committees, the crossbows, Gattling guns and smart missiles of our time, are rewriting the rules of political warfare. More and more corporations and trade associations are finding themselves drawn to the new weaponry.

This makes an accurate guide book to what PACs are allowed to do all the more important. The rules are getting more complicated all the time as PAC foes and PAC regulators alike move to impose every constriction they can via the Federal Election Commission, the Securities and Exchange Commission, the courts, shareholders and so forth.

Even though the ink is barely dry on the 1980 election returns, Washington observers are already picking up rumors of possible PAC restriction moves by the 97th Congress. It is unlikely, but not impossible, that anything serious will pass. If I had to bet on whether 1980 or 1982 would be remembered as the highwater mark of federal PAC influence, I would bet on 1982 -- but not with too large a stack of chips. After all, the political imbalance of Congress has been righted -- a pun, but also the truth -- and Capitol Hill ideology is not likely to shift too much farther. In the states, by contrast, where a growing percentage of business political battles will be fought during the 1980s, PACs should retain their running room. Piecemeal restraint will be slower restraint.

On the federal level, PACs will probably have one more election in the sun, thereby insuring the reasonably pro-business coloration of Congress during the early pivotal 1980s. Still, it is already possible to plot some of the restraints beginning to form a conceptual circle around the mid-to-late 1980s PAC operations.

In addition to the obvious possibility that a ceiling will be imposed on the amount of PAC money individual candidates can receive, it is likely that public funding pressure will grow, attempts will be made to shift the contributor dollar base back to individuals (perhaps even quintupling the present $1,000 per candidate individual contribution limit), and some reformers will continue to urge that candidates be funded through contributions to parties -- a process which would necessarily undercut PAC influence.

The Ralph Nader breed of activists, in turn, is already trying to get the FEC to force corporations to disclose every nuance of their PAC activities to shareholders. And in North Dakota, a referendum on the ballot in November 1980 to clearly authorize PACs in the state lost by roughly 55-45 percent, a circumstance that suggests PAC foes could begin to use the initiative device elsewhere.

There is also a larger threat: A growing body of U.S. opinion believes that our election process needs a massive wide-ranging overhaul. If that happens during the 1980s, PACs may well be restrained in the process.

And lastly, if business/government relations trends go the way many experts predict, then we are moving towards a national industrial policy and a business/labor/government partnership. Under those circumstances, it is hard to see how Washington could allow business to dominate the political processes through the rapid, continuing growth of corporate and trade association PACs.

Whatever the mid-range future, though, PACs have revolutionized U.S. politics in the last three to four years, and the short-term prospect is for more of the same. **PAC**

Kevin P. Phillips is a well-known and highly respected syndicted newspaper columnist with the King Features Syndicate (Hearst Corporation), where he has been since 1970. He also serves as a commentator on "CBS Spectrum" and is president of the American Political Research Corporation. Phillips is editor and publisher of two key publications, *The American Political Report* and *Business and Public Affairs Fortnightly*.

Phillips served as special assistant to the Attorney General in 1969-70. He was assistant to the campaign manager and chief political/voting analyst of the Nixon for President Committee in 1968. He has also served as an administrative assistant to a congressman.

Phillips is a well-known author. His books include, *The Emerging Republican Majority, Electoral Reform and Voter Participation* and *Mediacracy: American Parties and Politics in the Communications Age*.

I. CONGRESSIONAL

PERSPECTIVE

View From the House

Rep. Guy Vander Jagt (R-MI)
U.S. House of Representatives

Americans spent a total of 28 cents per person in 1976 on the campaigns of all candidates -- Republican, Democrat, Vegetarian, Independent -- who ran for the House of Representatives. That came to $60.9 million on all races -- primary and general election.

In the 1980 elections, we can expect that the final cost figures, when they are all totalled up, will be tens of millions of dollars higher. The money was raised in private contributions from millions of men and women who care about their government; who care about its quality, its well-being, its security; and who care about the policies their government promotes, the programs and services it provides and the parties that make their country's political system work.

Twenty-eight cents a person is a pretty small investment when seen in that light. It is even smaller when compared to the "investment" Americans make in other parts of their lives.

That same year, for instance, Americans spent almost 10 times as much, $575 million, or $2.67 for every man, woman and child in the country, on shampoo. One brand of anti-dandruff detergent, in fact, earned $84.4 million. That is more than one-third again as much as we spent to choose lawmakers who decide on questions of war and peace.

9

America sparkled, sizzled, flared and boomed with $240 million worth of fireworks last year. Their "oooohhhhs" and "aaaahhhhs" cost four times as much as they spent electing the House of Representatives.

We spent almost $4 billion ($17.95 for every American, regardless of age) on flower seeds for backyard gardens and potted plants for our homes and apartments. And Americans managed to pour another $295 million, five times the cost of electing the House, into just that share of women's hair coloring purchased for home use. That doesn't count all the hair dying done in beauty shops, where "only your hairdresser knows for sure."

With all due respect to the beauty of m'lady's hair, flower boxes filled with geraniums, and the pyrotechnics with which we mark Independence Day, the claims of those who contend Americans spend too much on politics just won't stand up under that kind of examination.

The average spending of a House candidate rose from about $70,000 in 1976 to about $90,000 in 1978. In the 1980 congressional elections, the average spending is expected to come close to $150,000 per candidate. And the average expenditures of a winning candidate are expected to be about $300,000.

There has been a startling increase, an increase brought about by the fact of inflation, the fact of stiffer competition between the two parties and soaring media costs. Half of that can be attributed to general inflation. But the inflationary spiral in politics during those years was even more severe because costs of the "Four Ps" of politics (people, paper, publicity and postage) skyrocketed far beyond general inflationary levels during that time.

Since 1976, there has been a substantial growth in political action committees, or PACs, which are organized to allow people with common interests to pool their funds and support a number of political candidates. PACs allow businessmen and women, physicians, educators, farmers, labor union members -- anyone with common interests and goals -- to pool their funds and support a number of political candidates. For instance, more than 70,000 physicians contribute an average of $11.50 each to their political action committee.

These are not "big money" contributions. But they are proving effective – and important – in meeting the rapidly rising costs of campaigns.

What does it cost in these days of the inflated dollar for a candidate to tell a voter where he stands? Consider the telephone: To install one phone in a campaign headquarters requires a deposit of two months telephone charges, in advance. Multiply that by the number of telephones required and you have some idea why campaign organizations must pay deposits of thousands of dollars to the telephone company.

The cost of your daily newspaper doubled in the past few years because the cost of paper has mushroomed. Just a few years ago it cost just six cents, then only eight cents, to mail a letter. Media costs in some markets have increased by up to 600 percent in recent years, and personnel costs have more than doubled.

Say a candidate wants to send a first-class mailing to every voter in his district. Count on at least $30,000 or $45,000 out of pocket, immediately. Neither the Postal Service nor the voters like "postage due" mail.

Or, say a campaign is given $100 by a voter backing the candidate. What can that contribution be in a district of a half-million people?

- About 500 bumper stickers.
- Or perhaps 10 cartops.
- Or 666 first-class stamps.
- Or letters to about 200 constituents.

Want to run a half-page newspaper advertisement? Count on up to $3,500 or so (not counting the art work involved) per paper. And don't forget to multiply by the number of newspapers covering the district. You don't want to miss any of the voters.

Incumbents, meanwhile, have almost all the advantages. The Americans for Democratic Action conducted a detailed study and came to the conclusion that the headstart handed congressmen running for re-election totals more than $550,000 a year in free mail, staff help and services – all courtesy of the taxpayer.

11

Against those kinds of odds, we need all the involvement of the general public that we can get. The American people *act* when they get mad, and the results of the 1980 elections prove that they were mad. PACs make it possible for people at all levels to organize for political involvement. We need PACs. We need you to become involved. **PAC**

Guy Vander Jagt, keynote speaker at the 1980 Republican National Convention, was first elected to the U.S. House of Representatives from Michigan's Ninth District in 1966, and won his eighth consecutive term in the 1978 election, recording 70 percent of the vote. In 1980, he was assured a ninth term in the House when he became the first Republican in 50 years to run for Congress in Michigan without major party opposition.

By unanimous vote, Congressman Vander Jagt was elected in 1978 to his third consecutive term as chairman of the National Republican Congressional Committee (NRCC). In addition to his important role in the House Republican leadership, Rep. Vander Jagt is a senior member of the powerful House Committee on Ways and Means. He is a nationally recognized speaker.

In his role as chairman of the NRCC, Rep. Vander Jagt has travelled more than 500,000 miles on behalf of the party, making more than 1,000 appearances in all 50 states. His effort is continuous, working during "off-years" doing ground-breaking work early in the election cycle which be believes pays dividends on election day.

View From the Senate

Sen. Wendell H. Ford (D-KY)
U.S. Senate

Political action committees have become a powerful force in the American political picture. The number of these committees has grown to more than 1,000 -- and more are coming on board all the time. They spent $4.3 million in the 1976 elections, $8.8 million in 1978 and contributed between $12 and $15 million in the 1980 elections.

No one could ever have predicted that these committees would grow so fast and become such an influence in the political process when the Federal Election Commission law was written. With this growth has come considerable criticism that the sudden surge – and impact – of PACs is unhealthy; that it upsets the balance of power and gives those groups an unfair advantage.

I cannot accept that argument.

I am a strong believer in the political action process. I think that PACs can and do have a positive and beneficial impact – as long as they do not cross the fine line that distinguishes special interest from selfish interest.

What do political action committees have to offer?

First of all, and most important, PACs can educate the public and get people involved. That is the real key to developing a more competent and

13

responsive government, because no matter what you say or think, our government is only as good as the people care to make it.

We have a serious problem in this country characterized by a growing indifference on the part of the American people to becoming involved with government. When that happens, the quality of government suffers as does government's ability to reflect the will of the people.

In the 1980 election, 47 percent of the nation's voting age population of 160.5 million did not vote. This is not a recent phenomenon, either. The percentage of indifferent voters has increased steadily over the past two decades. The 1980 figures were a full percentage point below the 1976 Presidential turnout rate of 54.4 percent and was the lowest nationwide vote since 1948. The same has happened with the mid-term elections. In the mid-term election of 1966, 45.4 percent voted; in 1978 it was down to 34 percent.

America's participation at the polls is the lowest of any industrialized democracy. And it's a shame.

PACs, by encouraging involvement and interest in the political process from the head of a company all the way down, can help transform indifference into concern. Involvement can come in many different sizes, shapes and forms. The most obvious mechanism is through contributions to the campaigns of various candidates. But involvement by no means has to end there.

There is a political action committee in Kentucky that brings a group of company employees to Washington every year to meet with their legislators and to discuss issues of mutual concern. Both legislators and employees benefit. We come away with a better understanding of what they expect from us. They go home, not only with a better idea of where we stand on those issues, but also with the satisfaction of making their views known.

I cannot overemphasize the importance of this form of direct communication, and I believe most of my colleagues feel the same way. That is why it is important that political action-oriented groups exist not only at the national level, but at the state and local levels, too. In this way, individual members become more politically-oriented and involved in issues which not only affect Washington, but state and local government as well.

14

Another way to promote involvement is to encourage good candidates, particularly those in your own business, to seek elected office actively.

Our system of government was conceived and is based on the premise that legislative bodies at the state and national levels are to be broad in base, to represent many different interests and are not to be just bodies composed of full-time politicians.

Something else political action committees do is to help make political contributions more understandable to the public by removing stigmas some people have attached to these contributions. PACs bring out into the open information about financial support for candidates, which is good.

I do not believe the public realizes just how much it costs to run for public office today. The cost of political advertising has soared out of sight. The simple fact is that running for office has become so expensive that only the well-to-do can afford the kind of expensive campaign it takes to win elections unless there is a broad base of financial support. The day may not be far away when candidates will be reluctant to seek and to hold public office because of the high cost of campaigning. The price of sinking their life savings into a political race, just so they can campaign at the same level, for instance, against an opponent who is independently wealthy is simply too much to ask. If the day should ever come when our legislative bodies are just a rich man's club, our country will be the poorer for it.

So far, this is exactly what you probably expected to learn about my perspective of political action committees. But there is another side to these groups, a side that is under continual examination by the media and other groups.

Many of these so-called "examinations" and reports have been less than favorable in context and have injected criticisms that need to be considered. You who are managers of business political action committees need to be in a position to respond to these opposing points of view. After all, you are accountable to your corporate boards, employees and stockholders -- and they may raise the very same questions.

The most common charge is that PACs have made a mockery of election reform laws which were supposed to signal an end to "special interest"

15

politics. To offset this criticism, PACs should have a broad base of support within their own organization -- a base that reflects a wide range of constituencies and broad public needs.

Another objection is that PACs make uncompromising demands on legislators. I do not agree with that contention, either, because any PAC worth its salt knows that a threat to contribute *only* if the legislator votes your interest on every single issue will be rejected lock, stock and barrel.

Certain groups have seen their effectiveness diminished in recent years because they want to take a strong, unbending position on every single issue that comes down the pike.

The best piece of advice I can give you is to decide what bills are most important to your interests, and to base your position on solid facts and persuasive evidence. In all likelihood, results will be favorable.

But remember: Your position alone, without supporting facts and justification, is not sufficient by itself for support on any given issue.

One more serious charge made about PACs is that they, through their campaign contributions, are trying to buy every single vote in sight. This allegation will be given credibility if your committees do not concentrate on policy issues and base requests for support on facts. Don't ever for a minute think that contributions alone can buy a vote, because no politician, at least one who wants to stay in office, will support a proposal that is counter to the best interests of those constituents to whom he is accountable.

A fourth criticism frequently expressed is that PACs make it impossible to create any type of national policy in Congress. While political action committees do tend to target, to say that they make it impossible to develop a national policy is a gross exaggeration of their power. As long as your concerns are on policy issues and not the sole effect on a given company or firm no credibility can be given to this point of contention.

Still another argument is that PACs can delay legislation which they want to block for unlimited amounts of time. That's true. But so can any other well-organized lobby. I can cite one example after another where this has been the case, and most of these groups were not political action committees. The key to offset this point is for PACs to act responsibly and use their committee as a vehicle to express your views, not to make demands.

The point I am trying to make, and this should not be a mystery, is that public perception of political action committees is most important. If the public thinks you are trying to pull a fast one, then it will not look kindly on either what you are doing or those candidates who support your views and positions. But if the public is on your side and understands the reasoning behind your actions, the motivation for your involvement, then you have won a strong and valuable ally.

After all, no matter how much money you invest in a political action committee or how much support you can offer to individual candidates, it is the public that always has the final say when all the votes are counted. **PAC**

Wendell H. Ford was the first Kentuckian ever to be elected to consecutive terms as Lieutenant Governor, Governor and U.S. Senator. He was elected to the U.S. Senate in 1974, and called shortly thereafter for the formation of a single Senate committee to handle all energy-related legislation. Two years later, the Senate complied. Since that time, Sen. Ford has been instrumental in drafting other energy-related legislation to come out of the committee.

As a member of the Commerce, Science and Transportation Committee, Sen. Ford is in a position to keep a watchful eye on the many regulatory agencies which come under the committee's jurisdiction – among them the Interstate Commerce Commission, the Federal Trade Commission and the Federal Communications Commission.

II. PAC BACKGROUND

PAC Overview

Joseph J. Fanelli
President, Business-Industry PAC

Business interests for too long were substantially inactive in the political arena, allowing a growing insensitivity to business conditions to flourish. This inactivity resulted in greater regulation and in policies which sharply inhibited business growth and which retarded normal channels of distribution of goods and services to the detriment of the entire economy. Through more effective legislative and political activity, business is finally beginning to free itself of some of that excessive regulation. The business PAC movement has helped to bring this about.

Business has strengthened its legislative impact largely through its involvement in the political process. It has become more effective in the halls of Congress because its legislative and political activities have reached a new level of sophistication. The political process includes, but is not limited to, involvement in congressional campaigns through direct contributions to candidates.

In focusing on the topic of business in the political arena it is important to distinguish between two separate kinds of corporate political activity: 1) those which can be, and are, financed out of corporate funds and 2) those which may receive corporate administrative backing but which are financed by the individual contributions of members of the corporate family. Understanding the difference is essential. It is also important to understand that many companies without PACs are not "second class citizens" nor are they sitting out the process.

Increasingly, corporate public affairs programs for employees (financed with company funds) include programs in the following categories: economic understanding, legislative information and action, and political information and action. Chief among these are efforts to educate employees about basic political processes. Such "civic action" programs teach employees how government works, how laws are made, how people are elected to public office, and how individual citizens may become active in the political party of their choice. Often, a basic part of the programs includes drives to encourage citizens to register and to go to the polls on election day. Obviously, such company programs cannot predict just how employees will vote on specific candidates, but they do encourage citizenship participation in the belief that it is good for the country.

GRASSROOTS LOBBYING

In recent years some very sophisticated mechanisms have been established within various corporations in which employees have been organized and mobilized to deliberate legislative issues and to communicate positions on the issues to members of Congress at the "grassroots" level. This has been a most effective technique — reaching legislators on their home ground through their own constituents. There is no better form of "lobbying." Certainly it is much more effective than having company professional lobbyists bear the full responsibility of communicating company and industry views to members of Congress on Capitol Hill. Such employee communications stress that the issues are important to their employment and well-being, and lawmakers recognize the sincerity of their views.

INTERNAL COMMUNICATIONS

Corporations also are permitted under the law to pay for various types of internal communications on political matters related to their business. Most often these include legislative reports to employees and/or stockholders about pending bills which would have a direct impact on their industry. Corporations may also expend funds to help approve or defeat ballot initiatives. There are no federal limits on how much a company may spend on these activities and there are no reporting requirements. Each state regulates activity as it sees fit.

In addition, corporations may expend corporate dollars to endorse candidates for political office at the federal level, including the president, vice president, United States senators and members of the House of Representatives. Such expenditures of over $2,000 must be reported to the Federal Election Commission and may take the form of communications to employees, stockholders and their families.[1] Although this little-discussed option is clearly outlined in the Federal Election Campaign Act, business failed to utilize it in the 1977-78 elections to any significant extent and preliminary reports suggest very little such activity in the 1979-80 elections. There is great potential in this prerogative, and each succeeding election should see its increasing use.

While the above-mentioned activities fall into the category of "corporate" and "political," it is the *political action committee* which is most frequently referred to in discussions. Whereas corporate public affairs activities have been undertaken for years with little outcry from critics of business, the PAC concept has met with different responses.[2]

Listening to some critics would lead one to believe that PACs are foreign to our way of government, that they are intrinsically evil, and that they ought to be tightly regulated because of their potential for harm. Critics lose sight of the constitutional basis of PAC activity. The fundamental expression of First Amendment freedoms through the phrase "assemble for the redress of grievances" applies to political action committees. PACs, in any segment of society, are nothing more than gatherings of individual citizens exercising their right to assemble. In other words, they are a more sophisticated and organized version of petitioners who used to write letters to King George III. PACs are as much an outgrowth of our political system as are the political parties.

Some who argue that PACs should be curtailed may not fully appreciate the deep, basic constitutional principle of freedom that is involved in the First Amendment. To them, the right of free speech and the right to assemble freely do not extend to political action committees in the same degree that they

23

extend to other forms of expression. Those of us who believe in PACs should take the opportunity whenever it is offered to refer back to these underpinnings of our activities, if for no other reason than to remind ourselves how precious is our right to join together for the purpose of electing our representatives.

Another key point to reinforce is that PACs do not derive their contributions from corporations. Rather, PAC contributions are derived from individuals — employees, stockholders and their families. It is well to keep pointing out, too, that all contributions are voluntary. Any fair observer would have to agree that corporate managers are meticulous in following the law. If there is any question about an activity which might give the appearance of being in violation of the law, the tendency is to go beyond the legal requirements to protect the company and the individual contributor from any hint of wrongdoing.

Surely, PACs will continue to face criticism from those who are hostile to the very concept of business involvement in politics. Perhaps little can be done to argue with these individuals other than to point out the inherent constitutional principles which are being implemented according to law. In my view, a far greater threat to PAC growth and performance comes from within the movement itself, from those who expect too much too soon or from those whose views of how PACs should operate are not fulfilled when looking at the record.

PAC MOVEMENT STILL TO MATURE

It is well to remember that most business PACs have been in existence less than five years. Many PACs of organized labor, on the other hand, have been active since the middle 1940s — giving them ample time to experiment with fundraising techniques, contributor relationships, communications, etc. While several corporate and association groups formed vehicles for political participation as early as the 1950s, it was not until the early 1960s that they attracted public attention. That was the period in which the American Medical Association and others formed state and national PACs. As with the labor unions, the medical community realized that their lobbyists could not expect a favorable audience with those who had been elected to Congress if the elected members had preconceived notions that were antithetical to the practice of private medicine.

Business-Industry Political Action Committee (BIPAC) joined the field in 1963 as an independent, nonpartisan organization representing the employees of business and individuals who support private enterprise. As a major departure from previous PACs (and most PACs existing today), BIPAC does no lobbying and takes no stand on specific legislative issues. Rather, its entire purpose is the election of a Congress oriented toward fiscal responsibility, reduction of the federal bureaucracy, and support of private enterprise.

The spurt in the growth of corporate and association PACs is traced to the Federal Election Campaign Act of 1971 and the 1974 and 1976 amendments to that Act. These acts, along with the implementing regulations, permitted explicitly the formation of corporate, association and labor union political action committees and further permitted the use of corporate dollars to organize and administer company PACs and the use of dues dollars for a similar purpose in forming association and labor union PACs.

GROWTH OF PACS

In 1974 there were 89 corporate PACs. In 1976 there were 450. In 1978 there were 821. As of November 1980, there were 1,226. In dollar growth, corporate PACs contributed $9.8 million to federal candidates in 1978. As of August 1980, they had already contributed $10.8 million to House and Senate candidates.

For the same time period, labor union PACs have also shown some growth. In 1974, there were 201 labor union PACs; 281 in 1978; and 318 as of August 1980. Their growth over 1978 represented about a 10 percent increase and a 50 percent increase over 1974. Labor union PACs gave $10.3 million in 1978 to federal candidates and were well over half-way to that mark at the end of June 1980, with contributions to House and Senate candidates of $7.5 million.

Through the time frame for which figures are available (January 1, 1979 through June 30, 1980), all candidates for the House and Senate had raised $125.8 million. All non-party political action committees accounted for $20.8 million of those receipts -- about 16 percent. Coincidentally, this was the same figure for the PAC share of all candidate receipts in the 1977-78 period.

Corporate PACs represented 6 percent of the total receipts of congressional candidates in 1978. As of the June 1980 reports, $7.4 million in PAC dollars would be about the same.

Thus, while corporate PACs are growing in number and in dollars, so are the other sources of candidate funds, primarily individual contributions. There is absolutely no evidence that PACs are crowding out the individual contributor, that candidates are turning to PACs for "easy" money, or that the average candidate's campaign dollars are inordinately made up of PAC contributions. The average corporate PAC in the 1979-80 period had contributed around $8,730. The average labor PAC had contributed more than 2 1/2 times as much -- $23,600 according to FEC reports as of June 30, 1980.[3]

Labor still sets the pace for the big givers. As of June, 14 of the top 20 contributors to federal candidates were labor union PACs. Not one corporation PAC made the list.

So why is there such a hue and cry today about the influence of business in congressional elections? The answer is obvious. It is that the gap is closing and that in some respects business PACs will out-perform labor unions when the final figures for 1980 are in. Given the continuation of that trend and the willingness for business to take more risks with their political dollars, labor will find itself playing a game of "catch up."

As in the 96th Congress, efforts could also be made in the 97th Congress to change the rules. However, in view of the 1980 congressional election results, punitive legislation aimed at business PACs will undoubtedly find an unresponsive atmosphere.

In the 96th Congress there was an attempt to have the federal government finance the election campaigns for Congress. Despite sponsorship of almost one-third of the House membership, the problems inherent in any such system became apparent. The Committee on House Administration resisted pressure from the White House, from some leaders in the House and some outside organizations, and it rejected that bill.

Thereafter, an effort was made to limit sharply the extent to which PACs could participate in campaigns with direct contributions. This was advocated by some, despite the fact that the inflation rate had already eroded by almost one-half what could be purchased with the contribution maximums which were set several years ago. Amid the propaganda drumfire about "special interests," the House passed (without hearings) the Obey-Railsback PAC limitation proposal, but it languished in the Senate without action. As was expected, many of the co-sponsors of the proposal and those who voted for it in the House nonetheless found it "necessary" to solicit contributions from PACs for their 1980 election bids.

GROWING IMPACT THROUGH "RISK" TAKING

If the real, rather than imagined, impact of PACs is to grow, it will be because PACs continue to take risks with their dollars aimed at improving the philosophical balance of Congress -- through the support of "pro-private enterprise" challengers with reasonable chances to win and in assisting similarly-oriented incumbents who are in danger of losing their seats. It would be as unproductive for a PAC to help all challengers without regard for their viability as candidates as it would be to help incumbents exclusively regardless of financial need.

Placing dollars in the most competitive races, or using dollars to make races more competitive, should be, if not the total goal of every business PAC, at least a substantial part of the premise on which contribution decisions are made.

THE "POLITICAL IMPERATIVE" OF COMPANY PACS

Anti-PAC individuals often will level special criticism at business PACs that show signs of utilizing some of their resources for obvious "lobbying" purposes; for instance, the support of a key committee chairman with little or no reelection competition.

While one may deplore the practice of some PACs in this regard, it appears that every PAC has the right to demonstrate support for those holding key positions on committees who have been helpful on legislation vital to the

27

company or industry involved and whose record demonstrates a sound understanding of that industry.

Current attempts to restrict free political association and involvement of some citizens should not be ignored. History has shown that limitations imposed on one group or one facet of activity are followed by restrictions on others. This, of course, could lead to the withering of not only our political system but of economic growth, prosperity and of our very freedom itself.

The argument that PAC financing is about to subvert the whole political process is spurious. The best guarantee of keeping the political process "open" so that all voices may be heard is to allow -- in fact, to encourage -- a maximum number of groups and individuals in all aspects of the process, including campaign funding. Efforts to restrict such free activity are counter-productive and of dubious constitutional validity.

Efforts to reduce or shut off campaign contributions likely will lead to increased "independent expenditures" by committees and individuals, and there are serious questions that the political process would be well-served by that alternative.

Restriction of corporate-related PACs, thus relegating voluntary associations of business employees to second-class citizenship, is particularly insidious. It would confer favored status on other PACs. Why should the ideological or single-issue PACs be considered more deserving to be heard than those with a business background?

PAC critics make one obvious error, apparently in a deliberate effort to exaggerate the potential influence of the business community. They regularly lump all of the trade association/membership/health PACs (using the FEC categorization) together with the corporate PACs as the "business" influence. Auto dealers, doctors and realtors have different objectives on the legislative scene, and for their PACs, than do the employees of a steel or food processing company. One has only to examine the lists of the various PACs' contributions to see that they cover a wide range of legislative performance. These groups have widely varying goals as well as significantly different strategies for achieving them.

Even within the hundreds of corporate PACs there are widespread differences about whom to support. In political action, business does not speak with one voice. It should not be expected to, considering the vastly different companies that comprise the list of over 1,200 firms with political action committees.

The corporate PAC movement is alive and well — and growing. Some further growth is expected and should be welcomed, but those who fear it will develop into an all-consuming monster have let their imaginations run wild. The views of those who join in such political action committees rightfully should be heard in legislative councils along with those of many other groups and individuals. Our nation is far more likely to suffer from unresponsive government when too few, rather than too many, voices are heard on Capitol Hill. **PAC**

FOOTNOTES

[1] The reporting requirement applies only to expenditures for internal communications having to do with support of federal candidates.

[2] It should be noted that there are political action committees sponsored by labor unions, trade and professional associations, and single issue groups of all sorts. For some reason the critics center their fire on those which are corporate-related as though they are merely seeking greater profits at the expense of the general public.

[3] A significant amount of campaign financing in 1980 came from the political parties themselves. The Republicans have been much more successful than the Democrats in this area, and G.O.P. committees were a major source of campaign funds in many challenger races. Continued growth of party support will, of course, dilute the influence of PAC money.

Joseph J. Fanelli is president of the Business-Industry Political Action Committee. BIPAC is a nationwide organization of individuals whose purpose is to help elect to the United States Congress those who advocate constitutional government and a free economic system. Through political education, BIPAC encourages political awareness and participation among the managers and employees of American business. BIPAC is nonpartisan and is not affiliated with any group or political party.

Prior to joining BIPAC in September of 1975, Fanelli was affiliated for thirteen years with the Chamber of Commerce of the United States, serving as manager of its Public Affairs Department for six years, with full responsibility for political participation and economic education programs. Before that he was a special assistant to a U.S. senator for four years and to a member of the U.S. House of Representatives for two years. He has been active in political organizational and campaign work on local, congressional and statewide levels.

Corporate PACs: Step-by-Step Formation and Troublefree Operation

Don R. Kendall
Political Consultant, Business-Industry PAC

The evolution of political action committees is clearly one of the most significant political developments of the past decade. A political action committee is a group of individuals voluntarily joined together to contribute money to candidates seeking elective office. These individuals have some purposes in mind which they believe will be served by the election of those candidates they support.

Assessments may vary as to whether PACs have a positive or negative influence on our political system, but few would question that PACs have become important factors in the political process.[1] In 1978 total PAC contributions to U.S. Senate and House candidates alone were over $35 million -- a figure which attests to their political clout.[1]

Of that total PAC involvement, corporate-related PACs contributed approximately 28 percent. The balance came mainly from PACs in the labor or association/membership/health categories and, to a lesser degree, from independent or non-connected PACs.

In retrospect, the increasing importance of political action committees in campaign finance seems almost inevitable, given the rapidly escalating costs of campaigns, the statutory restrictions placed on individual giving and the legislation which established the legal framework for PAC operation.

31

CAMPAIGN PRICETAGS

Nearly everyone decries the high costs of political campaigns, but no one knows those costs can be substantially reduced. Aside from increases caused by inflation, campaigns are more technical and professional than they used to be -- which means they are more expensive. Extensive use of television and other media requires considerable outlays; the use of costly polling techniques in campaign planning has become widespread. Today's candidates no longer rely on their relatives or business associates to run their campaigns; they know that harmful mistakes can be avoided by hiring experienced political operatives. Payroll costs for a campaign, which used to be almost nonexistent, are now a major budget item.

In 1978 the average House general election candidate spent approximately $107,000, and 80 of them spent more than $200,000, the latter in sharply contested races.[2] In the Senate, the average total expenditure per campaign was close to one million dollars, with several of them greatly exceeding that amount.

While candidates are obviously aware of the need to raise substantial funds for campaign purposes, their reaction to growing PAC involvement is varied. Some refuse to accept PAC contributions; others limit the amount they will accept from a PAC; most accept PAC contributions but seem rather embarrassed about doing so. The embarrassment is caused by the drumfire of insinuation, innuendo and allegation from critics of the PAC movement, directed particularly at corporate-related PACs, as if the contributions of business employees are somehow tainted and carry with them unwholesome obligations for the recipients.

THE PROLIFERATION OF PACS

Individuals have long known they could magnify their influence by pooling their resources and efforts. In some cases this led to the formation of so-called "single issue" groups, whether for or against gun control, abortion, tax limitation, etc. The effectiveness of these groups led others to see the possible advantages in banding together for specific purposes.

Although the term political action committee is new, some PAC-like organizations were formed in the '50s and early '60s. At that time companies offered their employees the option of participating in a "trustee plan" through which money was collected, kept in individual accounts, and disbursed to candidates only with the express consent of the contributor.

The years 1971, 1974 and 1976 were critical for the development of PACs. The Federal Election Campaign Act, originally passed in 1971, requires that all federal candidates disclose the source of their campaign contributions and itemize their expenditures. In the wake of Watergate, amendments were added in 1974 which limited the amounts individuals could give to federal candidates and even the amount of their own money which candidates could spend.

Then in 1976 the Supreme Court, in *Buckley v. Valeo*, (U.S. Supreme Nos. 75-436, 75-437 -- Jan. 30, 1976), declared the limitations on the candidates' own expenditures unconstitutional, as well as the overall limits on campaign expenditures. But the $1,000 limit on individual contributions to federal candidates remained. The rapid changes in federal election law gave validity to PACs as a political tool.

The 1974 amendments to the 1971 Act also created the Federal Election Commission (FEC). These amendments and subsequent FEC regulations laid down the groundrules for corporate PACs. Corporate executives approached these new regulations warily, but were glad to have the permissible corporate role clarified.

Responding to the possibilities which opened up, the number of corporate PACs has risen dramatically since 1974. Labor groups and some public interest organizations have viewed the corporate PACs with suspicion. Many business executives have welcomed corporate PACs as providing a counterbalance to the predominance of labor union political activity through COPE, the Committee on Political Education of the AFL-CIO, and similar groups. Operating since the 1940s, COPE has always been deeply involved in federal campaigns, and exerts a powerful influence on state and local elections in areas where a sizeable number of voters come from the ranks of organized labor. Total labor PACs number 226.

33

In recent years corporate-related PACs have grown to the point of near-parity with labor PACs. In 1978 corporate PACs contributed $9.8 million to congressional candidates; labor gave $10.3 million.[3] It is likely that total corporate PAC giving in 1980 will exceed that of the union PACs.

Also intensifying the growth of corporate PAC activity at the state and local level is the fact that the men and women elected to state legislatures this year will take on the important job of reapportioning House seats based on the 1980 census. Many state legislatures including such important ones as New York, Pennsylvania, California and Illinois, are now closely divided, and a shift of only a few votes could swing control. Corporate PACs will help decide on how these votes go.

THE EFFORTS TO CURB PACS

Faced with strong competition from business, the AFL-CIO and Common Cause joined ranks in an effort to stifle the PAC movement by supporting public financing of congressional campaigns. When the 96th Congress opened in 1979, the prestigious designation of H.R. 1 was given to the public financing measure. The bill had 132 cosponsors and was endorsed by Speaker of the House Tip O'Neill and President Jimmy Carter. A massive lobbying effort was mounted to get the bill out of the Committee on House Administration, but failed decisively.

The efforts to secure public financing of congressional campaigns failed for a variety of reasons. The committee could not agree on how much aid should be provided; some members were opposed to placing this extra burden on the taxpayers; some were awed by the mammoth monitoring resonsibility to be put on the FEC; some recognized that any such system would treat certain candidates unfairly. Backers of public financing will try again, but they still must settle the issues which the Committee on House Administration was unable to resolve.

Labor and Common Cause were also side-by-side in supporting another attempt to limit opportunities for PAC activity. The Obey-Railsback bill, which the House tacked onto a Senate-passed bill by a narrow margin, seeks to limit the overall amount of PAC contributions to any campaign ($70,000 from all PAC sources) and to cut the amount which any one PAC can give to any one candidate from a maximum of $10,000 to $6,000 -- despite the fact that inflation already has eroded the previous $10,000 limit by almost one-half. This effort currently is stalled in the Senate, but may be revived.

One may ask why organized labor, whose PACs have been very active, is now willing to support legislation which would curtail all PAC activity. The reason is that unions can conduct a number of "educational" activities apart from making direct contributions to the candidates they favor. For years the unions have carried out voter registration and get-out-the-vote efforts in areas where their membership is concentrated. They believe such efforts greatly benefit the candidates they support. Thus the unions are willing to reduce the opportunity for direct PAC financial contributions in which corporate-related groups are now competing on a nearly equal basis, while continuing their "nonpartisan" educational drives, which aid their favored candidates.

THE GROWTH OF CORPORATE PACS

As stated, the Federal Election Campaign Act of 1971 and subsequent amendments provided the basis for corporate political activity. Many corporate leaders were hesitant to utilize these new provisions in order to support candidates. Watergate revelations concerning the improper activities of a few corporate officials still affected policy in the mid-70s.

Gradually the commitment to corporate PACs grew: In 1974, there were 89; in 1976, 450; in 1978, 821. Today there are more than 1,000 corporate PACs, and the number is sure to increase.[4]

Similarly, the financial volume of this activity, at the federal level alone, has grown from $2.5 million in 1974, to $4.3 million in 1976, to $9.8 million in 1978.[5]

A few points about corporate PACs should be emphasized:

- Corporate-related PACs can be sponsored by a corporation to the extent that the company underwrites the administrative expenses of the PAC, but the money contributed to candidates must come from individual contributions made by PAC members (corporate employees and stockholders). Federal law prohibits corporate funds being spent in federal campaigns – a prohibition which dates from the Tillman Act of 1907. Present law allows the corporation to cover only the administrative overhead of PAC formation and operation.

• Those alarmists who project continued phenomenal growth of corporate PACs based on the remarkable increases since 1974 are jumping to conclusions. There is *potential* for growth, but many of those working in corporate public affairs believe the period of rapid growth is over. They predict a more moderate growth for corporate PACs in the next few years.

• Those who perceive corporate PACs as a monolithic political movement which will bend the Congress to the corporate sector's will and over-shadow other political influences should note that corporate PACs vary greatly in size, purpose and method of operation. By no means do they all support the same candidates. They have different goals and employ different criteria in assessing candidates. It is not unusual to find corporate PACs backing opposing candidates. Corporate PACs do not all want the same things; they do not all act the same way.

It is true that the 226 labor PACs also emphasize different issues and support different candidates. Nevertheless, there is much greater homogeneity among the labor PACs than among the corporate PACs. Indeed, labor gave an average of $1,231 to its candidates in 1978 compared to $485 for corporate PACs.

According to the classifications established by the Federal Election Commission, there is another major group of PACs – trade association, membership and health PACs. These PACs contributed $11.5 million to congressional candidates in 1978.[6] Understandably, they are considered a significant factor in financing congressional elections, but critics tend to lump them together with corporate PACs as sharing a "pro-business" philosophy.

These groups have greatly differing backgrounds and purposes. For instance, auto dealers and the management employees of a chemical company may share some general economic attitudes, but in terms of political activity, the two groups are likely to proceed along totally different paths. Is it really logical to assume that medical doctors and paper company executives are going to be seeking the same results from political action?

The case for lumping all of these groups together simply cannot be made, but those seeking to curtail PAC activity continue to do so.

The fourth major grouping of PACs by the FEC is the so-called independent PACs, which include PACs formed by people committed to a certain political ideology who have united to elect like-minded legislators. The Business-Industry Political Action Committee (BIPAC), for instance, seeks the election of more senators and representatives who are knowledgable about the workings of the free enterprise system and are sensitive to government policies which promote business and industry growth and opportunity.

PAC INFLUENCE IN PERSPECTIVE

Having established the major importance of the PAC movement in our political system, we must note that it still plays only a small part in the financing of congressional elections. In the 1978 congressional elections, only 17¢ of each campaign dollar came from all PACs – corporate, labor, trade and independent.

PAC contributions have been significant, but not overwhelming; probably influential, but hardly dominating.

Combined PAC activity was part of the 1978 congressional elections, but only a part – and that part encompasses a multitude of differing objectives and purposes.

A byproduct of the PAC movement is the involvement in the political process of many individuals who had not previously taken part. PAC managers report that many of their contributors never donated to a candidate or party previously.

37

PACs are composed of individuals who have grouped together to support political positions they share. They feel that as a group they can be more effective than as individuals, that a contribution in the name of their group will have more impact than scattered individual gifts. They seek to elect men and women who feel as they do on certain key issues. They do not think they "buy" votes by making contributions to candidates; rather they try to make their contributions to those candidates whose records or policy statements indicate views compatible with their own.

FORMING A CORPORATE PAC

Less than one-half of the Fortune 500 companies have political action committees; thousands of corporations have still not formed PACs. Some executives are leery of any political involvement; others are unwilling to devote any corporate resources to PAC administrative costs. But many have concluded that a PAC is protection for the corporation and a convenience for its employees.

Having a well-functioning PAC reduces the likelihood of a company's becoming a target for other types of political fundraising, some of which might be of a questionable character. A PAC should involve more executives and managers than only one top officer who merely collects checks from a handful of upper level colleagues. The structure and operation of a PAC must provide an easy way for many employees to participate in the political process.

Once the support of top management is assured, some basic choices should be made about the scope and operation of the committee. If the corporation has several plants and divisions, it must decide if it will have one or several PACs. Most corporations have found that a single PAC is the best way to proceed initially, while leaving open the option of creating additional PACs in the future.

Another basic question is: Will the PAC support only federal candidates, or will it extend aid to candidates for state and local office as well? Many companies feel that governmental decisions at the state and local levels are just as important to their operations as those made by the federal government, and therefore seek involvement at those levels as well. Separate regional PACs are then the best system, but this requires additional reporting to state agencies.

The size of the committee must be determined. The law currently requires that it have a chairman and a treasurer, but amendments requiring only a treasurer are being considered by the FEC. The committee can be composed of any number of members, but most PACs consider a limited number to be the most workable situation.

Under 1979 amendments to the FEC, a committee must file a statement of its organization with the FEC as soon as it is created. In addition, PAC names must accurately reflect the sponsoring organization.

A committee would be wise to adopt some form of bylaws which sets out its purpose, describes the duties and responsibilities of its officers, and outlines its methods of choosing the candidates it will support. A PAC can be incorporated for the purpose of relief from personal liability of those involved in formation, operations and contributions.

The criteria for supporting a candidate need not be set down in the bylaws in detail, although their general thrust should be. In practice, the committee members will have many key choices to make:

- Will they concentrate exclusively on those congressional districts and states in which the corporation has facilities, or look for interesting races everywhere?

- Will they make contributions to presidential candidates? To political parties? To any other PACs?

- Will their contributions be largely influenced by input from their Washington lobbyists, who have frequent contact with lawmakers?

- Will they disburse money so that some representatives of the PAC can attend fundraising events?

- Will they make post-election contributions to help ease a candidate's campaign deficit?

- Will they allow contributors to the PAC to earmark a contribution for a particular candidate or party?

In addition to direct contributions of money, PACs also can contribute "in-kind" services to a campaign, such as underwriting a mailing or some other specific campaign effort. Generally PACs prefer to make simple money contributions, and candidates prefer to receive unfettered cash.

A few PACs also have experimented with "independent expenditures" made in behalf of a candidate without his knowledge or approval. From the PAC viewpoint, the biggest hurdle to making this kind of contribution is that the law strictly prohibits contact between a representative of the PAC and anyone associated with the candidate's campaign in order to safeguard the independent nature of the contribution. Since active PACs are constantly in touch with various candidates, party officials, campaign managers, etc., an embarrassing allegation of improper contact might develop late in a campaign and hurt the candidate the PAC seeks to help.

Independent expenditures are still under review by many PAC managers. If Congress limits opportunities for direct contributions, taking the independent expenditure route may become an attractive alternative.

METHODS OF PAC MEMBER SOLICITATION

Methods of PAC member solicitation vary considerably, and some have proved to be more successful than others.

Most PAC managers agree that strong support from the chief executive officer (CEO) of the company is essential to PAC success. When solicited, management employees must know that the CEO personally supports contributions to the PAC. At the same time, it must be made clear that participation in the PAC is purely voluntary and has no effect on the employee's performance rating, chances for advancement, etc. Most PACs keep the list of contributors in strict confidence; the top officers of the company may have no knowledge of who is contributing or not. The chief executive's endorsement of such activity assures that those solicited give serious thought to contributing.

The CEO's interest is usually conveyed in a forceful letter addressed to those employees the PAC committee has selected for solicitation. That letter is often followed by one from another officer or from the PAC chairman. This follow-up letter includes detailed information about the organization of the PAC, its objectives, criteria for support of candidates and plans for informing the membership of its activities.

Sometimes a group meeting is used to supplement or substitute for the follow-up letter. Some companies have devised imaginative slide presentations and films to explain the need for political contributions. Some education work may be necessary at the outset to generate support from those employees who do not initially recognize the benefits of PAC involvement.

Virtually all PAC managers believe some personal solicitation is necessary to maximize results. Generally the solicitation is made by a colleague of approximately equal rank, in order to reduce any feeling of intimidation. The solicitor should, if possible, be someone committed to the PAC objectives and personally convinced of the effectiveness of the PAC program.

Most PACs suggest that the solicitation be made on an annual basis. Those who collect contributions through a payroll deduction arrangement have found it increases both participation and level of support.

PAC managers have discovered the necessity of developing a mechanism by which contributors can give their input concerning the committee's choices for support. Most contributors do not expect all of their suggestions to be followed, but if they are unable to offer them, their interest in the PAC quickly fades.

A few PACs have also built solicitation efforts around special events, sometimes inviting congressmen, candidates or others knowledgable about politics to address them.

PAC managers laugh at the allegation that employees are in some manner coerced to contribute. If this were so, they ask, how is it that only 20 or 25 percent of the employees solicited participate? Some PACs report a higher percentage of response, but generally they restrict solicitation to a limited number of executives who earn top salaries.

LIVING WITH LIMITATIONS

The legal restrictions on company sponsorship of a political action committee discourage some executives, who balk at the reporting requirements and the restrictions on solicitation. These restrictions can be troublesome, and any company considering the formation of a PAC must conduct full legal research on the matter. Nevertheless, most corporations forming PACs have found the regulations tolerable.

Deciding the appropriate level for employee solicitation has proven a problem for some companies. PAC organizers must draw some line between executive and non-executive, managerial and non-managerial employees. This tends to set up an unnatural caste system. To play it safe, some companies restrict their solicitation to only the very highest executive levels, thereby leaving a number of middle-management employees in a kind of no-man's-land between the union and top management.

The law allows companies to solicit stockholders, too; a few PACs have done so successfully. Those companies which have, however, had previously established a continuing relationship with their stockholders through public affairs newsletters and reports. PAC efforts at hitting stockholders "cold" have been disappointing.

The PAC directors of some corporations find restrictions on trade association solicitation very discomforting. Associations can solicit the management employees of member companies only after receiving approval from the companies; and member companies may authorize the solicitation by only one trade assocation per year. Most large companies are members of several trade associations which reflect various facets of the company. Each association has a different constituency within the member company. Thus, the solicitation by any one association is somewhat limited in its appeal.

Regulation has placed debilitating limitations on trade association PAC development. This is not apparent when one looks at the broad category of "trade/membership and health PACs" as defined by the FEC. But the associations in that group which have been successful are not those with company members, but rather those with individual members such as doctors and realtors.

PACs faced with difficult interpretation of the regulations can request an advisory opinion (AO) from the FEC. If the FEC agrees that the subject merits an opinion, the Commission will give its answer, and other PACs with identical problems can be guided accordingly.

PACS: A POSITIVE FORCE IN THE 1980S

In the coming decade, PACs are likely to continue to proliferate in the absence of any sharply restrictive legislation. Even if the FEC laws governing PACs are tightened, some similar form of political action is likely to flourish. If corporate PACs are shackled, the independent PACs may receive increased support. If limitations are placed on contributions to candidates, the PACs may resort to making independent expenditures to candidates.

Pushed in self-defense to take a more active role, business has now concluded that it should be politically involved. The proper functioning of the system demands that all voices be heard — and the business-industry voice is as legitimate as any other.

Those familiar with the PAC phenomenon believe that one of its most valuable byproducts is the personal involvement of the contributor in our political system. The PAC movement has perhaps done more to increase citizen activity in politics than any other recent development.

PAC support also can help candidates who lack the personal wealth to finance their campaigns strictly from their own resources: the growing cost of campaigns threatens to make politics a game reserved for only the very wealthy.

The more sophisticated PACs even help the candidates in managing their campaigns and budgets. Some PAC committees give support only to those who prove they are conducting effective campaigns; they refuse to assist poorly organized and shoddily run campaigns.

As Joseph Fanelli, president of Business-Industry Political Action Committee (BIPAC), stated in his testimony before a congressional committee:

> The attempt to tar all such groups with a reputation of greed and a disregard of the general good is unfair and unwarranted. It is true that such groups seek to determine which lawmakers are likely to vote most often as they would wish, and to give their support to those candidates. This is precisely what an informed, thoughtful individual voter does; and political action committees are merely a collective reflection of the same procedure.

> The end result is an amplification of views and attitudes, of assents and dissents. It increases the number of participants in the political dialogue; and it surely helps to ventilate issues which otherwise might have grown stale and musty in the closet of restricted debate.

With responsible management and given the chance, corporate PACs can be a positive force for democracy in the '80s. **PAC**

Reprinted with permission from
CAMPAIGNS AND ELECTIONS, Spring 1980.

FOOTNOTES

[1]Federal Election Commission, Press Release, May 10, 1979, p. 1.

[2]Michael J. Malbin, "Campaign Financing and the Special Interests," *The Public Interest*, Summer 1979, p. 27.

[3]Federal Election Commission, op. cit., p.3.

[4]Business-Industry Political Action Committee (BIPAC), "Summary of Political Action Committee Activity," May 1979, p. 1.

[5]Ibid, p. 2.

[6]*supra,* note 3.

Currently a political consultant to BIPAC, the Business-Industry Political Action Committee, **Don R. Kendall** previously has been involved in politics at the local, state and national levels. Kendall was the Republican chairman for Montgomery County, Maryland and later the Republican state chairman. He was the executive director of the Republican National Committee when Ray Bliss was the national chairman.

In the government, he was administrative assistant to a member of Congress for many years, the executive assistant to the Administrator of Veterans Affairs, and the deputy director of congressional relations for the Department of Transportation.

Kendall has taught classes in government and politics for the University of Maryland, and for eight years was a member of the Maryland Council for Higher Education.

III. CORPORATE PACS:
CASE STUDIES

The Corporate PAC Experience

Richard B. Berman
Vice President, Steak and Ale Restaurants of America, Inc.

Sir Winston Churchill once said, "Politics are almost as exciting as war and quite as dangerous, although in war you can be killed only once; in politics, many times." After suffering the frustration of legislative defeats, many of our corporate executives found Mr. Churchill's words particularly meaningful. Through the efforts of interest groups which had no offsetting influences, legislation had been passed and regulations adopted that were contrary to the best interests of our company and its employees as well as to the public in general. These decisions from Washington concerned and frustrated us. We realized the best way to have a positive impact on such policies was to help determine who held elective office. Capitalizing on that opportunity, we formed a political action committee.

Based on our own experience, a successful PAC is much easier to establish with genuine commitment from the top officers in the corporation. Endorsement is the key to opening the solicitation door. Without executive commitment, achieving a successful program must be far more difficult.

Top officers of our corporation were committed to invest company time in the process of solicitation. For example, in the early stages of the development of the PAC we held meetings for our restaurant managers expressly to explain the PAC. At these meetings we laid the foundation for our PAC on company time. This would have been impossible without implied endorsement from the top officers. Now that our PAC is off the ground, when a presentation is made in person, it is made as part of another operations-oriented meeting.

In meetings where we solicit, certain top officers often endorse the program without major speeches. For example, our CEO has expressed his support simply by standing to confirm his strong belief in the importance of the program. This creates a positive environment for solicitation.

Historically, our first attempt to solicit was by mail. We were unhappy with the 25-30 percent rate of participation we received. Although that rate might generate enough dollars in a larger company, we have such a small management base that we needed a greater percentage of participation for a meaningful PAC program.

We modified our approach and chose personal solicitation. In the first meeting, after they heard the presentation, we asked our managers and supervisors to indicate anonymously, in writing: 1) If they would be willing to contribute at the meeting, and 2) How much they would give. One hundred percent of the audience agreed to participate and the amounts of money were large, averaging several hundred dollars per person. We were obviously very pleased. At that time, our payroll deduction plan was not available, so we asked them to send their checks to the home office in Dallas. Nobody sent checks.

For the next presentation, we added a payroll deduction system and learned to get a commitment -- one way or the other -- before the meeting adjourned. The participation rate was over 90 percent with most people agreeing to a payroll deduction system.

In our meetings, we always ask for commitments to participate. We generally receive about 90 percent. If there is an objection to commit, we do not press for a decision. Instead, we ask the employee if he is comfortable making a decision at that time and we urge him to indicate that choice, yes or no. A negative response is important; it gives us a record of contact and an account of the decision. We avoid further contact which might appear to be harrassment to the employee. We also go to great lengths at the meeting to make people comfortable with a decision not to contribute. The entire presentation is geared to offering people a choice, *not* a demand!

50

Because an employee generally trusts and seeks his supervisor's opinion of the program, we make certain to begin the solicitation process at the top. In that way, a supervisor understands the PAC and its workings before his managers hear about it. We solicit down to the assistant manager level where his or her supervisory responsibilities and authority are the same as a manager when on duty.

In order to generate interest in the program, we tie the individual's and the company's fortunes together. The whole picture comes into focus for the employee: As the company's profits grow, there are increasing opportunities for the individual. Where there are cost pressures on the company, the availability of employee gains diminish. We stress that involvement in the governmental process is important to our future as a company and our future as individuals.

Illustrating strong participation gives credibility to the movement and encourages more participation. In the early, developmental stages of the PAC, several employees were reluctant to participate because they did not know if the PAC would be successful. We learned that new membership was more likely when we could cite a proven record. For example, during the first solicitation of managers, we stated that more than nine out of ten of our supervisors were already participating. At that meeting, 95 percent of the managers chose to participate. We used that figure at the next meeting, and the bandwagon was rolling. We always show an employee participation graph at our presentations. (See Diagram 1.) Because all of us enjoy being part of a winning effort, our growth and credibility have continued.

If employees approach the PAC apologetically or compellingly ("the corporation has decided this is something we should do"), it will not sell.

The presentation is, in our opinion, crucial in building a successful PAC. When we tell an employee that we have a good cause, we must be able to convince him that his effort will improve the political climate in which we do business. The presentation should be controlled by one who can effectively demonstrate his or her general political knowledge and create confidence. In convincing an employee of the program's importance, he must raise the comfort level so the employee parts willingly with his contribution and says, "Invest it in the system for me in a responsible way." Selling encyclopedias,

PAYROLL DEDUCTIONS
BY QUARTER 1976-1980

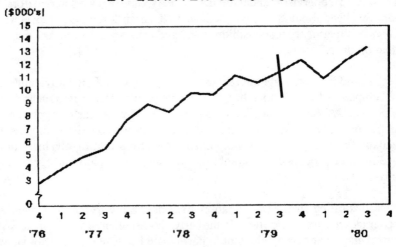

Diagram 1.

correspondence courses or political action committees has a common denominator. The "buyer" must be *comfortable* with the product and the worth of his investment.

We are reluctant to advertise or promote our "batting average." We do not want to promote a psychology where we are forced to support incumbents in order to maintain a good "win" record. Relating winners and contributions can lead to a loss in credibility. We do not think it is wise to encourage our contributors to believe that the only reason particular candidates won was our contribution. If we took this approach, our contributors might assume those who received our PAC dollars will do our bidding.

We do show how small contributions can make a difference. This is another incentive to be part of the process. If an employee can see how his contribution will *improve* the system, he is more eager to be involved. We point out how close some important congressional votes were and we note narrow margins in several congressional elections. In this way, we show that, if a few House or Senate seats had been different, significant legislation might have taken another direction.

Visual examples bring life to the presentation. When we show a campaign budget, the employees have a better grasp of the components that make up a political race and where PAC dollars are spent. After the 1980 elections, we plan to use actual campaign media in our presentation. This approach will enable us to graphically pin dollars to actual expenditures.

Annually, we hold three-day regional meetings for our supervisors and managers and their spouses. Although the main emphasis is operations management, we utilize this opportunity to communicate with the wives/husbands of management. One of our priorities is a full explanation of the PAC. We recap the PAC's activities and project the next year's undertakings. Our focus is an informative format centered around the PAC with a general discussion on current political affairs.

At this annual retreat are some new employees who have never been solicited; therefore, we include a solicitation. We give current contributors an opportunity to decrease or increase the last years' amounts. We have learned that, in some cases, initial contributions are token gestures. Our experience has proven that many of our employees grow more comfortable with the PAC over time. In our PAC, this upgrading process has often resulted in doubling and tripling initial contributions. In fact, a sizeable portion of the new dollars that flow into our PAC are generated from this source.

We supply our PAC members with a foundation for political awareness through educational opportunities. In various ways, we are successful in communicating how simple the political process is to our members. Published every six to eight weeks, our newsletter, with its short, newsy and sometimes humorous articles, transmits general information on political trends. Our newsletter has not only maintained reader interest, but has also increased it.

Our education program also includes tape cassettes on current political issues. These monthly tapes are produced by a conservative, bipartisan foundation. Corporate dollars make them available to our membership.

TIMING OF CANDIDATE CONTRIBUTIONS

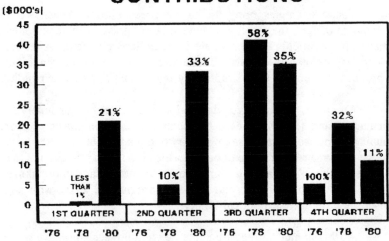

Diagram 2.

RESULTS OF 1978 ELECTION

Supported 64 Candidates $63,750

   63% of Candidates Won -- 73% of Funds $47,300

71% Were Non-Incumbents Receiving 73% of Funds

Republican Incumbents Supported ---- 22% COPE

Democratic Incumbents Supported --- 48%

Diagram 3.

Our PAC's contributions committee makes decisions regarding candidates and contributions. Originally, this body was composed of senior officers in the company. Through our efforts to expand its membership, today the committee is more representative of the entire list of contributors. We currently have more field employees than home office employees serving on the contributions committee. By shifting the emphasis of this membership, the PAC's credibility has increased.

We seek to place our contributions early in a campaign season (See Diagram 2.), so our research begins during the initial stages of a campaign. We have learned the importance of "early money," but we also know the power of incumbency. Unless an incumbent who has been a special friend is threatened in his election, we concentrate our money on "open seats" and challengers. (See Diagram 3.) If an incumbent's voting record and positions on selected issues are inconsistent with our philosophies, we develop early support for the challenger, if he meets our philosophical criteria and has serious potential for winning. In some cases, during the preliminary stages, we have found ourselves better organized informationally than the candidate we are supporting. After our research phase, we send contribution recommendations to our committee members who return, by mail, their agreements, disagreements or requests for additional comments. Unanimous consent is preferable, but the majority rules.

We have sought other uses for our corporate PAC dollars in campaigns. We hosted a luncheon in Washington for several candidates and invited other business PACs to expose the groups to each other. Since our PAC paid for the luncheon, this was reported as an in-kind contribution to the candidates. At other times, our PAC has paid for various expenses related to receptions for Senate candidates. These are ways that our PAC money has been used to generate other contributions for candidates and lever our interest in their election possibilities.

Locations of our units do not figure into our criteria for contributions. We have supported candidates in states and districts where we do not have units and the vice versa. We concentrate on supporting candidates who will make a pro-business change in Congress.

Although Pillsbury owns both Steak and Ale and Burger King, all three maintain independent political action committees. With the Federal Election Commission's limits on contributions, the three PACs are constantly in touch. But decisions are always made independently. Although uncommon, the PACs have at times supported opposing candidates.

Individual citizens and corporate leaders who assume responsibility can help determine the direction of our political system. When our corporation opted to support formation of a PAC, we believe we afforded our employees an opportunity to help make some of the decisions which affect them daily. Our growing PAC membership demonstrates a cooperation between the corporation and the employee to have a positive impact on how our government operates. **PAC**

Richard B. Berman is a vice-president for Steak and Ale Restaurants of America, Inc. of Dallas, Texas. His responsibilities encompass labor relations, government relations and legal affairs.

Prior to joining Steak and Ale in March of 1976, he was employed as labor counsel to the Chamber of Commerce of the United States.

He has also been employed as corporate attorney for the Dana Corporation, Toledo, Ohio and as a corporate labor attorney for the Bethlehem Steel Corporation in Bethlehem, Pennsylvania.

Berman currently serves as the United States business representative for Labor Ministers Conferences of the Organization of American States. He serves as a management co-chairman of an American Bar Association subcommittee, is a member of the Labor Relations Policy Committee of the National Chamber of Commerce, and has previously served as chairman of the Committee for Continuing Education for the labor law section of the Federal Bar Association.

DARTPAC: Successful Political Involvement

James Lindberg
Vice President, Dart Industries, Inc.

Since 1977, Dart's political action committee (DARTPAC) has become one of the largest corporate PACs in the country. DARTPAC has been included as one of the top ten PACs each year of its existence in categories such as receipts from contributors and contributions to candidates. For the 1980 elections, DARTPAC contributed over $245,000 to campaign committees and to candidates for federal office, experiencing a 72 percent success rate in the Senate and a 66 percent success rate in House races. These percentages are particularly significant since it has been the DARTPAC policy to give money early and to give mostly to challengers and open seats rather than only supporting incumbents.

GENESIS OF DART'S INVOLVEMENT

We consider 1974 a banner year in which businesses -- and Dart Industries in particular – began to recognize and understand the importance of becoming involved in the political process. Many business organizations such as the Business Roundtable, U.S. Chamber and NAM among others, began to generate convincing evidence indicating the need for their corporate members to take a more active role in the affairs of government. It had become a question of free market survival. Declining confidence in business from the public sector, the spiraling costs of government regulations and the government's encroachment over business and individuals were only a few of the many factors prompting businessmen to take the offensive in order to protect what was left of the private enterprise system.

Justin Dart, chief executive officer and chairman of Dart Industries, pioneered our involvement in the public affairs arena and he has been instrumental in its success ever since. Our political action committee is one of four programs that we commonly refer to as our "Total Package Concept." Our feeling is that DARTPAC is only as successful as the other three programs which include an Employee Economic Information program, Legislative Key Contact program and a Shareholder Communication program. Each program is designed to stand on its own but compliments the operation of the others and their ultimate success.

In 1977, it was obvious to us that no selling job could be persuasive enough to raise the amount of money we felt was necessary to run an effective PAC without appealing first to our employees' self-interest. Fortunately, our Employee Economic Information program, which was started as a test program in 1974, provided that tool. As a matter of fact, we feel the Employee Economic Information program, more than any other, has aided us in our fundraising efforts. We believe that any company with a PAC but without an Employee Economic Information program will raise far less funds than otherwise.

Justin Dart also played a premier role across the country encouraging other CEOs to follow Dart's example. In addition, he provided the initial funding to start the Center for the Study of Private Enterprise at the University of Southern California with the mission of institutionalizing and fine tuning company public affairs activities.

DARTPAC -- ITS OPERATION

As mentioned, Dart Industries established DARTPAC in July of 1977 in accordance with Federal Election Commission (FEC) regulations. DARTPAC officers were appointed by Justin Dart and given the responsibility to solicit voluntary contributions from legally allowable sources. The policy was established to support candidates to federal office who, regardless of political party affiliation, were fiscally responsible, were business-oriented and believed in preserving the private enterprise system.

DARTPAC has maintained by-laws even though the FEC does not require them. It is our belief that providing by-laws depicts our objectives and creates a greater credibility to our contributors.

DARTPAC's criteria for contributing to political campaigns is not always similar to other corporate PACs. DARTPAC officers do not give for access or for possible future favors from congressmen or senators. It is the DARTPAC philosophy that if the right people are elected, there will be no need to lobby.

It is a DARTPAC procedure that candidates are thoroughly screened to make certain they meet the criteria described. Personal interviews are included wherever possible. Their previous voting records (in the case of incumbents), stated philosophies, business backgrounds and electibility are all carefully considered factors. DARTPAC and its officers have maintained strict adherence to this philosophy and have seldom deviated from this policy. However, contributors may recommend candidates -- and many do -- but all must meet the strict criteria mentioned above. This year 20 percent of our contributions to candidates were based on recommendations from our constituents.

Some business PACs support incumbents who are important to their line of business or chair important committees regardless of their voting records. This parochial approach, in our estimation, is self-destructive in the long-run.

SOLICITATION PROCESS

DARTPAC is a management PAC with only management employees permissable under FEC regulations being solicited. This amounts to about 1,000 eligible employees of which approximately 22 percent participate in the program.

The process began in the summer of 1977 by sending an announcement, signed by Justin Dart, to all of these 1,000 executives and administrative personnel introducing DARTPAC and explaining the benefits to the country of making a contribution. Contributors understand why becoming involved in economic and political causes is in their best interest both as employees and as citizens of this great country.

In order to facilitate the fundraising process, general guidelines have been provided potential contributors. These guidelines are considered modest and do not go much below the $25,000 per year compensation level. At $25,000, it is suggested that a $100 contribution be made. There is a $100 tax credit on a joint return, so the net cost to the donor is only $50. The guidelines scale up gradually to $325 for $50,000 and 1 percent for those making $100,000 or more. It is required that those solicited be advised that they will neither be advantaged nor disadvantaged in any way by their decision to give or not to give or by the amount of their contribution. It is stressed that guidelines are merely suggestions. However, it is our experience that one-third of the participating employees meet the guidelines, that one-third gives above and that one-third gives less than suggested.

PAC COMMUNICATIONS

An essential ingredient to any successful fundraising activity is communication. Therefore, it is our policy to communicate on a regular basis with all potential eligible contributors and not just those who have contributed. We continually work towards widening our base. In so doing, we use a variety of communication vehicles. We publish a quarterly newsletter supplemented by periodic and needed legislative updates. In addition, a "Public Affairs Briefing" is published on special subjects pertinent to legislative and political events. Personal visits and group meetings with potential contributors also comprise an important part of our communication activities. To cap off communication, an annual DARTPAC report is provided all eligible employees to keep them intimately informed of where all their contributions were distributed. This is in addition to interim reports on this same subject.

When all is written about the 1980 election campaign, the important role corporate PACs played in the election process will be recognized. Hopefully this evidence will indicate the needs and benefits of greater business involvement. PACs provide an opportunity for business in general and individuals in particular to become more active in the political process. Our future welfare — corporate and personal — depends on helping to provide the kind of government that will keep economic and personal freedoms flourishing. Corporate PACs and all other special interest PACs are a vital part of the election process. **PAC**

James O. Lindberg serves as group vice president, public affairs at Dart Industries. He has served in the public affairs and management arena at Dart since August 1970.

Lindberg, a member of the board of directors for the Better Business Bureau, is chairman of the Western Region Public Affairs Task Force of the U.S. Chamber and serves on the board of directors of the Public Affairs Council. Presently he serves as deputy of the California Roundtable and vice president of the California Council on Economic Education. He is a member of the Public Information Committee of the Business Roundtable.

Lindberg retired as a Brigadier General from the U.S. Air Force in 1970. At that time he served as director of procurement policy at the Pentagon. Prior to that time, he held numerous positions in the logistics field. He retired after 29 years of military service.

Corporate PACs: No "Perfect" Formula

Michael Monroney
Vice President, TRW, Inc.

On the subject of corporate PACs, Congress and the Federal Election Commission have, in effect, set forth pretty much *what* companies can do. Neither, however, explained just exactly *how* to do it.

While FEC interpretations of the law sanctioning corporate PACs have permitted a number of ways in which companies can collect contributions voluntarily from certain employees, the "how-to-do-it" refers, in this case, to how the money should be dispersed.   In other words, which candidates to support.

It was entirely appropriate that neither Congress nor the Commission instruct corporate PACs on how to pick their favorite candidates, but the reaction to such a relatively novel decision-making process on the part of corporate America – accustomed to the much more precise science of business and insulated for far too long from the vagaries of the political world -- has bordered at times on schizophrenia.

The problem of "how to do it" has set off many a dispute within companies and between companies as industry has sought to perfect a formula for pumping its corporate PAC money into the political system.   And this search has led to a wide range of PAC policies.

62

Some companies have set rigid rules to govern their selection process, and they devote an inordinate amount of executive time applying these rules in analyses of one political contest after another before deciding where to put their money. Typically, such strict procedures involve support only for candidates with very high Chamber, NAM or ACA voting records (or for challengers against incumbents with very poor such ratings). At least one corporate PAC supports only challengers in races against incumbents who are considered anti-business.

Companies with these rigid PAC guidelines are usually confident they have found the "right way" which, if only the other PACs were smart enough to follow their lead, would result in a solid pro-business majority in Congress.

On the other hand, some PACs pay less attention to philosophical ratings and concentrate on candidates who hopefully, once elected, will remember the help and at least be more attentive to the company's views on certain issues. This approach is most often used by companies with a Washington-based lobbying team, and it frequently results in a defensive attitude on the part of the companies using it. They know they are not buying votes. As veteran Democratic fundraiser Bob Strauss has said, "If you can buy someone for $5,000, he isn't worth buying." But these companies are always worried that someone will think they are trying. (The corporate limit per election, incidentally, is $5,000.)

Now, the purpose of this article is not to condemn either method of selecting candidates – the rigid or the flexible. It is to suggest, however, that neither reflects the perfect formula. No one has found the "right way" to select candidates because there is not a "right way." There are too many "x" factors in our political system, too many variables, for any one candidate-selection process to be perfect.

Paradoxically, the widely divergent procedures used by corporate PACs in picking candidates for financial support may well have saved them from severe restriction by the 96th Congress. Even though this may no longer be true in the 97th Congress, it is worth further comment.

Those who oppose corporate PACs and fought the enabling legislation have charged -- and still do -- that business will use this political tool "to buy a right-wing Congress" or "to buy the Congress for the Republican Party." They will continue the attack, but it is sheer demagoguery. Business is not guilty of either charge.

Take a look at the facts. Of the roughly $350 million spent in 1980 by candidates for federal office, corporate PACs have contributed only about $20 million. And, of the $20 million, a significant portion was contributed to Democrats and moderate Republicans. This is not to say that the corporate PACs were not effective. But they could hardly be accused, for example, of insuring Republican control of the Senate. A more conservative American public, not corporate PAC money, was without question the key.

If there is a moral to this piece, it is not that PACs with strict procedures are "right" nor that those with flexible guidelines are "wrong." It is that collectively – divergent in approach though they may be – the political action committees of corporate America have probably hit just about the right balance. They have helped the cause of the private enterprise system without damaging the political system. Most significantly, the voice of the private business sector deserves to be heard in Washington as well as in the various state capitals. The PAC concept has thus far been utilized effectively and ethically toward this end. **PAC**

As vice president of government relations for TRW Inc., **Michael Monroney** directs the company's government relations program at both state and federal levels. In addition, he supervises TRW's Office of International Affairs which monitors both economic and political trends abroad and U.S. government actions pertinent to TRW's investments overseas.

Monroney is chairman of the Motor and Equipment Manufacturers Association's Governmental Affairs Committee, and secretary of the Alliance for Free Enterprise. He is a member of the Business-Government Relations Council and the Public Affairs Committee of the Machinery and Allied Products Institute.

Before joining TRW in April of 1973 as director of federal relations, Monroney served in Washington as a private government affairs consultant. From 1967 through 1970 he was special assistant and director of congressional relations for the president of Communications Satellite Corporation.

LTV PAC: Part of a Total Political Focus

Julian Scheer
Vice President, The LTV Corporation

Corporate political activity has become synonymous with the political action committee, and, subsequently, the political action committee has become synonymous with a single issue: pro-business. Few would deny that what is good for business is good for America (a familiar ring?), but, at the same time, there is some concern today with the rise of single-issue special interest groups at a time when we see a weakening of our two-party system.

Business must continue to become more and more involved in the political life of the nation and PACs should continue to be a major part of that activity. But the contribution/distribution effort exemplified by the PAC should be but a part of a corporation's total political sensitivity.

At The LTV Corporation we are pleased with employee participation in six political action committees and the positive effect we feel they have had in the support of a broad spectrum of political philosophy through candidate support. But more than that, we consider the political action committee only one part of our political focus.

Here is a brief case study of what we did in the 1980 political year, over and above the PAC contribution/distribution area:

Late in 1979 it took no crystal ball to foresee that 1980 would be "The Year of Politics": 30-odd primaries, two conventions, several (we thought) debates and a general election. We decided that the dialogue (particularly early on when the field of candidates would be large) would not touch on some subjects of interest to our employees, shareholders and the business community in general.

We designed a corporate mini-ad campaign for the *Wall Street Journal* in which we asked the candidates – remember when there was Dole, Bush, Baker, Kennedy, Connally and company? -- to give their views on business-related issues. We offered to send readers a book with a compilation of the answers and received more than 17,000 requests.

While we posted the ads in our offices and plants, the book was the kick-off to our employees' political education and awareness effort. All 80,000 employees received a copy of the book.

That was followed by a public television series, "Ben Wattenberg's 1980," an issues-oriented series which we helped underwrite. Our grant was not large, and we actually looked at it on a cost-per-employee basis. Had we produced and mailed a brochure, for instance, the cost would have been higher and the presentation far less vivid.

This effort was followed by a publication entitled "How to Pick a Candidate," produced by the League of Women Voters. We imprinted the booklet at a cost of only pennies per copy.

The League does such a good job in many areas that, as a side effort, we funded (again at incredibly low cost) a college campus registration and get-out-the-vote campaign designed and distributed by the League.

Additional materials developed during the period included a congressional handbook for PAC contributors, PAC newsletters for employees, a political calendar and an in-plant poster program.

We invited candidates to our facilities to meet and talk with employees. Our facilities became stopping-off places for both President Carter and President-elect Reagan as well as congressional and local candidates. As we reached the end of the campaign, Paul Thayer, chairman and chief executive officer, visited a number of our facilities and led get-out-the-vote rallies with employees.

Some of these efforts may be unique (such as an ad campaign), but the general thrust of coupling PAC activities with total awareness is workable and logical in many variations: One thing was clear to our employees: Management respected their judgment and felt involvement in the political process was of the utmost importance. **PAC**

Julian Scheer, senior vice president, corporate affairs for The LTV Corporation, divides his time between Washington and corporate headquarters in Dallas. He is also a director of Eastern Air Lines. The author of five books, Scheer is a former newspaper reporter, and was in charge of public affairs for the NASA space program from 1962 to 1971. He was a partner in the Washington communications consulting firm of Sullivan, Murray and Scheer prior to joining LTV.

The MAPCO PAC Experience

Paul E. Thornbrugh
Chairman, MAPCO PAC, MAPCO Inc.

Having been denied the right to participate in the political arena and in the process of electing public officials to all levels of government for more than 30 years (25 years behind organized labor), the business community finally got its chance with the passage of the 1974-1975 Federal Campaign Act. The act and subsequent amendments permitted corporations to form political action committees, bi-partisan in nature, permitting them to solicit employees, stockholders and their families for contributions, and in turn, to channel funds to candidates seeking election to federal office, specifically, the United States Congress.

MAPCO Inc., an energy company, was one of the early business corporations to form a PAC – called the MAPCO PAC. With strong CEO and top management support, the PAC was formed in 1975 and became a multi-candidate committee in 1976. The PAC has a five-member PAC Committee. The PAC's stated objective is to identify, select and support candidates on a bi-partisan basis whose stated philosophy or proven record demonstrates their commitment to the free enterprise system, sound energy policies, fiscal sanity and less government restraints.

Robert E. Thomas, chairman of the board of MAPCO Inc., put it in its proper perspective from the beginning when he said that too many Americans and American businesses, while highly-concerned over our personal freedom and preservation of the American free enterprise system, have done little more than wring their hands and complain, thinking it hopeless. It was not hopeless, he said. Something can be done -- and MAPCO was doing just that in the formation of the MAPCO Political Action Committee, providing our employees, stockholders and their families with the opportunity to participate in the financial support of the PAC. It, in turn, would channel funds to candidates who support the concepts of good government.

The MAPCO PAC, from its inception, has solicited all stockholders and all employees, exempt and non-exempt. It is the only business corporation PAC in the nation to do so. Stockholders have contributed approximately 45 percent to the total PAC income. In 1978 the MAPCO PAC contributed approximately $50,000 to 81 candidates for the Senate and House, including a substantial number of open seats and challengers to anti-business incumbents. The MAPCO PAC has had a win record of 64 percent.

In 1980, $53,000 was contributed to 112 candidates with an impressive 71 percent win rate and a record of having contributed to all but one of the new members elected to the United States Senate.

Candidate evaluation is of extreme importance to the MAPCO PAC. It determines where the PAC dollars -- contributors' investments -- go. MAPCO uses four major criteria in determining candidates who will receive MAPCO PAC money. After all, when a PAC gives money to an incumbent or an unknown challenger, it is endorsing his or her political philosophy.

First, the candidate has to show he or she would support a free market solution to our energy problems. Second, the candidate has to show he or she would be fiscally responsible with tax revenue. Third, the strength of the candidate's campaign organization and his or her need for money must be evident. Finally, his or her electibility must be established.

Following these criteria, the PAC prioritizes its candidates who will receive financial contributions, identifying:

1. Pro-business incumbents who need protection against anti-business challengers.
2. Pro-business challengers to anti-business incumbents.
3. Open seats.

Candidate evaluations take time and research, but they pay great dividends. Information used by the MAPCO PAC includes:

Step I: For Incumbents

A) *Almanac of American Politics* -- gives group ratings, key issues and voting records.

B) *Congressional Directory* -- free from your congressman or senator -- gives committee assignment -- seniority.

C) Developing key issues:

- Affecting the economy and free marketplace;
- Regulatory concerns and regulations imposed on business;
- Special matters affecting company operations in key constituency areas.

D) Key issues affecting business and candidates' votes on these issues -- a voting record from organizations who follow congressional matters like the U.S. Chamber of Commerce, NAM, National Association of Business, API, Public Affairs Council and others.

E) *Congressional Quarterly* -- gives continuing reports on votes on the key issues before Congress and explanations of what the measures voted upon mean.

F) In developing the key issues, an important process to follow is

- Determine the "key players" involved in those issues, and
- Determine the key people who can influence these players.

71

Step II: For Challengers

A) Candidate campaign material, brochures, literature and campaign position statements.

B) Newspaper items, news poll reports, personal letters to and from the candidates, or information available from such organizations as NABPAC, etc., or from the Republican and Democratic national committees.

Step III: Setting Up Candidate File

A) Set up permanent file for every candidate from whom requests for financial support is received. The file becomes a complete history of the candidate which includes:

- All correspondence to and from the candidate, campaign material and letter soliciting funds.

- Biographical material -- photo of candidate.

- Campaign organization and staff of candidate.

- Budget and breakdown of campaign expenditures.

- Group ratings -- voting records on key issues or campaign issues and positions.

- Name and address of campaign and finance chairman, name of committee as registered with FEC.

- News items, polls.

- Correspondence transmitting PAC contribution, receipt acknowledgement by candidate or his committee.

- Identifying plant and facility locations by candidate's congressional district.

Step IV: Preparing Report for Review and Distribution of Funds

A) Priority races:

- Pro-business incumbents needing protection;
- Pro-business challengers to anti-business incumbents;
- Open seats.

B) Candidate evaluations on issues.

C) Candidate chances of winning and need of money, where it could make the difference.

D) Suggested amount of contributions ($500-750, House; $1,000-1,500, Senate).

Step V: Transmitting Contribution to Candidate

A) Correct name and address of committee as registered with FEC.

B) Letter setting out basis of contribution.

C) Information about PAC or company.

D) Ask to be kept informed as race and issues develop.

Step VI: Keeping Employees and Stockholders Informed

A) Annual report.

B) Citizenship involvement programs.

C) Bring members of Congress in to visit employees — a continuing part of the program and objectives of the MAPCO PAC to bring government and some congressional insight to MAPCO employees.

What of the future impact of business political action committees? What is their potential? It is, in a word, *unlimited*. As business PACs like MAPCO approach the level of sophistication already reached by labor PACs, they will become even more effective. As the administrators of business PACs become more familiar with our political system, their understanding of it will increase and fewer mistakes will be made, particularly in the area of candidate support. Many of us, myself included, have found ourselves contributing to candidates of whom, in retrospect, we were not very proud. You will, I predict, see less and less of that. To describe it in a phrase we all understand, business PACs are becoming hard-nosed in their selection of candidates to support.

The candidates who will receive support in the future will be those worthy of it. The elections of 1980 show clearly that corporate business PACs like MAPCO have come of age as a viable force in the political process.

PAC

Paul E. Thornbrugh is presently manager of tax and government affairs as well as corporate coordinator of government relations for MAPCO, Inc. in Tulsa, Oklahoma.

Thornbrugh serves as chapter president and member of the board of directors of the National Association of Business Political Action Committee (NABPAC). He is also chairman of MAPCO's political action committee (MAPCO PAC). He serves on two important boards of directors: Oklahomans for Energy and Jobs, Inc. and Oklahoma State Chamber of Commerce.

Thornbrugh is the former chairman of the Tulsa County Republican Committee, a delegate to the National Republican Conventions in 1972 and 1976, and a presidential elector for the Republican Party in 1980.

Loctite Corporation: The Making of a PAC

D. Craig Yesse
Director of Government Affairs, Loctite Corporation

Loctite Corporation has a successful record as a growth company. As a small company, we pioneered a new technology. We created jobs. The world needs jobs, and we have added them at a compound rate of 30 percent per year over the last twenty years. We went abroad with enthusiasm. Then, in 1978, we began to take note of and investigate the reasons for the sharp decline of the United States in the highly competitive global economy during the last two decades.

THE PROBLEM

We found that our free enterprise system and the basic scale of values that served this land so well for three centuries, even liberty itself, were under assault by a vicious ideology that allows big government to feed and to fatten on its productive citizens under the guise of compassion for the unproductive. We found ourselves in the middle of a war of ideas, which pits the advocates of cradle-to-grave centralized planning by big government against those who believe in individual freedoms and responsibilities.

Literally thousands of rules, regulations and laws were being issued every year at all levels of government mandating what you can and cannot do, usurping individual authority and responsibility to plan and run our own lives and infringing more and more each day on the managerial authority to run our own business.

Government, once our servant, had become our master. An army of bureaucrats, not elected by or responsive to the people, controlled more and more of our daily lives at our expense.

At issue was the survival of the free market system, and, with it, the survival not only of the managerial authority to run your own business, but of your individual freedom to run your own life. It was that specter that pushed us into developing our political action committee. In our own small way, we decided to do whatever we could to turn the situation around and return to those values and principles that brought the U.S. from a backwoods colony to the leader of the free world in the brief span of 180 years.

ESTABLISHING A PAC *at Loctite*

A planning task force was established to investigate the feasibility of beginning a political action committee. This group, the Public Affairs Steering Committee, gathered data regarding the laws and regulations on PACs and addressed the question of membership: Should it be open to all employees, or only to management? At the time, many self-appointed "public interest" groups were clamoring for public financing of election campaigns. We believed public financing amounted to an unwarranted tax on all citizens. People interested in the political process demonstrated that interest by working for candidates or a political party, or by contributing to campaigns. We felt that disinterested people should not be forced to participate by having their tax dollars finance election activities. Therefore, the decision was made to open PAC membership to all levels of employees, since all were affected by the economic consequences of political decisions and should have a voice in the process.

We spent a good deal of time learning about political action committees, how they were formed, what they could do and what we could expect from a PAC. We came to realize that although on the surface a PAC is simply a vehicle for assembling campaign contribution dollars, in reality a PAC can be much, much more. It can serve as a rallying point around which politically

76

active employees and shareholders can gather. They could interview candidates for office, assessing their positions on issues relating to the free enterprise system, and, in fact, determining which candidates should be endorsed and supported financially.

WHO DECIDES?

One of the most difficult questions we wrestled with was that of who should decide which candidates warrant financial support from the PAC. It appeared from our research that the vast majority of corporate political action committees reserved that decision for an executive committee, usually appointed by the senior management of the corporation. We decided to run our PAC somewhat differently.

We started from the point that a PAC is more than simply an extension of corporate campaign clout; it is a tool for political education. In fact, by combining it with a participative economic education program, a broad-based communications program illustrating the perils facing our free market system and our personal freedoms, we became more and more confident that employees, more often than not, would select the same candidates that top management would, based on the candidates' positions on the issues.

So we established our PAC in a way that the membership determines which candidates are to be supported in a democratic manner. Treating the decision-making process in this manner generates trust, commitment and greater allegiance to the company, because it shows employees they have much in common with the company.

THE INITIAL SOLICITATION

Prior to our first PAC solicitation, we asked ourselves who our major constituencies are. Which groups do we have the most in common with and which are most likely to take active roles in the political process? Our first major constituency, of course, is our employees. We solicited all levels of employees in our Connecticut location, totalling some 450 people, from hourly wage-earners to top management, and listed 94 employee members, just over

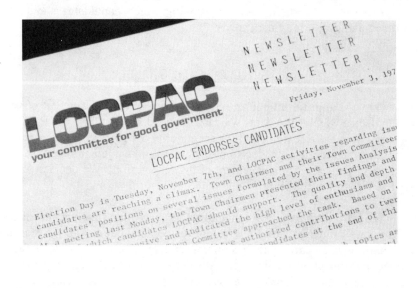

NEWSLETTER
NEWSLETTER
NEWSLETTER

Friday, November 3, 197

LOCPAC ENDORSES CANDIDATES

Election Day is Tuesday, November 7th, and LOCPAC activities regarding issu
candidates are reaching a climax. Town Chairmen and their Town Committees
candidates' positions on several issues formulated by the Issues Analysis
At a meeting last Monday, the Town Chairmen presented their findings and
which candidates LOCPAC should support. The quality and depth
gressive and indicated the high level of enthusiasm and
Committee approached the task. Based on
authorized contributions to twen
candidates at the end of thi
topics a

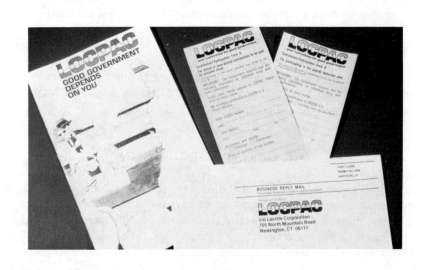

20 percent. The average employee contribution was $92, and we were surprised at the fairly high participation rates of the hourly wage-earners and lower level administrative personnel. It appeared we had hit on something.

Our next major constituency was our shareholder group. We decided to solicit only our individual shareholders and excluded our institutional shareholders. The response to our initial solicitation of shareholders was, to say the least, a little discouraging. Out of a group of slightly over 3,000 shareholders, our initial returns amounted to only 45 members with an average contribution of $22. So it was back to the drawing boards to try and determine how we could create more interest in our political action committee and in the political process in general.

THE RESTRUCTURING OF LOCPAC

We restructured our PAC. We got more people involved. We set up an *Issues Analysis Committee*, responsible for developing and investigating issues that affect our company, our employees, our stockholders, our customers and the free enterprise system in general. Of course, the members of LOCPAC determined our PAC's position on the issues thus generated.

We developed a *Candidate Profile Committee*, with the responsibility for assessing the voting records of candidates and their positions on issues generated by the Issue Analysis Committee. Candidate questionnaires were developed to pinpoint accurately the candidates' positions.

We set up *town committees* for each of the towns in which our employees resided. Members of these town committees held "Get To Know Your Candidates" cocktail parties and backyard barbecues, where they and their neighbors got a chance to meet the candidates, and, more importantly, the candidates had the opportunity to listen to their constituents. Each town committee was responsible for recommending to the LOCPAC general membership which candidate should be endorsed and why, usually citing the candidate's percentage of favorable responses on the issues that matched LOCPAC positions.

79

This increased employee involvement seemed to work well. During the 1978 elections for Connecticut's General Assembly, the town committees recommended and the PAC membership approved 26 candidates for endorsement and financial support. Those employees who interviewed the candidates personally delivered the campaign contributions. Thus the candidate saw the employee representing LOCPAC at least twice. Of the 26 candidates, 17 won their respective races and the face-to-face recognition and the numerous references to LOCPAC have enabled those employees to continue to serve as conduits of information to those 17 representatives.

All this activity was accomplished on the employee's own time and the total of the 1978 campaign contributions was a modest $4,500, demonstrating that a PAC truly can be a political force far in excess of the funds it disburses simply be getting people involved in the process.

We also established a *Political Education Committee* responsible for specific mailings and conducting meetings of the LOCPAC membership to update them on issues and to hear invited guest speakers discuss various political topics. This group also had responsibility for our non-partisan *Voter Alert* program in which all employees were involved.

A final committee set up was our *Newsletter Committee*, which was responsible for maintaining high interest levels by keeping communications going on a timely basis. In addition to keeping the PAC membership informed, the newsletter became an ideal vehicle for recognizing employee participation in the political process.

NO STEAK WITHOUT THE SIZZLE

Every good advertising man knows that you cannot sell a steak without the sizzle. We learned that you don't just form a political action committee, send around a note on company letterhead announcing its creation, and expect big things to happen. You must *merchandise* the PAC.

We developed a little booklet entitled "LOCPAC – Good Government Depends on You," which explains the details of membership and the general objective of our PAC. This was mailed to all employees and shareholders as part of our second solicitation. It is also given to all new employees on their first day of employment.

SUPPORTING THE PAC

In addition to beefing up our PAC activities, we also established a *Shareholder Activist Network*. We mailed to all shareholders a prepaid postcard asking if they would be interested in becoming active in letter writing and personal contact activities with state and federal elected officials. We received slightly under 2,000 responses. Of that group, nearly 500 volunteered to become activists and another 1,000 wanted us to continue sending them information but did not wish to be actively involved at that time.

We then began mailing *issue summaries* to those 1,500 or so shareholders outlining issues of importance to the free enterprise system. Then, as a particular legislative item began to surface, either in committee or on the floor, we sent out action alerts advising the activist group whom to contact and why. This simple procedure unleashed thousands of letters, phone calls and personal visits to elected representatives. It is effective because it represents true grassroots involvement. It is the senators' or congressmen's constituents who are speaking, not some paid lobbyist.

Following those two actions (the beefing up of our PAC and establishing our Shareholder Activist Network) we went back for our second solicitation. The results were reversed this time. While our employee PAC membership did not jump significantly, shareholder membership more than doubled, and the average contribution increased to nearly $65. All of this took place over the twelve-month period beginning June 1978. Since then, we have added three more facets to our public affairs activities which complement and reinforce the goals we hope to accomplish with our political action committee.

CORPORATE PHILANTHROPY AND THE WAR OF IDEAS

Corporate philanthropy can be a big weapon in the battle for men's minds. There are many institutions that serve to shore up the foundations of our freedom, including our economic freedoms.

These institutions have articulate, well-trained staffs which could be rapidly expanded, and this is one case we have found where money, by itself, can be effective. The amount of money that corporations can give to such institutions is limited only by the IRS rule that puts a ceiling on deductible contributions of five percent of domestic income before tax. However, the Conference Board says that corporations average only 12 or 15 percent of that amount, so the ceiling has no practical significance.

According to the Institute for Educational Affairs in New York City, total corporate philanthropy is running around $1.5 billion per year. By increasing corporate contributions only one-half of one percent of domestic pre-tax income, business can deliver an extra billion dollars a year for our side of the battle. In fact, if all business met the 2 percent of domestic income before taxes target of the Filer Commission Report on Corporate Philanthropy, we would have an extra $2 billion a year for this purpose. At Loctite, we currently dedicate two-thirds of our corporate contributions budget, or about $350,000 a year, to support those institutions which favorably influence public opinion on behalf of freedom and free enterprise.

CORPORATE ADVERTISING

The corporate advertising budget is another powerful resource at business's disposal. It represents part of the problem and part of the solution. The top 600 ad agencies place over $22 billion worth of billings each year. With that much pure economic power at hand, it appears that American business must insist that, in the process of selecting advertising media, attention is given to the editorial policy of the media used as an advertising vehicle as well as simply to cost-effectiveness in moving a product.

Ask yourself, where the media which belittles our way of life and undermines our personal and economic freedoms gets its operating funds. To be sure, a few operate on their sales income, but the vast majority rely on business advertising dollars to live from issue to issue or from one week to the next. Without those advertising dollars, quite simply, they are out of business. Thus, we find the business community feeding the very mouths that bite us. We not only pay for the executioners ax, but we supply his salary and pension as well!

A hard-hitting no-holds-barred weekly confrontation in which leading figures debate business and economic issues

The sparks fly as some of the most provocative arguments you're likely to find fill the TV screen on "It's Your Business." Produced by the Chamber of Commerce of the United States, the program pits leaders from business, labor, government, and the professions against one another. They argue their differing viewpoints on the day's biggest business, economic, political issues. Result: the kind of hard-hitting and informative half-hour that attracts audiences to the TV screen . . . and builds awareness of the Loctite products carried in your area.

Check your TV listings for the day and time that "It's Your Business" is on locally. It's worth looking into!

it's your business

Loctite Presents "It's Your Business" on Nationwide Television

A prime consideration in our advertising program is to maintain a careful balance between moving products and supporting those institutions and media which promote the benefits of our free enterprise system.

EMPLOYEE INFORMATION PROGRAM

The fifth plank in our platform of public affairs activities is our employee information program. This is a program where economic education is interwoven throughout. It is a broad-based communications program which illustrates the perils facing our free market system and our personal freedoms.

Topics are normally free enterprise-oriented and include business, economics, government, consumerism, defense and world issues. Media used varies from pamphlets and books to films, videocassettes and guest speakers. The key to such programs is to take an issue which is international or national in scope and focus on its impact and meaning to the individual employee, whether its ramifications are felt in the pocketbook through higher taxes or more inflation, or felt in the mind and heart as a social issue. Employees are people, and people have a natural thirst for information. An employee information program fills that need and provides additional benefits.

We really *are* in a war of ideas. The fundamental problem is the erosion of the traditional values on which rested the broad acceptance of capitalism. We found that an economic education program could be the starting point in helping to win this war of ideas.

Benefits are two-fold. First, by providing a better understanding of the free enterprise system and its relationship to personal freedoms, you obtain a group of employees with higher morale, greater productivity and a sounder base for making economic decisions, even those "economic decisions" as to which candidate the PAC should support. Second, employees discover quickly that they have many more interests in common with the company than not. You can effectively compete with union leaders for the allegiance of your employees!

LEADERSHIP: WHY PACS ARE NECESSARY

At issue in the war of ideas is survival. The issue is survival of our free market system as well as our managerial authority to run our own businesses. But it also includes the authority of the individual to run his or her own life. That is why PACs are necessary. That is why a shareholder activist network is necessary. That is why business management, employees and shareholders need to get involved more and more in the political process. So often we hear disparaging talk about the lack of leadership in government, and we may very well agree with that. But the fact remains that it is up to us to fill that vacuum of leadership.

Let's show the public some leadership from the business community. We have the talent. We have the know-how. We have the incentive. Let's fill the leadership vacuum and show the public that business is not the problem; business is the solution. As the true custodians of benefits to the average citizen, business not only has the right but the responsibility to be politically involved. The danger to the business community by not becoming active is that management's task will soon become nothing more than that of a "compliance supervisor" receiving instructions from Washington.

That is why we at Loctite took these five simple steps: 1) a political action committee, 2) a shareholder activist network, 3) selective placement of corporate contributions, 4) balanced use of corporate advertising dollars, and 5) an employee information program.

Is it working? Only time will tell. However, in addition to those successful candidates LOCPAC supported in the 1978 elections for Connecticut's General Assembly, there are now 23 more state legislators who believe in and support the principles of freedom and free enterprise. In the 1980 elections LOCPAC endorsed and supported 34 candidates, many of them challengers, with the result that seven state senators and 16 representatives espousing traditional values were elected. They won, in large part, because an active, informed group of employees, coupled with modest financial contributions, took the time and the effort to become involved in the political process.

As a company looking to become involved in public affairs and the political process, we decided we could best aid our side of the battle by bringing to bear the same talents and resources to the political problems facing our nation as we would traditionally bring to solve a sagging earnings picture or an unprofitable plant situation. To my way of thinking, this is corporate social responsibility in its broadest sense. And if all American businesses do not get involved soon, we will certainly never see the renaissance of the American economy. **PAC**

D. Craig Yesse is director of government affairs at Loctite Corporation in Newington, Conn. A graduate of Eastern Connecticut State College, Yesse's responsibilities include analysis of proposed legislation and regulations, management of external economic education programs and directing Loctite's public affairs program.

He is a member of the International Management and Development Institute and the Smithsonian Institute, and president of the Conservative Media Group. Yesse serves on the boards of several conservative political organizations.

Rexnord's PAC

Marion A. Youngers
Director of Taxes, Rexnord Inc.

The concept of political action committees is not really a new idea from the 1970s; they have been around for a good number of years before that, although they were used mainly by organized labor. The business community, for a variety of reasons, seemed not to be interested. For example, as early as the 1950s, labor PACs contributed many millions of dollars to friendly candidates in election after election. At that time, certainly no one had heard of a business PAC or a trade association PAC.

The current status of PACs is, of course, a result of events in the 1970s, starting with the 1971 Federal Election Commission legislation, and it is a very interesting story. It is necessary to review this historical background to understand how we got to where we are today. It is more important, however, that we understand these events to evaluate what we think the future role of PACs should be in the political process and how to prevent scandals and abuses of major proportions which may already be ticking like a time bomb.

HISTORICAL BACKGROUND

The 1971 legislation was the result of an earlier Justice Department indictment of some low-level union officials for allegedly violating federal election laws. They were accused of coercion in collecting contributions from union members. (Even then, PAC contributions were required to be voluntary.) They were later convicted, and the Supreme Court in 1971 agreed to review the case. The union at this point, became concerned that PACs might be outlawed entirely. To reinforce their position, the labor lobby approached Rep. Orval Hansen of Idaho, who agreed to introduce an amendment to the election bill then pending on the House floor. The amendment was introduced with very little attention paid to it by anyone except organized labor. Consequently, there was little debate. There was no input from the corporate community, presumably because of lack of interest. The Hansen amendment passed, entirely the result of organized labor's input, and laid the foundation for what we see today -- a groundswell of activity in corporate political action committees. The Hansen amendment provided:

- The right to provide members with information on candidates and issues,

- The right to conduct nonpartisan registration campaigns,

- The right to sponsor get-out-the-vote drives,

- The right to solicit voluntary contributions from their members, through PACs which did not have to be independent from the union's leadership.

Since the Hansen amendment needed some support of moderate legislators to assure its passage, all of the above rights were extended to corporations as well as to organized labor. The union lobbyists were not much concerned about this at the time. They did not feel that companies would take advantage of these provisions since they had always shown such little interest.

Labor was right! There was little activity in companies' board rooms to take advantage of these changes. Of course, there was still some uncertainty as to the extent of permitted corporate political activity.

The next relevant piece of legislation was the 1974 amendments, thanks again to the influence of organized labor. This time, Congress felt a need to reform the election laws as a result of the Watergate abuses and scandals of illegal corporate contributions. The primary objective of Congress was the elimination of the role of the "fat cats," by imposing a limitation on individual contributions to $1,000 per candidate and $25,000 overall. But PACs came out better with a limitation of $5,000 per candidate per election cycle and with no aggregate limitation at all.

The most important admendment for the business community, however, was the change allowing government contractors to establish PACs. Prior to 1974, government contractors were not allowed to make political expenditures. Thus, there had been some concern that government contractors may also have been prohibited from sponsoring PACs. This uncertainty was a considerable restraint to business when one considers the large percentage of corporations doing business with the government. Although labor lobbied for this amendment, it has been obviously more beneficial to corporations than to organized labor.

But it was not until late 1975 that corporations realized the potential of these new laws. The event kindling the interest of the business community was the FEC decision in the now-famous SUNPAC case. The FEC ruling in that case was the final event ushering in the new era of the corporate political action committee. To briefly review this decision, Sun Oil Company requested the FEC to rule that:

- Corporate funds could be used to organize and to pay administration costs of a company-sponsored PAC,

- A company PAC could solicit employees as well as shareholders (the 1971 legislation was unclear as to whether it was limited to solicitation of shareholders only), and

- Employee contributions could be made through a payroll deduction plan to either a PAC or directly to candidates.

The FEC voted 4 to 2 in the affirmative on all three of the above issues.

This was the impetus needed by business. The Rexnord PAC was started almost immediately thereafter, making us one of the early entrants. According to FEC records, about 150 corporate PACs were started in the six month period following SUNPAC -- more than doubling the number of PACs in existence up to this time. This has since mushroomed to somewhere in excess of 1,100. The labor unions? Less than 300, little changed from where they were when it all started.

WHY REXNORD WANTED A PAC

Shortly after the SUNPAC decision, Rexnord management agreed to organize the Rexnord PAC. It was a relatively simple process, and we were in business by February of 1976. The establishment of the Rexnord PAC was a natural extension of the Rexnord public affairs efforts. During 1975, Rexnord had launched a very extensive public affairs program. The public affairs program is open to all employees. It established, among other objectives, two important goals:

First, the company implemented an educational program whereby employees of the company become more aware of the effects which the growth of government at all levels and the numerous federal and state regulatory agencies have had upon each of our lives and the extent to which this growth and regulation has impared the ability of our free economic system to function effectively and efficiently.

A second goal of the public affairs program is to aid employees of the company to express themselves more effectively and to be heard and be represented in the various political processes of our country. As an outgrowth of this second goal, it was decided that the establishment of a political action committee would afford an easy opportunity for our employees to participate, in an economic sense, in achieving these objectives. Accordingly, the Rexnord Political Action Committee was established, and in its Articles of Organization, set forth its purpose as follows:

"The exclusive purpose of the PAC is to influence the nomination or election of qualified candidates to public offices. Particular emphasis will be given to candidates who have demonstrated that they are favorably disposed towards the private free enterprise system."

One of our major concerns from the outset was to assume that employee contributions would be completely voluntary and there would absolutely never be any coercion or even hint of any arm twisting. We felt that it was absolutely essential that no supervisor would solicit a subordinate. In this connection the SUNPAC decision made it very clear, in allowing Sun to solicit employees, that there should not be any coercion or semblance of coercion. Although it did not prohibit solicitation of a subordinate by a supervisory employee, it definitely frowned on this practice. It set forth some very strong cautions on the inherent dangers of such a course of conduct.

In addition to prohibiting such solicitation, we made it very clear that PAC records relating to employees would be kept strictly confidential. In this regard, our PAC brochure states:

> "By law, the treasurer of the PAC must keep detailed records of the individuals who make contributions and the amounts. Periodic reports of these contributions must be filed with the Federal Election Commission and the various states where the PAC is qualified. Committee records may also be made available to an outside auditor. *The records will not be disclosed for any other reason.* However, reports are filed with the Federal Election Commission and are available for purchase from the Federal Election Commission, Washington, D.C."

As a result this very firm policy on solicitation and confidentiality of employee information instituted from the very beginning, we have never had a problem at Rexnord in assuring that the program is completely voluntary. The PAC contributions committee, comprised of top corporate officers, has never requested, nor would it receive, any information on an individual contribution. No supervisor has ever requested, nor would he or she ever receive, any information on any individual, subordinate or otherwise. Of course, the FEC itself makes this information accessible since the reports required to be filed with the FEC are available for purchase from the FEC. To my knowledge, no employee has ever requested copies of our reports from the FEC.

It should be mentioned that the Rexnord PAC is a low-keyed operation. This is in accordance with our original intentions. Our primary objective is not to raise huge sums of money to dole out to political candidates. Naturally, we would not object to receiving more contributions. However, our primary objective is involvement and participation in the political processes, not raising funds. We think that if an employee gets involved in an economic sense, he or she will be more active and more interested. That might mean that an employee makes contributions directly to a candidate's campaign rather than through the PAC. He is also encouraged to do that. The PAC is made available as *another* method for involvement. This idea is communicated to employees in our question and answer fact sheet where the question is presented: Why should an employee contribute to the PAC as opposed to making a direct contribution? We give the following answer:

> "It may be desirable to do both.
>
> "The PAC has the ability to evaluate candidates for elective offices in the states in which Rexnord operates. This will identify where the money can get the best results. In addition, by combining employee contributions, the money will have a greater impact.
>
> "However, for personal reasons, an employee may feel strongly about making a contribution to a particular candidate. Employees are encouraged to make contributions directly if they wish.
>
> "The important thing is that employees should participate. The PAC offers an alternative not available before."

In keeping with our principal objective of involvement, we encourage the payroll deduction method as an easy way to participate. Since we only solicit employees in the FEC defined group (professional, supervisory and management employees) one might think that huge sums of money would be raised by encouraging a monthly payroll deduction. As a fundraising endeavor, however, the PAC would be considered a failure. The typical payroll deduction is about $5 per month. The number of contributors has never exceeded 25 percent of those solicited and that is during peak periods of election year interest. We solicit once a year primarily to remind employees of the PAC's availability and to make new employees aware of its existence.

Because we encourage payroll withholding, we also cooperate with the various unions which represent Rexnord employees in helping them use the payroll withholding system. While the FEC allows the company to make a charge for providing this service, it seems prudent not to do so. After all, the union lobbying efforts made the whole thing possible so it is the least we can do to show our gratitude. Seriously, the cost is minimal. And, more importantly, if our goal is involvement, we should not restrict our encouragement only to employees that we perceive to be in agreement with our particular political philosophy. Again, such information is treated confidentially within the company. Of course, the information must be furnished to union treasurers so that they can file the necessary reports with the FEC. It is interesting that the payroll withholding system is used very little by union employees.

HOW TO INCREASE EMPLOYEE INVOLVEMENT

One of the things we are doing to increase employee involvement is to "divisionalize" the PAC. What this means is that we transfer the responsibility for solicitation and collection of funds to the local operating level. They also then have their own contributions committee to decide who should get those funds. We have found that this increases employee involvement where we have tried it. Also, local employees probably are more knowledgable about local candidates than we would be at corporate headquarters.

We attempt to favor contributions to candidates in areas in which Rexnord has plant locations. When this is done from corporate headquarters, we must rely heavily on wishes and requests from divisional employees. They are sometimes reluctant to make their wishes known, and localizing PAC operations overcomes this problem. We still only have one PAC, of course, inasmuch as there is no advantage in having more than one. (The FEC requires all PACs of an affiliated group of companies to essentially be treated as though they were one PAC.)

Since the divisions' activities are part of the Rexnord PAC, they must furnish us the information necessary to file the FEC reports. This has the advantage of eliminating burdensome compliance requirements at the operating level where they have more important things to do. We also clear their proposed disbursements with the corporate contributions committee to avoid FEC violations and inconsistencies in candidate support which might otherwise arise between divisions.

There are at least two potential problems with this arrangement. The first is that divisions invariably want to contribute to state and local candidates. This means that we have to register with the particular state involved and file additional reports. It is conceivable that in complying with state election laws that conflict can arise between differing state requirements.

The second problem can be potentially more serious – that solicitation is not coercive, that participation is voluntary and that records are confidential. We attempt to watch and warn, but it may not always be possible to prevent a well-meaning but over-zealous plant manager from overstepping the rules. This takes continual oversight. Some things to watch for:

- A higher level of participation than you would normally expect compared to other locations.

- Similar contributions from employees of equal rank suggesting a formula arrangement.

- Across-the-board increases in participation levels.

SOME THINGS TO CONSIDER

One of the continuing objectives which cannot be overemphasized is keeping PAC participation voluntary. A coerced employee becomes an unhappy employee and not an "involved" employee. It should also be stressed that a PAC is only one factor in what employers can do to stimulate employees into becoming active and involved citizens. It is shameful that participation by eligible voters in the electoral process is less than half what it could be. A reason typically given by non-interested citizens is that all the candidates are unqualified. But we believe that if more people are involved, the candidates will get better and government will become more responsive. That is why political involvement is more important than the political philosophy of those we attempt to motivate.

Another suggestion for improving PAC effectiveness and credibility is to change the composition of the PAC contributions committee to include lower level employees. This should make the committee more responsive and representative and encourage participation. It may also remove a large area of potential abuse through imprudent use of funds by corporate executives.

CONCERNS FOR THE FUTURE

It is ironic that the election law reforms of the 70s resulted in a potential for abuse larger than the abuses corrected. The media refers to business PACs as though those funds were business funds – not individual contributions, generally small, from a large group of employees. (It is important that transmittal letters to political candidates stress the source that made these funds possible.)

But is the media to blame when some business executives treat these employee funds as their own private bankroll to be dispensed at will to "buy" a politician from whom they want a special favor? These former "fat cats" who were curbed by the FEC law reforms may now be fatter cats on somebody else's money. Several newspaper articles over the last few months indicate that this may already be happening in some isolated instances.

Coupled with this philosophy, of course, is the possibility of all kinds of abuses in the employee solicitation process which could lead to public financing -- removing an important area of free choice from the individual to some far off bureacracy in Washington. L.L. Gordon wrote in a *Business Week* editorial two years ago about these problems in words that are even more relevant today:

> "Heavy-handed solicitation is not only likely to cause a backlash within the company. Sooner or later it will erupt into a major scandal. And business simply cannot afford another scandal.

> "It will take only a few corporations breaking the law – putting pressure on their employees to contribute to politicians the employees do not want to support -- to touch off an

explosion of headlines, congressional hearings and prosecutions. When that happens, it will not be an acceptable public explanation to talk about a few rotten apples in the barrel."

The concluding sentence of his editorial is also an apt conclusion here:

"The risks of dabbling in political action committees are too great a risk for a prudent businessman to accept."

Whether that advice turns out to be true is up to us. **PAC**

Marion A. Youngers is assistant secretary/director of taxes with Rexnord Inc. in Milwaukee, Wisconsin. He has been with Rexnord since 1969. For the past five years Youngers has also been secretary and treasurer of the Rexnord Corporate Political Action Committee, giving him an excellent perspective for writing about corporate PACs.

Youngers is a member of the Virginia State Bar and the Taxation Section of the American Bar Association. He is chairman of the Tax Committee of the Wisconsin Manufacturers and Commerce.

Youngers has developed notable expertise on political action committees in his five years with Rexnord's PAC.

IV. ASSOCIATION PACS:
CASE STUDIES

FOODPAC: Effectiveness and Efficiency

Robert E. Bradford
Vice President, National Restaurant Association

The political action committee established by the Food Marketing Institute on behalf of the nation's food distributors has become one of the most effective in the business community.

With a membership exceeding 1,100 retailers and wholesalers, the Food Marketing Institute represented tremendous untapped political potential. Members were scattered throughout the nation, with stores in virtually every congressional district.   The challenge facing FMI was to galvanize the grassroots in order to make the industry's political action arm a viable tool for political involvement. Complicating the task was the diverse nature of the food distribution business, which includes liberals and conservatives, Democrats and Republicans.   But all members have one element in common – a dedication to keeping America's food distribution system the most efficient in the world.

NEED FOR A PAC

Many member companies of the Food Marketing Institute realized that the time had come for a change in their traditional way of dealing with government. Business in general, and the supermarket industry in particular, had not taken an activist political role in the past. Business leaders seemed content merely to respond to government legislative and regulatory initiatives, rather than working to modify proposals or lobbying for helpful ones.

But during the past two decades, everything changed. Business people were forced to take a hard look at their public image and the results were sobering. Only one out of five Americans expressed confidence in business institutions. And only 20 percent of college students considered business executives to have acceptable moral or ethical standards. The free enterprise system clearly was in trouble.

Government got into the act as well, in 1964, with the establishment of the National Food Commission set up to investigate these charges. After nearly a year and volumes of testimony the industry was cleared but the damage had been done. For supermarkets, this attitude culminated in the consumer boycotts of the early 70s. Consumers vented their frustration at sharp jumps in food prices, especially beef products, by picketing and accusing the industry of "profiteering."

Supermarkets realized they had not done the job of explaining to the public why food prices rise or fall. The food retailer was seen as villain, not victim. The public and the government alike failed to realize that the local supermarket was merely the most visible link in the total inflationary chain. When prices are high consumers can forego a new car or cut back on the clothes budget, but for most people food-shopping is still a weekly event. Effects of inflation are seen immediately on supermarket shelves.

The nation's food distributors decided to set the record straight. FMI Chairman Donald Schnuck explained that "the biggest business in Washington is government. The second biggest business is trying to influence what the government does. That's where our political action committee comes in."

FMI PAC FUNCTIONS

FMI realized that when adverse legislation is enacted, it usually is because legislators fail to take into account its effect upon certain industries. The problem is not hostility to that industry, but simply lack of knowledge. The mission of FMI's political action arm is to support candidates for federal office who are willing to listen to our industry's viewpoint.

In today's complex world, running for office is a complicated and expensive proposition. Although it is still theoretically possible to rise from a log cabin to the White House, anyone who attempts it is going to need a lot of dollars along the way. Money is needed to hire staff, rent office space, buy radio and TV time, print and distribute publicity and travel throughout the district, state or nation. Helping a candidate fund his campaign is a legitimate way of participating in the political system. Only a few people can personally contribute substantial amounts to candidates of their choice. But individuals can pool their resources and provide impressive support to candidates of their choice. This "pooling" is the basis of a political action committee.

Federal election laws permit an individual to contribute up to $5,000 a year to a single campaign and up to $25,000 in total contributions yearly.

Every FMI political action committee contribution is computerized. The individual's name, address and occupation are stored. This is helpful when filing the required Federal Election Commission's forms.

OVERCOMING OPPOSITION

When an organized PAC was first proposed, many members were not enthusiastic. In the wake of Watergate and various "slush fund" scandals, PACs were seen as slightly tainted. FMI had to assure its membership that political action committees were governed by strict rules of the Federal Election Commission. Reporting, record-keeping and disclosure requirements are spelled out in detail.

For the first two years, it was not easy convincing chief executive officers and boards of directors of the legal nature of political action committees. They needed constant reassurance that PACs were authorized by Congress and completely legal. FMI decided that more education was necessary to establish proper awareness.

EDUCATIONAL ACTIVITIES

Articles on political action committees were included in the *Issues Bulletin*, the Institute's monthly newsletter, and an FMI representative was made available at meetings to discuss how PACs work.

FMI's government relations division was involved in producing a short film called "A Washington Fable." This film explained how the federal government works, and it included a discussion of the role of political action committees. PACs were described as a necessary complement to the public affairs activities of trade associations and a legitimate way of participating in the political system.

The film was shown over a period of time at nearly every major industry meeting. Every time it was shown, it generated enthusiastic response – and this interest was the opening the FMI staff needed to build on in explaining the nature of PACs and the benefits to the industry.

Staff members also found that many of the supermarket industry's top executives were already involved in politics on the local level, but they were not familiar with federal campaigns. FMI initiated a series of meetings to help clarify federal election laws, explain again the way political action committees work and emphasize the potential strength of the food distribution industry.

Education efforts were effective as more and more CEOs became committed to the program. The Food Industry Good Government Committee (FIGG) was born.

HOW FMI'S POLITICAL ACTION COMMITTEE WORKS

The first step involved is selecting the PAC chairman. FMI staff approached a member of the executive board who had expressed an interest in the program and who was known for his integrity and his contributions to the industry. Then, regional vice chairmen were appointed throughout the country. FMI has developed a strong regional network. Regional chairmen can help contact companies in their area to urge support of the association's activities. They also provide a good source of information on candidates running in their districts.

To proceed further, FMI must receive an answering authorization letter, which is kept on file. If no response is received, a second letter is sent, asking the CEO to reconsider. If there is still no response or if a negative answer is given, FMI will not pursue the issue.

Once we have an authorization, a letter is sent out under the chairman's signature to the chief executive officers of each authorizing company, explaining PAC goals and operations. The letter also hits heavily on the fact that unions distributed a million dollars through their political action committees to support their choices in recent elections. The initial letter includes a promotional brochure on the PAC that FMI can supply in quantity for distribution to management staff. It sets out the annual dollar goal and asks that a particular company's management designate Food Marketing Institute's political action committee as the sole PAC allowed to solicit.

The Institute's PAC can either solicit the management staff directly or provide materials for the CEO to take the lead. Even if FMI contacts other executives directly, the CEO is asked to lend his support to the concept by mentioning it at the next staff meeting, or whenever convenient, and explaining that he is behind the effort. This is an extremely effective technique. As one member said, "If the CEO plays golf, everyone plays golf. If the CEO is involved in PACs, everyone gets involved in PACs." But FMI emphasized that there can be no coercion, nor can employees be rewarded or punished for their decision.

Some companies choose to set up their own political action committee. While an association PAC is prohibited from soliciting a corporate one, there are no restrictions on accepting contributions from a corporate PAC.

CONTRIBUTIONS

Donations must be personal funds and preferably on personal checks. We will accept cash, but checks provide for ease of accounting and auditing of records. Checks received range from $5 to over $1,000.

One of the most innovative features of the food industry's political contribution efforts is the establishment of the President's Club and the Capitol Club. Membership in the President's Club is open to those who give at least $1,000 annually. The Capitol Club is for those contributing at least $500 but less than $1,000 per year.

President's Club members receive two tickets to all fundraisers, with reserved seating, and a free subscription to the newsletter. Capitol Club participants are given one ticket to fundraising events, with additional tickets available at a discount, and a free subscription to the newsletter. Club members take pride in playing an important part in contributing to our industry's goal of political awareness.

NEWSLETTER

FMI publishes a newsletter for PAC contributors, approximately six times a year. It is designed to keep participants up to date on how much has been raised, what the "hot spots" are in Congress and how the fund is being used. A recent issue pointed out that FMI PAC contributions had backed winners about 74 percent of the time in the most recent elections.

FUNDRAISERS

FMI sponsors four breakfast meetings each year, in conjunction with our public affairs conference, mid-winter executive conference, annual meeting and the meeting of the Western Association of Food Chains. The price of admission is $100, up from the original fee of $50.

Anyone who attends a breakfast must complete a form, certifying that his or her participation is strictly on a voluntary basis. He or she need not have contributed previously. An individual remittance form is completed for each attendee.

These breakfast meetings have featured an array of bi-partisan speakers such as former Senator Edmund Muskie of Maine, former President Gerald Ford and many others. All of them, whether Democrat or Republican, have shown at least a willingness to listen to the concerns of the industry and consider the complex issues at stake from FMI's point of view.

FIGG BECOMES FOODPAC

After FIGG's first two years of existence, the Federal Election Commission, bureaucratic watchdog of PACs, ruled that the name of the sponsoring organization must be included in the title of any political action committee. FIGG became the Food Marketing Institute Political Action Committee (FOODPAC). This necessitated a new educational effort by FMI just as identification with and understanding of FIGG was growing stronger.

CONTINUED PROGRESS

In its first year, FMI's efforts resulted in nearly $10,000. The next year the total reached $50,000. In 1980, FOODPAC will have raised about $150,000, short of its $250,000 goal, but an impressive amount. For the first time, FOODPAC will be in a position to make meaningful contributions to congressional candidates. Support for FOODPAC has grown more enthusiastic every year, as members realize that they can have an impact on government decision-making. **PAC**

Robert E. Bradford joins the National Restaurant Association with over 20 years of experience in public affairs. He was executive vice president of the Food Marketing Institute prior to accepting the position of executive vice president at the N.R.A. Bradford joined the Food Marketing Institute as vice president for government relations when it was founded through a merger in January 1977. He became executive vice president in 1979.

Bradford has held senior staff positions with the U.S. House of Representatives, the U.S. Senate and a major federal agency. He was administrative assistant to U.S. Representative Richard Poff (R-Va.) for 10 years. From 1971-73 he served as administrative assistant to U.S. Senator William Brock (R-Tenn.). He was appointed director of congressional affairs for the Federal Cost of Living Council in 1973.

Bradford also served as executive director of the Illinois Republican State Central Committee, and before joining the Food Marketing Institute, was manager of government affairs for Firestone Tire and Rubber Company.

REALTORS© Political Action Committee (RPAC)

Jack Carlson
Executive Vice President, National Association of Realtors

The Realtors Political Action Committee (RPAC) of the National Association of Realtors© is the largest individual member trade and professional PAC in the nation. As of November 1, 1980, 87,828 members of the 746,000-member association, whose average income is only $20,000, contributed an average of $11.07 for a total RPAC income of $936,120. This, combined with the $886,003 contributed in 1979, made for an aggregate total of $1,849,123 available to RPAC for contributions to federal candidates in 1980.

Yet, none of these contributions was directly raised by the national association headquartered in Chicago. These donations were obtained through voluntary solicitation at the more than 1,800 local boards of realtors and at the 50 state associations of realtors.

In this way, RPAC is unique. Through written agreements with all 50 state associations, all solicitations for RPAC funds are made at the state and local board levels. From these collections, 40 percent of all "hard" dollars or personal contributions are forwarded on to the national RPAC. The remaining 60 percent plus any "soft" or corporate dollars (where allowed by state law) remain at the state and local board levels to be available for contributions to local, legislative and statewide candidates. In this sense, RPAC is truly a "grassroots" political action committee.

Formed in 1969, RPAC has grown from a small "political education committee" to the nation's largest political action committee in a very short period of time. This growth has been the result of forward-looking leadership that has stressed the necessity of involving the association and its members in the political process of our nation at all levels.

Through a growing political education effort and success in impacting upon public policy, the membership has responded -- not only with contributions of money to RPAC, but with contributions of personal time. Members have demonstrated that collectively, through RPAC, they can influence policies which help elect better representatives who will vote for better policies for the country and for improving people's work and lives.

How does RPAC work? As indicated, contributions are collected at the local level on a volunteer basis. The ultimate responsibility for the decisions concerning the disbursement of RPAC funds lies with a board of trustees. Appointed by the president of the National Association of Realtors, each of 18 trustees serves a staggered three-year term which insures continuity on the board.

In an election year the trustees will formally meet as many as seven times to review requests for contributions and to determine where best to make RPAC contributions. The trustees look to several sources for intelligence and information on candidates and campaigns.

First of all, and most importantly, the trustees seek out the opinion of realtors at the local and state boards. In most cases, the local board or state association will itself initiate a request for a contribution for a candidate that has realtor support at the local level.

Secondly, information on the candidate or incumbent's voting record on real estate-related issues is sought from the Washington association staff and evaluated. Beyond the voting record, any other positive (or negative) legislative role the incumbent has played in regard to real estate-related legislation is reviewed.

Third, a field report prepared by a political field staff reviews any information relevant to the "winability" of the campaign such as polling data, financial status of the campaign, skill level of the campaign management team and strengths and weaknesses of each candidate and campaign.

After reviewing this information, the trustees decide upon the course of action to be taken. Once the trustees have authorized a contribution to a candidate, the RPAC check is issued and sent back to the local board for presentation to the candidate by local realtors. A report on this presentation is then made back to the national level. This approach combines both the judgment of local and national realtors to make democracy work better.

The key to the success of RPAC lies in its "grassroots" nature — providing the opportunity to every member of the National Association of Realtors© to participate in the political process by contribution at the local level. Our PAC generated requests for contributions from the local level, giving each member the opportunity to indicate support for a candidate. It also places decisions in the hands of a cross-section of realtors responding to the input of fellow realtors at the local level. And, finally, it insures that local realtors make the contribution directly to the candidate.

By stressing this approach, through educational programs, and demonstrated successes in impacting upon public policy, RPAC has doubled its number of members in the last three years and plans to double again within the next four years. **PAC**

Since June 1979, **Dr. Jack Carlson** has been the executive vice president, chief administrative officer and chief economist of the National Association of Realtors, the largest trade association in the United States with over 700,000 members.

From 1976 to 1979 he was vice president and chief economist of the Chamber of Commerce of the United States.

Carlson has served each United States president during the last 20 years, and has been chairman or member of several U.S. delegations to international meetings in Europe, the Middle East and Asia concerning business, economic, energy and defense policies.

Developing Contributions Criteria: AGC PAC

Richard C. Creighton
Executive Director, Congressional Relations,
Associated General Contractors of America
with Roberta D. Kimball

Long before Associated General Contractors Political Action Committee's (AGC PAC) governing body, its contributions subcommittee, adopted formal contributions criteria, its three loosely defined guidelines for decisions were financial need, reasonable chance of victory and philosophic agreement with construction industry goals.

For making these decisions, it clearly was necessary to get reliable information about U.S. Senate and House candidates and about elections in states and congressional districts across the nation. The bulk of this information was and is provided by an internal National AGC membership lobbying system called "the legislative network," which pre-dates AGC PAC.

Like many such membership networks, AGC's is pyramid-shaped. The apex is a prominent national member (currently, a respected past president) who serves as chairman of an interlocking triumvirate: AGC PAC and its 25-member subcommittee as one entity, a legislative network and National AGC's 29-member legislative committee as the other two.

Next on the pyramid are the eleven regional coordinators who also share positions on the three interlocking entities. Supporting them are a legislative network and PAC state chairmen for each state, usually the same individual.

The state chairmen appoint contractors as key legislative contacts for every senator and representative, and they appoint contractors to be PAC representatives to each of AGC's 113 chapters.

There has been an additional benefit to relying on an existing membership network, already accustomed to political involvement, to provide PAC information. Contractors found themselves more personally involved in political campaigns, came to know more candidates more personally, developed more in-depth knowledge of campaign funding needs and became more enthusiastic about political action committee fundraising.

When these politically-active contractors began requesting contributions for their favorite candidates, the need for a more formal set of contributions criteria became evident.

Rather than re-invent the wheel, AGC PAC looked at the contributions philosophies of ten of the largest (in April, 1978) trade association political action committees. This research was memorable for the mildly startling diversity within the "business community" of Washington.

"Look," one pro reasoned, "I don't care what anyone says about decentralization of power on Capitol Hill. It's still those committee and subcommittee chairmen you've got to take care of. Pick out your most important committees, about four each for the Senate and House. Remember every Democrat on those committees may eventually be a chairman. Give those guys all they need, all you've got."

Another issue-oriented politico warned, "Forget about broad-interest ratings like those of the American Conservative Union and the U.S. Chamber of Commerce. You're stuck with the 'special-interest' label; you just take care of your own special interests. Watch those floor votes. Demand that legislators vote consistently 'with' you on your slate of issues."

Yet another: "Whatever you do, don't form an ideologic 'litmus test.' You'll just alienate candidates. Remember, you sometimes have to face them *after* the election, too."

And, from almost everyone: "Ignore party labels. Don't give directly to all those multi-candidate congressional committees with names like 'Democrats from Corn States.' Make sure you know where every penny from every dollar goes before you write the check." There were widely differing, fiercely defended ideas about when, if ever, to "cover your bases" by contributing to more than one candidate in a given election.

The contributions subcommittee used some of these ideas, and others tailored to AGC members' specific concerns, to form the AGC PAC contributions criteria.

AGC PAC CONTRIBUTIONS CRITERIA

The following criteria must be considered in all AGC PAC contributions subcommittee decisions concerning contributions to candidates for federal office.

Criteria for Incumbents

The past voting record of incumbent candidates will be an important consideration in contributions decisions. The history of votes cast on the floor of the chamber may be tempered by recorded committee votes and additional considerations, where information is available.

Those incumbents holding leadership positions in subcommittees, committees, or the chamber as a whole, will be eligible for special consideration.

Open Seats

Special emphasis may be placed on candidates campaigning for seats in elections where there is no incumbent candidate. Candidates will be evaluated on the basis of philosophical agreement with AGC and future support of legislation of importance to the construction industry. Campaigns may also be evaluated on the basis of current and historical demographic, economic and political variables.

113

Criteria for All Candidates

Except in very unusual circumstances, as defined by the AGC PAC contributions subcommittee, contributions will not be made to more than one candidate in any given election.

Candidates must have a realistic chance of success in the election as demonstrated through survey or analytical evidence of the popularity of the candidate and/or the effectiveness of the campaign organization.

Contributions will not be made to candidates whose opinions on legislative or philosophical issues of importance to the construction industry do not differ substantially from those of their opponents.

Contributions will not be made to those candidates receiving substantial support from groups whose interests directly and consistently conflict with those of the construction industry.

The AGC PAC contributions subcommittee will seek out and consider the opinions of members or staff of the appropriate AGC chapter(s) when considering candidate contributions.

Later, the subcommittee adopted its primary election contributions criteria.

AGC PAC PRIMARY ELECTION CONTRIBUTIONS CRITERIA

No contributions will be made to candidates in primary elections unless:

- The filing deadline for the primary election has passed; *and*

- The election is essentially single-party, with the primary winner essentially being the general winner; *or*

- There is a clear philosophical difference on industry issues between the leading candidates in the race.

Because AGC's primary business is to serve its members, flexibility was built into the guidelines. Note, however, that throughout there is an emphasis on information. Before requesting an AGC PAC candidate contribution, a contractor will research the candidate's election (filing deadline, number of opponents, recent local survey information) and positions on industry issues (common situs picketing, highway funding, Alaska lands restrictions, to name but a few).

Locating the PAC operation in AGC's Washington headquarters allowed use of other local and valuable information resources. Each national political party has three independent campaign fundraising arms: the national committees (both Democrat and Republican), the senatorial campaign committees (again, both parties) and the congressional committees' campaign divisions (both parties).

The six separate staffs of these groups each has an individual responsible for raising business PAC money for its candidates. These staffers will not only provide accurate and timely information and evaluation of their candidates (occasionally, and understandably, a bit slanted by omission or emphasis), but they will also schedule their candidates to talk to representatives of the larger PACs in the PAC's offices. This allows direct, face-to-face discussion with the candidates without interruption in a relaxed but business-like environment.

These personal meetings not only insure that the PAC can measure a candidate against its criteria; they also establish within the future legislator's mind an image of the PAC's parent organization and its industry's concerns. This has benefited AGC's lobbying efforts substantially. The Washington location also provides easy access to the volumes of information on file at the Federal Election Commission.

AGC PAC makes two basic types of contributions. Ticket purchases for Washington receptions of incumbent legislators account for about 10 percent of AGC PAC contributions. These purchases are based on a review of committee and floor voting records, and are determined within the Washington office.

The remaining 90 percent of AGC PAC's funds are contributed in minimum amounts of $1,000 for House and $5,000 for Senate campaigns. It should be noted that these contributions are personally given to candidates by association members who serve as the legislative network contact in the case of the incumbent, or a member who will serve in that capacity if the candidate is successful.

These large contributions are made under the direction of the subcommittee, and are considered at the impetus of a request by an AGC member contractor in the candidate's state or district. Informing candidates of this fact has resulted in the enjoyable situation of listening to future legislators *request* to be introduced or directed to AGC contractors.

Usually, however, candidates already know one or more politically active AGC contractors, and are happy to learn of the affiliation. This also lets the future legislator know who his or her contractor-constituents use as Washington eyes and ears. Further contractor/PAC ties are established by the AGC PAC policy of requesting that contractors personally deliver large contributions to candidates, as noted above.

Contributions decisions will always be complicated by the competing desire to pick all winners (some call this "not wasting your money") and the desire to create really good friends by making the "first" or "only" or "largest" PAC contribution to more obscure but solid candidates.

In its first entire election cycle (1980), AGC PAC sent about 40 percent of its large contributions to incumbents (about 90 percent of the incumbents running for re-election generally win); about 20 percent to candidates in elections where no incumbent was involved (such elections frequently have predictable outcomes); and about 40 percent to candidates running against incumbent legislators (about ten percent of whom usually win).

AGC PAC's overall "success rate" for these contributions exceeded 70 percent. This record was attained by balancing the desire to pick the winners and to help the long-shots, while being responsive to and relying upon information supplied by AGC member contractors. **PAC**

Richard C. Creighton is executive director of the Associated General Contractors of America. He joined AGC in 1965 as assistant director of the Highway Division. Soon thereafter, he assumed responsibility for AGC utilities construction operations, a position he held until being appointed director of the Highway Division in 1967.

Since 1977, Creighton has devoted full time to AGC's legislative activities. He was named executive director for congressional relations in November 1980. Issues he has covered include manpower and training, open shop and government services, Davis-Bacon, labor, safety and health, EEO, industry advancement programs, pension reform, AGC's National Employee Benefit Trust and ethics.

Roberta D. Kimball is with the Legislative Division of the Associated General Contractors of America. She serves as the manager of Associated General Contractors Political Action Committee (AGC PAC), as well as working in a legislative capacity on those issues affecting PACs and federal elections.

Starting a National Association PAC

Dick Fisher
General Manager,
National Federation of Independent Business

Most small business people are too busy running their businesses to get involved in running the country. But more and more small business owners are realizing what labor unions have been aware of for years: If you want friends in Congress, you have to help them get elected. For this reason the National Federation of Independent Business, an association with more than 625,000 small and independent business members, decided in 1978 to form a political action committee. The short history of the NFIB PAC demonstrates very well the major degree of interest that small contributors have in the political process. In 1978 the NFIB PAC raised some $12,400 and contributed modest sums to a handful of House and Senate races. But by the 1980 election, the NFIB PAC had raised nearly $200,000 and contributed to over 200 House and Senate races.

NFIB is a general business association representing all types of independent and small business, with members in every state and congressional district. Thus our decision to form a political action committee was not taken lightly. We have a large membership and a significant presence in Washington. We saw the formation of a PAC as a good way to enhance and to further the interests of our members in Washington, and to remind candidates for Congress that small business has an important stake in congressional actions.

A FIRST STEP

The decision to form the PAC was made by our Board of Directors in 1978 after NFIB participated with the U.S. Chamber of Commerce, the National Association of Manufacturers and the University of Southern California Center for the Study of Private Enterprise in a series of conferences across the country highlighting the importance for business of PAC involvement. During the preparation for these PAC conferences, we became convinced that NFIB would be ignoring an important and effective tool for political involvement if it did not form a membership PAC. However, since as an organization we had no personal experience with PACs and had over 600,000 active members, we felt we should proceed in stages in order to work out a smoothly run PAC organization.

As a start, NFIB organized an employee PAC. We felt the experience with our 600 employees would give us a good indication of the level of interest within the small business membership of NFIB for a political action committee. Organization of the PAC was announced through in-house publications and through separate mail solicitations of employees at their residences. Employee response was encouraging: A significant number at all levels within the organization made contributions. Interested employees could contribute directly or through a payroll checkoff.

Personal contacts between employees regarding the PAC were minimal or nonexistent. Participation in the PAC was encouraged solely through written solicitations and in-house publications. NFIB is an organization devoted to the political betterment of small business, so the political awareness of our employees was already high. The successful experience with our employee PAC made the decision to form a membership-wide association PAC much easier.

CHOOSING THE CANDIDATES: INCUMBENTS

Of greater importance to our Board of Directors was whether we could organize a PAC with legitimate guidelines for contributions which fairly reflected the interests of our small business membership. We had to establish firm operating guidelines to assure ourselves and our members that the power of the PAC would be used carefully, and that the many individual contributions would be prudently invested on behalf of small business candidates.

Fortunately, our primary PAC guidelines evolved as a logical extension of NFIB's traditional congressional rating. NFIB, at the end of every Congress, publishes and distributes to each of our members a rating of how senators and members of Congress voted on issues which were particularly important to small business.

These ratings are based on the 15 to 25 significant small business votes in each Congress. The small business positions on these votes have been determined previously by NFIB members through a poll conducted in our newsletter for members. The issues selected cover a broad range; not just Small Business Administration legislation. Each Congress' rating usually contains several votes on labor, tax, energy and regulatory issues. We do stick strictly to business-related issues in the rating; there are no gun control, busing or other such emotional issues included.

In compiling the rating, votes are selected which the NFIB lobbyists had emphasized to the Congress before the vote. During a session a member of Congress can track what we consider important votes and know, even before we publish any scorecard, what his particular NFIB record is likely to be. At the end of the Congress, the voting records are published with percentage support scores based on the key small business votes we have followed.

To heighten the importance to a member of Congress of his NFIB rating, we give a "Guardian of Small Business Award" to every member of Congress who scores 70 percent or better on our voting record. In September of the election year we present the awards at a Capitol ceremony and make available a photographer and press releases tailored to the particular congressional district or state. At the end of the 96th Congress, NFIB presented "Guardian of Small Business" awards to 208 congressmen and 30 senators. In most cases the award winners were only too happy to avail themselves of our photographer and press releases to their home district media.

The small business voting scorecard and resulting awards are the key to the NFIB PAC decisions. We strongly believe that we have a very well thought-out, fair, broad-based system for rating the Congress. When faced with the challenge of allocating NFIB PAC funds, it was clear to us that our own voting record of small business support should be the most important factor in identifying suitable recipients for PAC contributions.

Thus in the congressional elections the NFIB PAC uses a "70-40" rule to make most of the preliminary decisions on whom to support. Any incumbent who is a Guardian winner, that is, has scored more than 70 percent on the NFIB rating, is automatically eligible for an NFIB PAC contribution.

Conversely, any incumbent whose NFIB voting record rating is below 40 percent is automatically eligible to have contributions made to his challenger. And in most cases, the NFIB PAC does not get involved in the races of those incumbents whose scores fall between 40 and 70 percent.

This system has worked very well for us. It is an objective standard which can be uniformly applied and simply explained. Every office of every member of Congress is familiar with our "Key Small Business Vote Cards" which telegraph to the member the fact that we will likely use a particular vote as a basis for the rating. Knowledge of the NFIB rating gets around fast, as does awareness that our NFIB PAC decisions are based primarily on our rating.

We have had disputes, to be sure, with candidates over this system. However, the conflict usually is over some particular vote in the rating. We have had little or no conflict over the procedure of using the rating as a uniform yardstick on which to predicate PAC actions. Candidates generally seem to respect the fact that a PAC operates with a clearly set out system, although they may disagree with what that rating system happens to say about them.

Obviously the "70-40" rule does not answer all our questions. We still have to choose among candidates who do qualify, determine amounts of contributions and determine what to do about open seats.

In 1980 the NFIB PAC did not give money to every incumbent who qualified or against every incumbent whose NFIB rating was less than 40 percent. In making these sorts of decisions, we have found that plain legwork and direct contact with the candidates is our biggest help.

If our "70-40" rule is the NFIB PAC's first law, then our second law is only give money to candidates who need it. That is, of course, easier said than done. Before reviewing the various races, we have our Washington staff try to get a reading on the status of every eligible incumbent's campaign. In most cases this is a simple matter. Our strong supporters on the Hill are usually the people our Washington staff is regularly in touch with anyway. And in those cases where we do not have a good contact within an office, we can usually rely on a senior colleague from the same state or area to give us a reading on the status of the various campaigns in a particular area. With the more active "classes" of the last few Congresses, we can also go to a class leader and find out how his colleagues are faring.

CHOOSING THE CANDIDATES: CHALLENGERS

When an incumbent member of Congress is plainly not a supporter of small business, the NFIB PAC frequently contributes to challengers. The decision on contributions to challengers is an inexact art.

Much more than incumbents, challengers are moving targets in terms of their potential. A campaign may be alive in April but dead by November; or it may catch fire in the last month against a sleepy incumbent.

Our first move in assessing the challenger is to visit the national campaign committees of each party. Even a year before a congressional election, it is starting to become evident where the big races will be. As the election draws nearer there will be multiple inside tips about various "hot" races. But there is really no substitute for our PAC, which looks at every congressional race in the nation, to spend a few hours with Republican and Democratic party staffers nine or ten months before the election getting a good overview of what's coming up. Even though we may not get the latest confidential readings from the party people, the nationwide information from the two parties dovetails very well.

We do strongly believe it is our responsibility to support challengers to low-rated incumbents. A major factor for deciding to support a challenger is probability of success. If we feel that an attractive and able candidate can make a credible campaign against an incumbent, we are not dissuaded by any leadership or majority status of the incumbent.

A good example was the 1980 victory of Jack Hiler over John Brademas in the Indiana 3rd District. Hiler was a politically active young businessman, an active NFIB member and an impressive candidate. Brademas was the veteran House Democratic Whip, with a consistently terrible score on NFIB ratings and with no particular instances of helping small business with his leadership position.

The NFIB PAC contributed early and generously to the Hiler campaign, long before it became a subject of national speculation. Rather than shying away from the Brademas race, we felt the incumbent symbolized a too common insensitivity to small business. Hiler was a viable challenger and we were eager to support that challenge.

How did we determine Hiler was a good candidate with a chance? Important information always comes from a personal meeting with the candidate. We are anxious to see any candidate in any race who wants to visit us and sell us on why we should support a campaign. It gives us a chance to size up the person and their ideas. And it also lets us remind the candidate of the importance of small business issues and of our membership in his particular area.

Typically candidates visit Washington months before their election and will make the rounds of potential PAC contributors. Often the national parties arrange or recommend the visits. There are also inevitable meet-the-candidate fundraising receptions, but with the crowds and necessary socializing we do not find this the most effective way to get an accurate impression of candidates.

In the Hiler example, as in most other races where we supported challengers, we also relied greatly on advice and information from Indiana and from the Washington political community. Active NFIB members and employees often contact us about races, and serve as a sort of informal field network. Our Washington staff also checks the opinions of political professionals and other association and business representatives who are following particular races.

CHOOSING THE CANDIDATE: OTHER FACTORS

There are some other factors which we find useful to consider in deciding to whom and how much the NFIB PAC will donate to in a campaign. We use a loosely applied "committee" strategy to insure careful consideraton of all the races of members of congressional committees we regularly work with on small business issues.

Membership on a particular committee does not dictate any automatic NFIB support. On the contrary, we feel it is important to judge every incumbent on his entire small business voting record. But when our Washington staff is in the position of working with certain committees on a regular basis, the PAC tries to make an especially informed decision on those races. It's easy to tell someone of your support, but you must have good reasons to explain to a member you work with consistently why you are staying out of the race or contributing against him.

Where contributions against powerful legislators are clearly dictated by our ratings and other factors, we do not shy away from a race because of committee assignments of the incumbent. Senator Gaylord Nelson (Wis.) was chairman of the Senate Small Business Committee. In the 96th Congress, Senator Nelson's NFIB rating was the lowest in the Senate. When the ratings were published, the Nelson rating provoked intense interest and controversy in Wisconsin, where he was running for re-election to his fourth Senate term.

The issue was clear to the PAC board: Should we stay out of this race against a tough incumbent who wields tremendous political influence over critical legislation to NFIB? Or, should we back up our congressional rating system with a PAC contribution againt Senator Nelson, whom we all agreed was not a strong friend of small business or NFIB, despite his committee position?

Our rating system, which is the basic standard of our PAC, dictated the decision. We made the maximum contribution to Senator Nelson's opponent. NFIB was denounced on the floor of the Senate and in numerous other forums as well. However, the PAC did not feel that Nelson's powerful position should be any cause for the NFIB PAC deviating from its own consistent guidelines. In the Nelson race, there was some indication that the NFIB PAC contribution encouraged other contributions to the Nelson challenger, Bob Kasten. The election results, fortunately, rewarded our PAC consistency in the Nelson race.

In the case of the Nelson campaign, our PAC contribution was bolstered by our history with Senator Nelson. He has never scored particularly high in our ratings. If Senator Nelson had a consistently better record with us, and merely dipped down in the most recent rating, the PAC might have made a different decision. We do take into account the long-term record of a candidate, particularly in the Senate where an incumbent runs on a six-year record.

CHOOSING THE CANDIDATE: OPEN SEATS

The NFIB PAC looks at every congressional and senate race, as we have members in every district in the nation. Analyzing the candidates and races for the November elections is a big challenge. For that reason we have chosen not to get the PAC involved in primary or run-off campaigns.

There are always strong suggestions to the contrary, usually from candidates in a tough primary. The argument for primary involvement is that in some areas one party is so strong that the primary result is tantamount to final election.

NFIB succumbed to this pitch once, and we will not again. In the 1980 campaign for senator from Florida, Senator Dick Stone, an NFIB Guardian Award winner, was in dire financial straits and solicited our PAC's support. The PAC contributed to Stone's campaign just before the primary. He had argued that since he would have been eligible for a general election contribution, the money was much more important before the primary. History records that not only did Stone lose the primary run-off, but a Republican won the Senate seat. The primary win was clearly not tantamount to the election in Florida and is not in very many other areas as well.

In analyzing open seat races, it is especially important to get local opinions of the candidates and their background. The NFIB PAC tries to supplement information which the candidates themselves provide with input from our local members and state lobbyists. In many races, candidates will have records from state or local government which provide good indications of what the issue orientation of the candidate will be.

The committee also determines how much money to give each recipient. Some candidates receive as much as $5,000, the maximum amount allowed by law. But before they get any of it, they are asked if they need the money. If they don't, we ask them to let us give the money to races where we can make a change.

Some candidates are not so concerned about the amount but want more to make the point that they are being financially supported by a well-known and highly-respected small-business organization. This attitude about the NFIB PAC is remarkable because a lot of members don't want to publicize contributions from other PACs.

When the time comes for a vote on the distribution of funds, the majority of our PAC executive committee rules. The committee is carefully comprised of three small-business owners who also serve as NFIB board members and of two NFIB personnel, including NFIB's general manager and the organization's treasurer. An advisory committee assists in the decision-making process. Included on that committee are, among others, NFIB's chief lobbyists.

Our system is hardly perfect, but it works well. The PAC has a clear philosophy which it tries to apply consistently. We have a good record of picking winners, but that is not the primary purpose of our PAC. Besides wanting to buy access, some PACs just want to show a good win record. A lot of PACs like to invest in incumbents because the incumbent has a tremendous amount of power in the election.

The NFIB PAC philosophy is just the opposite. It is not the end of the world if we lose a race, as long as we plant the seed and help to attract high caliber electable candidates. That is the excitement of our PAC: We are not afraid to investigate the challengers and give them our support. After all, good people cannot get to Washington if they are never elected. **PAC**

Dick Fisher is general manager of the National Federation of Independent Business, a 650,000-member organization representing small, independent business people throughout the United States. The main function is to serve as a business lobby for the small business community. NFIB has registered lobbyists in all 50 states as well as a Washington office which serves as the base for federal legislative activities.

Fisher has been in the association management field for 21 years. During those years, he has served on literally dozens of committees of both the Indiana and California Societies of Association Executives as well as the American Society of Association Executives (ASAE). He has also served on the board of directors of both state organizations.

Using the NAM as a Political Resource

Helena C. Hutton
Manager, Political Research,
National Association of Manufacturers

By the end of June 1980, political action committees had spent over $27 million in direct contributions and independent expenditures on House and Senate races and the presidential primaries. An official of the Federal Election Commission has estimated that PAC contributions for federal, state and local campaigns could reach $125 million this year, compared to $77 million in 1978, with most of it coming from corporate and ideological PACs. FEC data shows that business groups are giving almost as much to Democrats as to Republicans – an indication that corporation PAC managers support the two-party system but wish to replace "unfriendly" incumbents with people more in agreement with business objectives.

Looking at the FEC figures on the distribution of the amount spent up through the election, the logical conclusion is that most corporate PACs made relatively late contributions. There was a flurry of spending as the general election neared, with PACs deploying nearly $10 million in a mere three weeks – mostly in connection with House and Senate races. While certainly helpful to the candidates, these contributions may not have affected the ultimate balance of power in the Congress as significantly as those made early on.

In many districts, a candidate must run for two or more years to challenge an incumbents, and many potential voices for business are lost because the early money just was not there. The flip side of the coin is the problem faced by PAC administrators as they give their contributions the final report – they would like to have more wins than losses.

Another problem faced by PACs is limited resources – not enough information about challengers and not enough time to gather it; not enough money to spend and too many races where it could be spent wisely.

If political action committees face many problems, they also offer a number of advantages. The National Association of Manufacturers supports the continued growth of PACs for the following reasons.

- Political Action Committees – corporate, union or association – are a legally established, acceptable device for raising and distributing political campaign funds. As such, the PAC protects both the corporation and the contributor to the PAC. The concept is addressed in the law and the process is defined by Federal Election Commission regulations. Replacing earlier methods – conduit, trustee systems and other -- PACs are the centerpiece of a legal system for corporate political activity.

- Private financing of political campaigns continues. While advocates of public financing continue to push their proposals, they have never been successful in passing legislation. Even so, none of the bills that have been seriously considered would totally eliminate private financing or negate the importance of PACs. And, in addition to hard-dollar contributions, there are the areas of in-kind contributions and independent expenditures -- areas largely untapped today by corporate PACs.

- The requirements of establishing and operating a PAC are reasonable, understandable and low cost. There is little substance to complaints that the requirements of the Federal Election Commission are complex, burden-some and costly.

- A PAC is a convenience. It provides for the creation and management of a legitimate fund for political contributions from which to meet worthy requests for support. A PAC is also convenient for contributors because someone else does the crucial research necessary to make intelligent decisions on how best to make expenditures.

- A PAC spreads the burden of responding to political solicitations beyond the top executives of a company -- the handful of top officers who are the most prominent and available targets for political campaign solicitations. Further, contributions to and through corporate committees offer a means for political participation by corporate executives and employees who will volunteer for no other political activity. Most corporate executives and, indeed, most employees simply will not involve themselves in the fundamental aspects of a campaign -- ringing doorbells, manning telephone banks, stuffing envelopes and working at the polls. But many of the people who will not do these things *will* contribute money to the candidate or party or committee that interests them.

- The establishment of PACs provides for the disclosure essential to open, honest elections and campaigns. Disclosure of who gave how much to whom, and who received what from where, is an accepted protection of our political process.

- Contributions through a company-sponsored committee help the company make its views known. They give the company recognition with the recipient, and insure that he knows of your interest in him, in his legislative performance and in his election or re-election. It gives the legislator greater interest in listening to ideas.

- A PAC can serve as a management tool for building the company's self-image. While it is making the corporate view known to candidates and public officials, it can

130

perform a similar function with the company's own employees and stockholders. When presented properly, the PAC can build trust and inspire confidence in the corporate philosophy. Citizen involvement in the political process is essential to make our system function properly. Through its PAC, and complementary actions like registration drives and candidates' visitations, the company is filling its obligation to benefit the community by promoting and encouraging active individual involvement in politics.

● And finally, PACs and their contributions support the competitive enterprise system. They help to elect candidates who support the system -- as opposed to those who do not or who do not understand it -- and they help provide access to legislators by businesspeople seeking to secure understanding of particular issues or goals. Electing officials who understand the goals of the business community is more cost-effective than lobbying to change the minds of those who do not. In the 1980 elections, corporate PACs outspent labor in backing challengers -- the goals being to change the composition of the Congress rather than to buy access.

The NAM recognizes the problems faced by members in establishing and maintaining an effective political action program, and has the resources to provide needed assistance. Personnel trained in the intricacies of political action committees and with broad exposure to various corporate programs are available both at NAM headquarters in Washington and in field offices across the country.

Before making any political contribution, a corporation must first organize a political action committee -- often an arduous and frustrating experience. NAM staff can sit down with a new PAC and answer questions ranging from how to fill out a Statement of Organization to what solicitation techniques to use. It is not unusual for a public affairs director to bring together members of experienced PACs and new ones for a "meeting of the minds" on what worked and what did not.

Political research is an on-going process, with public affairs representatives across the country advising division offices and headquarters staff on developments at the local level. During an election year, NAM staff interviews candidates of both parties in order to provide specific information to PACs as they go through the evaluation process. In some instances, it has been possible to match candidates and PACs who share common concerns. In April 1979, the Public Affairs Department began publishing *The PAC Manager*, a monthly political journal that analyzes key races and political trends.

In addition to campaign-related activites, the NAM monitors PAC-oriented legislation and took a strong position against the Obey-Railsback bill. Through staff and *The PAC Manager*, NAM members received a great deal of information that was useful in lobbying against the bill.

The National Association of Manufacturers provides the services of a political data bank to any member who needs them. Whether a company chooses to become involved early in the campaign cycle or to play it safe and contribute in October, the goals remain the same -- the election of a Congress that is fiscally responsible, one that understands and appreciates the needs of a productive, growing economy that will provide jobs for all, and one that will preserve our basic personal freedoms. **PAC**

Helena Hutton is political research manager for the National Association of Manufacturers and serves as a liaison between corporate PACs and the NAM. She meets candidates and follows the elections. She also edits *The PAC Manager* newsletter. Prior to joining the NAM, she worked for the House Republican Policy Committee and the Health Insurance Association of America.

Guidelines for Association PACs

Jerald A. Jacobs, Esq.
Leighton Conklin Lemov Jacobs and Buckley

This chapter provides associations with some basic guidelines for the establishment and operation of PACs. The guidelines only apply to PACs concerned with federal elections. Associations that support local or state-level candidates should consult local and state laws and regulations.

These federal guidelines are only an introduction to a comprehensive understanding of the requirements of the Federal Election Campaign Act and the regulations of the Federal Election Commission and the Internal Revenue Service. The requirements are complex, are subject to updated interpretation, and their violation can result in civil or criminal sanctions. Therefore, any association contemplating the formation of a PAC or already operating one should be closely advised by legal counsel familiar with this specialized area.

LEGISLATIVE HISTORY

Political action committees have existed for years, but, prior to 1971, corporations and unions were prohibited from making political contributions. The Federal Election Campaign Act of 1971 for the first time sanctioned the use of corporate funds to institute and maintain political action committees.

Clarifications of the act were set forth in the Federal Election Campaign Amendments of 1974. Under the Amendments, it became lawful for corporations, including incorporated associations, to use their own funds to establish and maintain political action committees for the purpose of channeling campaign contributions from employees, members and shareholders to federal candidates. The 1974 Amendments also established the Federal Election Commission and provided for public financing of presidential campaigns.

The constitutionality of the 1974 Amendments was challenged in *Buckley v. Valeo*, 424 U.S. 1 (1976). The Supreme Court affirmed some parts of the amendments and required changes in other parts. Provisions concerning corporate and association political action committees were not affected.

Congress incorporated the changes required by *Buckley* in the Federal Election Campaign Amendments of 1976. These Amendments set forth some of the rights and responsibilities of association PACs and imposed additional limitations on PAC solicitations and expenditures. Technical changes in the law were made in the Federal Election Campaign Act Amendments of 1979. Of general importance to PACs is that reporting obligations were reduced; and of specific concern to association PACs is that the name of the sponsoring entity must be included in the official name of the PAC.

While it remains illegal for incorporated associations to use their own funds for campaign contributions, the federal election legislation allows association funds to be used to organize and operate PACs. The PAC then solicits campaign contributions and directs them to candidates. Limitations on the use of these funds are set forth in the election and tax laws.

WHY FORM A PAC?

There are numerous reasons for an association to establish a political action committee. The first is that by directing campaign funds to candidates for federal office who support certain association goals, a PAC assists in effectively presenting its positions in government.

Second, an association's own PAC serves to counter the influence of campaign funding and lobby groups already taking strong positions contrary to those of the association on various legislative matters.

Third, an association-sponsored PAC gives notice that the association is interested in affecting the legislative process generally or with respect to specific issues.

Another reason for forming an association PAC is to take advantage of the higher limits on PAC contributions to candidates than are allowed individual contributors. Additionally, the PAC provides a convenient and direct method for association members to support campaigns while recognizing significant tax advantages.

And finally, PACs actively involve association members in the political process.

WHY ARE PACS SUCCESSFUL?

Association PACs have been successful in soliciting and distributing campaign contributions as part of an overall association effort to effect federal legislation. By contributing to the campaigns of candidates sympathetic with the association's positions, PACs are advancing the association's interests. The following reasons are advanced to explain why numerous PACs are meeting success.

First, there have been conscientious attempts to organize and administer PACs in strict accordance with the federal requirements. This enables association members who become PAC contributors to be assured of the legitimacy of the operation. Also, through professional solicitation of association members, long-term goals for the desired level of PAC financial activity are being met. Additionally, PACs are achieving their desired goal of furthering the legislative aims of the associations by systematically distributing PAC contributions to candidates who support the associations' objectives. By pacing their activities, PACs are insuring that momentum is carried from election years through non-election years.

Finally, in soliciting contributions, PACs have pointed to the substantial income tax advantages available to contributors. This results in increasing amounts of PAC solicitations and contributions.

PAC BYLAWS

Federal laws do not require an association to adopt a governing document, but an association with a PAC is well-advised to do so. Such a governing document, usually in the form of bylaws, should set forth the organization and management structures of its PAC. An administrative manual detailing methods of solicitations, contributions, expenditures, reports, record keeping and other operation matters can also be developed as guidelines to the PAC's officers and staff.

The following provisions are often included in the bylaws of an association PAC:

1. The name of the PAC and the identity of the sponsoring association and any other political committee to which it is related.

2. The general purposes of the PAC (e.g., to solicit and contribute funds to political candidates who support the views of the PAC) and any specific purpose of the PAC.

3. The structure of the PAC as a voluntary, nonprofit political committee comprised of individual, noncorporate members (if the PAC has members) who might be described as those who contribute to the PAC.

4. The authority of the PAC to solicit and distribute campaign funds under federal election campaign laws and according to the procedures set forth in the bylaws and any administrative manual.

5. The procedures by which the PAC solicits, receives and distributes campaign contributions.

6. The composition and responsibilities of any governing board that the PAC may establish. This may include the number of governors, their method of appointment, the length of their terms and the provisions for voting.

7. The number, method of appointment, terms, duties and authority of the officers of the PAC. This should include a chairman, treasurer, vice treasurer and assistant treasurer.

8. Requirements for meetings of the PAC members, governing board or officers.

9. Provisions for amendment of the bylaws.

It is often a good idea to distribute a copy of the association's PAC bylaws to association members when their contributions are solicited by the PAC. This acquaints members with the structure, purposes and goals of the PAC.

PAC ORGANIZATION

Federal election and tax laws play a large role in determining the methods and procedures involved in organizing a PAC. Numerous requirements must be met to qualify as a tax exempt, bona fide PAC. The following discussion sets forth the major requirements to be met in organizing a PAC.

The name of the PAC must include the full name of the sponsoring association. That name must be included in all documents pertaining to the organization of the PAC, on all reports and as part of any legal notices required on solicitations. In place of the full name, the Federal Election Commission has approved the use of an acronym on letterheads and checks of the PAC. For example, the National Widget Association (NWA) would name its PAC the National Widget Association Political Action Committee. On its letterhead or checks, the PAC could use a recognizable abbreviation or the acronym NWAPAC.

A PAC must be registered with the proper office within ten days of its formation. Generally, the registration is filed with the Federal Election Commission. But if only candidates for the Senate are to be supported by the PAC, the registration is filed with the Secretary of the Senate. And registration forms are filed with the Clerk of the House if only candidates for the House of Representatives are supported.

The registration form, supplied by the government, must include the following information:

- Name, address and type of political committee involved;

- Names, addresses and relationships of any connected organizations or affiliated committee;

- Name and address of the treasurer of the committee;

- List of all banks, safety deposit boxes, or other depositories used by the committee.

Upon receipt of the registration statement, the PAC will receive an identification number which must be indicated on all subsequent filings. Whenever information filed previously has changed, an amended registration statement must be filed within ten days. The Federal Election Commission permits, but does not require, PACs to incorporate. But incorporation can only be for the purpose of protecting the PAC from liability. Nevertheless, treasurers of PACs remain personally liable for their duties under the law.

Federal income tax laws require that for the PAC contributors to receive personal income tax credits for their contributions, the PAC to which they contribute must be organized and operated for the exclusive purpose of furthering the nomination or re-election of candidates for public office. The IRS further requires that a PAC refrain from engaging in general political, educational or legislative activities if it intends for its contributors to be eligible for tax benefits.

This does not preclude an association from involving itself in political activities outside of furthering the election of candidates. But in order to avoid

139

jeopardizing the tax advantages given to PAC contributors, the association should conduct such activities outside of the PAC.

A PAC may exist as a tax-exempt entity if it is organized and operated primarily to accept contributions and make disbursements intended to influence the selection, nomination, election or appointment of individuals for public office. When a PAC meets this test, income received in the form of contributions is clearly exempt from federal income taxation. The Internal Revenue Code and regulations governing "political committees" detail the other kinds of income which are exempt from taxation. An example of other income which is *not* exempt but rather is subjected to a $100 specific deduction, is interest received by a PAC on its deposited funds.

While association funds cannot be used as contributions to the PAC for distribution to candidates, the association may use its money to establish and administer the PAC. This maximizes the amount of PAC funds that can be distributed to political candidates. Administrative costs that can be paid from association funds include:

- Printing, mailing and other expenses for PAC solicitation;

- Salaries of PAC employees or association employees assigned to PAC administrative activities;

- Rent and other expenses of maintaining PAC offices; and

- Fees of attorneys, accountants, political consultants, direct mail consultants or other professional advisors to the PAC.

PAC SOLICITATIONS

Association PACs are subject to complex federal laws concerning their ability to solicit campaign contributions. An association PAC may solicit contributions from:

1. Specified corporate member executives and stockholders *after receiving advance approval* from the member corporation;

2. The association's non-corporate members, without restriction; and

3. Specified association staff executives, without restriction; but from its other employees only twice a year.

It is noteworthy that a PAC may not solicit or accept contributions from any corporation.

The advance approval required from a corporate member before solicitations may be made to that member's executive and administrative employees or stockholders (or their families), must be "separate and specific." FEC regulations also require that the approval be in writing. Other corporate member employees may not be solicited for PAC contributions.

A member corporation can grant solicitation approval to only one federal-level, association PAC each year. If a separately incorporated subsidiary, branch, division or affiliate of a member corporation is itself a member of the association, it can also approve solicitations by one association PAC each year. For purposes of the advance approval requirement, whether an association member is a "corporation" is determined by state law.

In seeking advance approval for PAC solicitation from an association corporate member, one copy of sample solicitation materials may be mailed or given to the corporate member representative with whom the association normally deals. Since prior – not simultaneous – approval is required, solicitation in newsletters reaching persons where written approval has not been given, is prohibited. FEC has taken a restrictive position that articles about a PAC which might provoke an individual to make an unsolicited contribution are to be viewed as actual solicitations. FEC has allowed an association to publish in its newsletter a form for advance approval for solicitations to corporate members; however, FEC has at the same time required that a careful explanation be published along with the approval form. An association must approach PAC articles in newsletters with caution lest the articles be considered by FEC as solicitations.

Once advance approval is received, the PAC may solicit contributions from administrative and executive employees or stockholders (or their families) of the association member corporation as often as is desired and whether or not the corporation has set up its own corporate PAC. However, the corporation, in its approval, may limit the manner and frequency of association PAC solicitation.

Advance approval is not necessary for PAC solicitations made to individual association members who are not employees, or to stockholders of a member corporation. Solicitations may not be made to family members of these individuals.

Solicitations for PAC contribution may be made to the association's own administrative or executive employees (or their families) without restriction. But solicitations to other non-executive association employees may be made only twice a year by a letter mailed to the employees at home. These solicitations must be made in such a way that the association and the PAC remain unaware of who makes single contributions of $50 or less, multiple contributions aggregating $200 or less, or who makes no contribution at all.

The PAC must keep records of all association members that have approved solicitations or which do not require advance approval for solicitation (if any). The advance approval documents must be kept by the PAC for three years.

Mail solicitations may be addressed only to individuals for whom advance approval has been obtained or for whom approval is unnecessary because they are non-corporate members. Subject to the advance approval requirement, there is no prohibition against including solicitation materials with other routine association mailings.

Oral solicitations and distribution of solicitation materials at association seminars, meetings or conventions attended by corporate member executives or stockholders may be made only if the association PAC has received advance approval for solicitation from the corporate members in attendance. However, the FEC has stated that under certain conditions an association may maintain a PAC booth at meetings attended by association corporation member executives to make solicitations and receive contributions. Some suggested procedures for these PAC booths are:

142

- The PAC booth should be staffed by personnel familiar with the laws and regulations.

- Reference to the PAC booth should be avoided in pre-meeting publicity by the association; during the meeting, no announcements should be made about the existence of the PAC booth or its location.

- Simple signs directing meeting delegates to the PAC booth and a simple sign at the booth are acceptable.

- Any meeting delegate inquiring at the booth can be offered a PAC brochure explaining its purposes and outlining the advance approval requirement for executives of association corporate members.

- Written advance approval for solicitation of association corporation member executives should be accepted only from authorized corporate members.

- Solicitations for contributions to the PAC should only be made to meeting delegates who are executives of association corporate members that have given advance approval for the solicitation.

Solicitations for contributions to the association PAC, whether by mail or at association meetings, *must* include: 1) a statement that the PAC is organized for political purposes, and 2) a statement that the solicited party may refuse to contribute to the PAC without fear of reprisal by the association or by the employer.

Written solicitations for contributions *must* include the following language: 1) paid for by (association PAC); and 2) not authorized by any candidate or candidate's committee.

Solicitations for contributions *may* include: 1) a statement that no corporate funds will be accepted by the association PAC; 2) information on the tax advantages of contributing to the PAC; and 3) the fact that single contributions to the PAC of more than $50 or multiple contributions exceeding $200 must be reported to the government in detail.

PAC RECEIPTS AND EXPENDITURES

Federal laws set forth numerous limitations on contributions to PACs and expenditures to candidates for federal office.

Individual contributions to association PACs are limited by law. An association may not accept cash contributions of more than $100 from an individual. Nor can an association accept contributions in excess of $5000 from any individual in one year. Additionally, individuals may not contribute more than $25,000 in a calendar year in total political contributions.

An association PAC cannot accept contributions from corporations. If a doubt exists as to whether a particular contribution is corporate or individual, the PAC must determine the status before accepting it. Furthermore, association PACs cannot accept contributions from non-U.S. citizens, individuals contributing on behalf of a third party or a corporation, national banks, government contractors, or federally incorporated firms.

Contributions designed to be given by the PAC to a particular candidate or campaign committee are called "earmarked" contributions. The following special rules apply to such funds:

- The intended recipient must be informed of earmarked contributions made through the PAC when the contribution is passed on to the recipient;

- The intended recipient must be given any earmarked contributions made through the PAC within ten days of when the PAC receives them, together with the identity of the sources of the earmarked contributions; and

- Earmarked contributions must be described by the PAC separately in its regular reports to the government.

All contributions accepted by an association PAC must be deposited in the PAC checking account. All expenditures of the PAC, other than petty cash disbursements, must be made from that account.

A receipt for contributions to an association PAC may be necessary for the contributor to receive any tax benefits. Generally, the IRS will accept an individual's cancelled check as evidence of a PAC contribution. However, IRS has the discretion to require the production of additional documents on the nature and purposes of the PAC and the contribution. Therefore, it may be advantageous for the PAC to provide a receipt stating the name of the PAC and the fact that it supported candidates for federal office in the applicable year; the amount and date of the contribution; the name of the contributor; and the signature of an authorized PAC agent.

For contributors to receive tax benefits, the PAC must support at least one candidate during the year of their contributions. For a contributor of earmarked funds, the designated candidate must be supported by the PAC during the year of the contribution. Unspent contributions may be retained by the PAC to support candidates in future elections, but must be spent "within a reasonable period of time," according to IRS regulations.

An association PAC may not contribute more than $1000 to any one candidate in any election (primary and general elections are counted separately). This $1000 limit is increased to $5000 per election when the PAC qualifies as a "multi-candidate committee" by 1) being registered for at least six months, 2) receiving contributions for federal elections from at least 50 individuals and 3) making expenditures to five or more federal candidates.

An association PAC may give no more than $15,000 in a calendar year to a national political party.

145

No contribution may be accepted nor expenditure made by an association PAC without the authorization of its treasurer. However, the treasurer may delegate to another (orally or in writing) the authority to make expenditures.

There are no requirements that PAC expenditures be bi-partisan or otherwise balanced among candidates of differing political philosophies or persuasions.

PAC REPORTING AND RECORDKEEPING

Certain reporting and recordkeeping is required by federal election and tax laws.

For each contribution received, records must be kept of:

- The name and mailing address of each contributor from whom contributions totaling more than $50 are received in a year;

- The name, mailing address, occupation and employer's name for each contributor from whom contributions totaling more than $200 are received in a year; and

- The date and amount received.

For each expenditure made, records must be kept of:

- The name and address of the individual to whom the expenditure is made;

- The date and the amount;

- The name of the candidate; and

- The office sought by the candidate.

For expenditures in amounts of more than $200 for whomever receives the expenditure, the PAC's treasurer must obtain and retain a "receipted bill," which may be a check or invoice, that states the name and address of the recipient, the date and the amount spent, and the purpose of the expenditure.

All of these PAC records must be kept for at least three years.

Various election campaign reports must be filed at specified times with the FEC, or with the Secretary of the Senate or the Clerk of the House of Representatives if only candidates for senator or representative are supported.

The PAC must file semi-annual reports during non-election years and quarterly reports in election years. Or in the alternative, it may file monthly reports regardless of whether an election is being held that year. Additionally, a pre-election report must be filed by the twelfth day before a primary or general election and a post-election report must be filed within thirty days following a general election.

These reports must be filed on the appropriate government forms. They must contain cumulative information on all contributions received and expenditures made by the PAC. Specifically, the reports must disclose the following:

- Cash on hand at the beginning of the reporting period;

- The name, mailing address, occupation, name of employer, date and amount for each contribution received from contributors who gave the PAC more than $200 in the current calendar year;

- The total contributions received by the PAC in the reporting period, other than those listed separately;

- The name, address, date and amount of each expenditure made to a candidate or PAC of more than $200 in the current calendar year;

147

- The total expenditures made by the PAC in the reporting period and the calendar year; and

- Other information such as loans, debts, ticket sales, investment income, contributions or expenditures of goods or services, where applicable.

Association political action committees are subject to numerous detailed requirements under the federal election and income tax laws. However, where a PAC is properly-organized and administered, compliance with the federal requirements is not overly burdensome. Most associations that have PACs agree that their significant benefits — particularly the opportunity for an association to channel members' political contributions to federal candidates chosen by the association — far outweigh the efforts required for compliance with the federal requirements. **PAC**

The author acknowledges with appreciation the assistance of Ellen Kahn in preparing this article for publication.

Jerald A. Jacobs is a senior principal in the Washington, D.C. law firm of Leighton Conklin Lemov Jacobs and Buckley. He received undergraduate and law degrees from Georgetown University.

Jacobs is a specialist in antitrust and trade regulation matters, and is active in his firm's representation of nearly fifty national trade and professional associations. He has been involved on behalf of association and corporate clients in all of the legislative changes to federal election campaign requirements since 1970.

Jacobs' handbook on legal aspects of trade and professional associations will be published by the Bureau of National Affairs, Inc. in early 1981.

DSAPAC: The Advantages of a Small PAC

Neil H. Offen
President, Direct Selling Association
with Stuart Byer

If one were to examine Washington trade groups and the size of their constituencies, the direct selling industry's 150 corporations and the more than four million independent contractor (non-employee) salespeople might strike an impressive note.

With this large a number of individuals whom we serve, it might seem that the Direct Selling Association Political Action Committee (DSAPAC) could generate enormous sums of money. Anyone familiar with the Federal Election Commission law governing trade associations, however, would immediately realize that only the 150-member corporations are solicitable (if they so permit), and that the complexity of rules surrounding solicitation by trade associations makes it quite difficult to raise substantial sums of money.

The four million salespeople affiliated with our member-firms do, however, represent potential political clout for they are, for the most part, of voting age and are more politically aware than the general population. They are active throughout their communities because they sell directly to customers in the customers' own homes. In addition, based on Lou Harris' survey data, direct salespersons call on three out of every four households every year, and 23 percent of all households contain an individual who now sells for our firms or once did (8 percent and 15 percent). Potential grassroots clout is therefore truly staggering.

Since moving to Washington, D.C. from Winona, Minnesota in 1968, DSA has been a group aware of the importance of access to opinion leaders in both the executive and legislative branches. Following the historical Federal Election Commission act which permitted business to establish separate segregated funds to contribute to individuals seeking federal office, the first rumblings calling for creation of DSAPAC surfaced through the association leadership and staff. However, wary of any "access buying" mechanism following the Watergate debacle, association-member companies felt it best that industry maintain a low profile in the political contribution area.

Another factor opposing the creation of DSAPAC was the fear that, due to associations' heavy lobbying activities before state legislatures and city and county councils, requests for funds would be received from numerous non-federal legislators with whom DSA worked. Such requests could not be met and it was considered safer to have one only for federal candidates.

It soon became apparent that an effort to sensitize the industry to the need for political involvement was needed, and the association launched a "Washington Caucus with Government" program. Simultaneously, recognizing the necessity for a greater congressional involvement, a "Calling on Congress" program also was initiated through the association's government relations committee.

The Washington Caucus with Government brought top-level corporate executives to Washington where they were briefed by Cabinet-level officials and leading members of Congress on issues of importance to the industry. In conjunction with this event, an annual award was presented to the Direct Selling Association's "Champion of Free Enterprise," and a congressional reception and dinner were held where all executives in attendance were expected to invite and host their elected officials. DSA staff executives invited government officials as well. These programs are still ongoing.

With a new awareness of how "buttons are pushed" in Washington brought about by these programs, the need for a PAC became evident, and DSAPAC finally got off the ground in 1977. Our first year we raised an unimpressive $1,100. Faced with the fact that we would never be able to raise enough or as much money as we felt we needed to expend, DSAPAC quickly learned that through innovation and intelligent management we could maximize our exposure.

The size of the PAC is really of less importance than its ability to establish realistic goals, to grow and to meet new fundraising objectives each year. Of comparable importance is the manner in which funds available are allocated. Certain key friends of the industry received disproportionately large shares of our contributions. Also, DSAPAC encourages formation of member-company PACs and coordinates efforts within the four- to five-member company PACs now in existence.

DSAPAC has also chosen to invest proportionately large sums of its treasury in political party-sponsored organizations. These groups, including such DSAPAC-supported organizations as the National Finance Council of the Democratic National Committee, the Republican Congressional Leadership Council of the Republican Congressional Campaign Committee, the Democratic House and Senate Council of the Democratic Congressional Campaign Committee and the Republican and Democratic Congressional Campaign Committees, are themselves important entrees to the power centers of the federal government and Congress.

Through functions sponsored by these organizations for their members, representatives from large and small PACs can approach "equal access" to Cabinet members, members of the House and Senate and Democratic and Republican party officials. It is at such functions where association interests can be discussed informally, with plans made for follow-up meetings. Of critical importance, however, is the individual in attendance at such functions. A staff member politically naive will accomplish nothing, while one that is politically savvy can make friends for the industry.

Being a small PAC does have its advantages. By necessity, DSAPAC is an "access" PAC, not a philosophical PAC. We do not have the funds to effect major philosophical changes in Congress, but we are able to contribute to a broader range of candidates due to our need for across the board access.

Also, direct selling is more a method of marketing than an "industry." Therefore, our interests are extremely varied and not limited to one or two consumer commodities.

We also are able to support candidates whose political views may be out of step with those of the larger business community. These views will be consistent with DSA's self-perceived role as a consumer advocate and

151

wom&n/minorities opportunity voice within the business community. We consider ourselves a progressive organization seeking to serve the public interest in ways that many other business organizations either do not pursue or do not share our viewpoint. Accordingly, in weighing support for a candidate we consider positions relating to consumer protection, equal opportunity and corporate ethics as much as our more narrow industry interests.

It has been our experience that supporting proponents of such legislation lends a certain credibility to the DSAPAC with groups which otherwise might be our adversaries (or adversaries of the remainder of the business community). This pays unexpected dividends at times, and has helped us win the battles in states and cities which otherwise might have been lost, e.g., having a state consumer organization vouch for us and make introductions to legislators and regulators who might otherwise refuse to listen to our presentations.

Making contributions of this type requires support from our PAC audit or advisory committee, i.e., members of the association's Executive Committee of our Board of Directors. The chairman of the PAC must have the respect and trust of the membership to be able to make quick decisions and, at times, to give contributions to persons who are generally unpopular with the business community. (The DSA president, i.e., chief staff executive, is our PAC chairman.) These decisions must, however, be marketable to the membership when it is time to solicit funds.

DSAPAC's method of raising funds naturally conforms to the guidelines set forth by the FEC. At times, the membership of the association believes the FEC restrictions placed on DSAPAC solicitations border on an infringement of their First Amendment rights. We must continually impress on them the importance of complying with seemingly unfair requirements and burdensome forms necessary for compliance.

Recently, it was decided that DSAPAC would attempt to project a more formal and organized image in the hope that it would produce a higher, more positive rate of response during our fundraising drive. We designed a brochure describing the process of soliciting "permission to solicit." On the back of each brochure was a detachable form giving DSAPAC permission to contact the executives that the corporation listed. Our response rate did not increase and we spent $1,000 printing the brochure.

We did, however, mail it to each association member that we normally do business with, as permitted by FEC law, although most of the individuals could not grant permission. Enclosed with the request for permission to solicit was a sample solicitation. We did raise a total of $23,134 in 1979 and $10,806 in 1980 and distributed all but $1,000 to 45 candidates, almost 84 percent of whom were incumbents. We contributed heavily to members of the committees handling legislation of greatest concern to us such as the House Ways and Means Committee and the Senate Finance Committee.

We also spent several hundred dollars setting up a PAC booth at DSA's annual meeting in 1980. The FEC restricts the operation of the PAC booth to such an extent that it proved to be a waste of time. The solicitable class of people at the meeting was so small that the operator of the booth could speak to most individuals only in very general terms concerning the PAC.

For a small PAC, there are a number of ways to maximize clout. It is basically helping out in any way you can when you do not have the hard cash to contribute. DSA and DSAPAC routinely utilize all of the following:

1. We distribute reprints of *Congressional Record* inserts placed by friendly congressmen on issues of concern to the industry. Member companies, in turn, often distribute the reprints in quantity to their executive and administrative personnel. Often, expenses in this area can come from the association, but whenever there is doubt, we let the PAC pay for it.

2. We set up debates between candidates in order to expose their positions to our constituencies. We estimate that we have well over 7,000 salespeople in every congressional district.

3. We encourage member companies to report on favorable votes to their employees, independent contractors and executive and administrative personnel through their in-house organs.

4. We ask members of Congress whom we would like to thank for their support, to speak at DSA luncheons, dinners, conventions and committee meetings and provide honoraria and expenses for those members who desire to accept them. Again, association funds are often used for these events.

5. When we receive a fundraising invitation that we are unable to attend, we send it out to the members of the association who live in the appropriate district or state and encourage them to attend or contribute. We also encourage our corporate member PACs to support their friends at these times.

6. We are willing to lend DSA staff members who take vacation or unpaid leave time to campaigns, with DSAPAC paying for their ongoing association fringe benefits, i.e., health insurance, pensions, etc., as an in-kind contribution.

7. Individual DSA executives help set up and organize fundraisers as well as lend their names to lists of individuals supporting particular candidates.

Political awareness must continually be built within the potential group of PAC contributors. They should receive copies of thank you's and personal notes to members of Congress and administration officials, and copies of correspondence from these individuals in government to your own constituents. Make sure that they know you are working on their behalf to get to know the individuals whose decisions affect their livelihood.

DSAPAC's goal, of course, is impact on the DSA membership and, more importantly, on the decision-makers. We want to enhance this impact by encouraging member-companies to form their own PACs and/or to get involved in their local and state government. The stronger they are, the stronger we are, and the greater our visibility in the nation's capital.

We are competing with thousands of other voices for the attention of a very small number of people. To be without a PAC and to expect to play in the big leagues of national politics cannot be done. A $150 contribution has impact, albeit not as much as a $1,000 or $5,000 contribution. Without a PAC, even the $150 checks would not be written, and minor league status would be a real possibility in the eyes of federal decision-makers. **PAC**

In February 1971 **Neil H. Offen** joined the Direct Selling Association (DSA), the national trade association for leading manufacturers and distributers of products sold in the home, as staff legal counsel. He eventually rose to the position of senior vice president and legal counsel prior to becoming president of the association in February 1977.

Before joining DSA, Offen was a legislative and administrative assistant to a U.S. congressman and, prior to that, was a federal management intern and a Latin American program analyst for the Department of State's Agency for International Development (AID).

Offen serves on the National Finance Council of the Democratic National Committee. He also serves on the board of directors of the American Retail Federation and as secretary-treasurer of its Central Council of National Retail Associations, as well as chairman of the Federation's Trade Regulation Task Force.

Offen serves on the Citizen's Choice National Commission on Taxes and on the IRS. He is a member of the National Council of the Federal Bar Association, of the Government and Regulatory Affairs Committee of the Chamber of Commerce of the United States, and of the Legal Committee of the American Society of Association Executives.

Stuart Byer, now with Fraser/Associates, was formerly with the Direct Selling Association (DSA) where he was manager of government and consumer affairs. His responsibilities included orchestration of grassroots and national lobbying campaigns ,formulation of association positions on issues affecting the industry and legislative monitoring and analysis. He was also secretary of the Direct Selling Association Political Action Committee.

Prior to joining DSA , Byer was involved in two presidential campaigns coordinating logistics and scheduling for press and field staff. He also served on the staff of Rep. Christopher Dodd, now a member of the U.S. Senate.

Toward an Effective PAC:
What to Do and How to Do It

Robert J. Wager
President, American Bakers Association

Corporate trade association PACs have become an important force in the political process. From just a handful in 1974, they have grown to more than 400 in just six years. They contributed over $5 million to House and Senate candidates in 1979-80.

Trade association PACs face different problems in soliciting and distributing their funds than do corporate and individual membership PACs. Let's look at how one trade association PAC raises and distributes its funds to maximize its effectiveness in advancing the economic interests of the industry it represents.

THE PURPOSE OF THE PAC

At the outset, it is important to understand clearly the purpose of the trade association PAC. The objective of the PAC should be to protect and promote the interests of the association in the legislative and regulatory processes of government. The executives of member companies will give, and continue to give, only if they believe the money is being used wisely on behalf of the economic interests of their companies.

Members of the PAC board or committee should take the view that they have a fiduciary obligation to the contributors to use the money to further *their* interests. Thus, a PAC representing the maritime industry should not contribute substantial sums to candidates or members of Congress whose primary interest is in agriculture. The watchword of the PAC should be "help your friends and defeat your enemies." Politics is a two-way street. If an association wants to be an effective force in Congress, it must aid those who have supported its positions at campaign time. The ultimate value of the PAC contribution is that it shows the association remembers its friends and supports them.

It is equally important to understand what the PAC receives for its contribution, and what it does not. In the aftermath of the Watergate era scandals, there was a common belief that senators and congressmen were "for sale." This was false. A PAC cannot "buy" voters; it cannot even "rent" them. What the PAC wants, and what it should receive, is timely access and a sympathetic hearing for the views it represents from those who accept its contributions. This enables the association to present the facts and arguments on its side of an issue before a vote. That is all a PAC can legitimately ask.

THE "PHILOSOPHY" TRAP

It is common today in business PAC circles to hear that contributions should be based on "political philosophy." When asked to explain what this means, advocates of this view respond that contributions should go to "conservatives," "fiscal conservatives" or "pro-business" candidates. When pressed to identify such candidates, the answer usually is that you can tell them by analyzing their voting records -- high scores on the Chamber of Commerce and NAM charts and low scores on COPE and ADA records.

There are several fallacies in this approach to PAC contributions.

First, most issues are not philosophical; they are pragmatic. In the 96th Congress, the House took more than 1,200 recorded votes. In the Senate there were nearly 1,000 votes. Seldom are these votes a matter of "either-or." Most of the time the issue involves balancing closely competing arguments and reaching a decision on which side better serves the public interest. Organizational litmus tests cover only one or two per cent of all votes taken. They reveal more about the biases of the organization selecting the votes than they do about the senators and congressmen.

Second, issues selected by the Chamber, COPE and others are not those which concern most associations. Only a few groups have a major interst in cargo preference legislation, common situs picketing rules or the Energy Mobilization Board. The result is an ideological screening which is irrelevant to a large majority of trade associations.

Third, these votes never indicate how the member will vote on the specific issues important to your association. In reality, it does not matter whether a senator or congressman is conservative, moderate or liberal. The only thing that does matter is how he or she votes on *your* issues. It does not benefit the association if a congressman meets every "conservative" test, yet votes against the association's interests most of the time.

Fourth, business interests are not monolithic. Often there is conflict in the business community over an issue. For example, on the natural gas legislation in 1978, industrial users favored one policy, while agricultural users supported another. Moreover, it is not always clear what the "conservative" position is. Should the Energy Mobilization Board have broad power to set aside state laws and regulations? Conservatives split over the issue.

Fifth, the philosophical approach makes floor votes the only criteria for contributions. But every practical politician knows that most issues are decided in committee. This method of evaluating candidates totally neglects this important fact. Thus, it gives no credit to the member who casts a key vote in committee or persuades another member to support the association position.

Sixth, it is a romantic delusion for any PAC to believe that its ideologically motivated contribution will make a difference in a closely contested race. The $1 million House and $4 million Senate campaigns are a reality. Every knowledgeable observer of the political scene predicts that campaign costs will continue to zoom upward. Thus, no PAC can play a decisive role in any major race. All it can realistically hope to achieve is timely access and a sympathetic hearing for the views of the association.

Finally, the ideological approach takes a static view of the political process, when in fact it is dynamic. Members of Congress realize there is a conservative trend in the nation. Since the first law of politics is to be reelected, the members will tend to be more conservative, especially if they believe business PACs will recognize the change and support them.

It is in the interest of trade associations and their PACs to do so. Statistics show that incumbency is a powerful advantage. More than 90 percent of all senators and congressmen who have sought reelection in the past decade have won. Thus, it is much easier to change an incumbent's view than to defeat him.

Rising costs of campaigns reinforce the conservative trend in the nation. Members must look outside their states and districts for financial support. This helps to make them more receptive to association arguments. Accordingly, smart associations will utilize their PACs to help persuade key members of Congress to their point of view.

The key to success for any PAC is to take a pragmatic approach which emphasizes effective action on behalf of the economic interests of the association.

These seven reasons conclusively demonstrate the fallacy of the philosophical approach to campaign contributions. Following this path leads only to wasting money, with no benefit to the association.

Business PACs must understand that, ultimately, politics is persuasion, not philosophy, because successful politicians are pragmatists, not philosophers. Thus, timely access, a sympathetic hearing and strong, solid arguments are the keys to success in the legislative arena.

FUNDRAISING

Trade association PACs face a more difficult task raising funds than do corporate- or individual-member PACs. Under the 1976 FECA amendments, before trade association PACs can solicit the executive and administrative personnel of a member company, they must obtain written permission to do so from the corporate member. The company may approve solicitation by only one trade association PAC per year.

This severely restricts trade association PAC solicitation. BreadPAC and two other PACs are challenging the constitutionality of these restrictions. We contend that they violate First Amendment guarantees of free speech and association. The case is currently before the Supreme Court for decision. Until these limitations are invalidated by the Court, or changed by Congress, trade association PACs must follow them. Thus, mail solicitation and fundraising events in connection with association meetings are the principal ways a trade association PAC has of raising money.

BreadPAC has found that the cocktail party with a headline political speaker, as part of our semi-annual association meetings, is an effective fundraising device. It also serves to remind members of the close relationship between the association and the PAC.

DISTRIBUTING THE FUNDS

From what has been said, it should be clear that disbursement of funds should be closely tied to the legislative and regulatory aims of the association. The PAC board or committee should fully understand the major issues facing the association, its positions on the issues and the names of legislators who will be influential in deciding them.

At BreadPAC we have found that, with these considerations firmly in mind, it is most effective to distribute the money in accordance with well understood, objective criteria. This helps assure contributors that the PAC is being run in their interest, and blunts any criticism that the PAC board or committee is using the money to support their own personal favorites.

BreadPAC has developed five objective criteria for its contributions:

1. Closeness of the race – projected at 55 percent or less. Key senators and congressmen who do not meet this criteria can be aided in another way. The association

can invite them to speak at its meetings, and provide an honorarium which may be paid from corporate funds.

2. Need for the money.

3. Voting record on association issues. It is essential that the PAC maintain its own voting record on important issues to the association. Do not use the Chamber of Commerce, NAM, COPE or other outside record. As pointed out above, these organizations emphasize issues important to them. They will seldom be the same as those vital to your association. Even when they are, sometimes the Chamber or NAM will take positions contrary to those of your association.

4. Committee position. Does the member serve on a committee which has jurisdiction over important matters to the association? If so, is he or she a subcommittee chairman or ranking member?

5. Overall attitude toward association legislative and regulatory goals. This is a catch-all category which allows the PAC to take into consideration other actions by members of Congress, such as intervening on behalf of the association in an agency regulatory proceeding. It also enables the PAC to make a "missionary" contribution to a member with whom the association wants to develop a closer political relationship.

These criteria work well with incumbents, but how should the PAC judge candidates for open seats and challengers? At BreadPAC, we have developed a separate set of questions to help us allocate our funds in these situations:

1. Who is the campaign manager? Is the person an able, experienced professional or an amateur learning the political ropes?

2. What is the campaign budget and how much has been raised? Where is the remainder to come from? Two key indications of a viable campaign are an ample budget and significant early progress towards raising the target amount.

3. Who is doing the campaign polling and what are the latest results? Is the firm a respected organization with a reputation for accuracy?

4. Who is doing the media? Again, is this vital area in the hands of a competent professional or an inexperienced person?

5. What is the candidate's first choice for a committee assignment? If the association is interested in agricultural policy, the PAC should not contribute to someone who plans to go on the Judiciary Committee, unless the PAC especially wants to defeat the incumbent in that race.

6. What are the candidate's views on at least three issues of importance to the association? The PAC should support only those candidates who are in accordance with its position on major issues.

Using the answers to these questions, Bread PAC has found that we can separate potential winners from likely losers, and those who will support our positions on committees important to us.

Results of recent elections show that political winds can change very swiftly, so it is essential that information on individual races be kept current. At BreadPAC, we use every available public and private source to learn the latest campaign developments. We have found that the House and Senate Republican and Democratic campaign committees, local political writers and members of our own association are good sources of information.

Once the PAC has applied its criteria, in the case of an incumbent, or has answers to the key questions about a challenger or open seat race, its conclusions must be implemented pragmatically. The final decision is not simply a matter of arithmetic. Nor is each criteria or question equally important. For example, a few years ago a certain congressman scored poorly on the majority of our criteria, but had interceded on our behalf in an important case before a regulatory agency. This proved very valuable to the association. Accordingly, we gave him a substantial contribution.

At BreadPAC, our experience has proven it is best to keep a bipartisan balance in our contributions. Both Democrats and Republicans should know that contributions will be given on merit, without regard to ideology or party labels. This assures that the association will have friends in both parties.

The PAC should reserve 10-20 percent of its funds for contributions during the last two to three weeks of the campaign. Most candidates find themselves in a tight squeeze for media money at the end of the race. Last minute contributions to meet these needs are always well-remembered. The PAC can earn many credits for the association if it is prepared to move quickly. No long, involved authorization procedure should be used during this period. The PAC treasurer should be authorized to make the contributions promptly, with approval of the PAC chairman.

Whenever possible, the check, or a copy of it, should be personally delivered by the treasurer, or an association member to the candidate. This is even more effective if the PAC treasurer is the association's chief lobbyist. That assures the PAC contribution will reinforce the lobbying effort.

To sum up, an effective PAC is one whose contributions are closely tied to the legislative and regulatory goals of the association. The PAC should make contributions in accordance with its objective criteria on a bipartisan basis, so that the association has allies on both sides of the aisle. Proper implementation of the pragmatic approach outlined here should enable the PAC to select winners over losers with at least a 2:1 ratio. If the PAC does not, contributors will soon lose confidence that their funds are being used wisely.

Some will argue that the results of the 1980 elections proved that giving for philosophy works; that it can change the balance of power in Congress. But that theory is far from proven. Analysis of the returns from many states shows that, for the first time since 1964, a presidential candidate had real coattails. There will be no such effect in 1982, and 1984 is far in the future.

It may equally be argued that double digit inflation, high unemployment in basic industries, the hostage stalemate and a widespread desire for more effective management in Washington were larger factors in the election results than ideology of the candidates. PACs must not gear their policies to the most recent election results or they will find themselves in the position of the proverbial general always preparing to fight the previous war.

For the long run, corporate and trade association PACs cannot rely on adverse economic conditions, foreign crises and presidential failures to elect senators and congressmen who will support their interests. They must mobilize all their resources and those of the business community to protect and advance their legitimate economic interests. **PAC**

Robert J. Wager has been president of the American Bankers Association since January 1974. He is also treasurer of that association's political action committee, BreadPAC.

Wager came to ABA from the staff of the Senate Subcommittee on Reorganization, Research and International Organizations. He served there as staff director and general counsel from 1970 to 1974. Prior to that, he served as an assistant to the deputy chairman of the Democratic National Committee, and was assistant counsel to the Special Equal Rights Committee of the DNC. Wager has extensive experience with the legislative process and national politics. He is well-known for his sophisticated association management.

V. PAC BUDGETING

Careful Budgeting for PAC Success

Jerry Rapp
Government Relations Consultant

One of the most difficult – yet most fundamental – of PAC problems lies in *how* to budget the funds it collects. For all of the decisions made on when, where and how to solicit PAC contributions, just as many must be made on how to disburse the money. And in a dynamic environment of ever shifting political power and soaring campaign costs, a political action committee must be prepared to make those decisions wisely and quickly for maximum effectiveness.

PURPOSE

A well-researched, thought-out budget allows a PAC to respond quickly to requests for contributions, contribute early money in key races, maintain a consistent purpose and deny requests on the basis of a thoughtful process. It is easier to deny a request made difficult by philosophy or dollar amount expected if you can refer to a budget. The impersonality of a structural obstacle is often preferable to more personal or "emotional" obstacles.

A carefully constructed budget helps a PAC to develop or maintain continuity of purpose. Just as any planning lends itself toward consistency, so does a good budget. It is an established structure from which "newcomers"

169

can learn and upon which "old timers" can rely. A good budget, adhered to by the PAC decision-making body, helps the PAC to establish a theme or character. But the budget cannot be rigid. Dynamic political and legislative climates demand flexible budgeting.

STRUCTURE

A PAC budget cannot be definitive for obvious reasons: the prospects of re-electing or defeating an incumbent change, open seats develop, and you cannot calculate with certainty what total PAC receipts will be. But a budget is an essential guide, and two elements incorporated in it can compensate for the uncertain components.

First, place a minimum and maximum dollar figure for each seat to which you expect to contribute. Then contribute within that range based on the success of your fund solicitations and the prospects and financial requirements of your chosen candidates. Second, include in the budget a discretionary fund to allow for flux and last-minute opportunities.

Before developing a fund disbursement structure, a PAC must determine what the budget decision-making body will be. The best organization seems to be a two-tiered PAC committee. The first tier is composed of representatives of all major operating divisions of the PAC. This allows for broad-based participation in the budget forming process and insures varied inputs and a more representative output. It also enhances the PAC's ability to raise funds from the various divisions the committee represents.

The second tier of the PAC committee is a smaller disbursement committee composed of, maybe, five individuals. The disbursement committee expedites contributions by allowing a few individuals -- guided by the established PAC philosophy and budget -- to approve contributions. The selection of this smaller committee could be done any number of ways, depending upon the individual PAC. The purpose of the two committees is clear, however. The larger committee allows broad involvement. The smaller committee responds to initiatives of the larger committee and gets things done. Both committees operate with an agreed upon budget structure so that disbursement decisions do not result in a virtual "free-for-all" as election time nears.

DECISION-MAKING CRITERIA

PAC budgeting requires a careful selection of candidates or seats prior to setting maximum/minimum contributions guidelines. The key to good budgeting is the ability to pare down your spending categories to a manageable size, then set your budgeting limitations for each option.

Basically the categories a PAC of any size must review include:

- All Senate seats up for re-election;

- All House seats where the PAC has a facility or constituency;

- All House seats where the incumbent serves on key committees, and especially subcommittees, which have jurisdiction over issues of importance to the PAC;

- Any state legislative or executive races the PAC may be interested in.

- Any political party contributions the PAC may want to make;

- A discretionary fund set aside to meet the aforementioned unexpected developments.

Determining which candidate the PAC would support once these categories are established include:

- Voting record of incumbent to date;

- Candidate's attitudes toward corporation/association positions on important issues;

- Probability of electing the favored PAC candidates.

CONCLUSION

There is no way to insure winning campaigns in every race. In fact, most PACs are not primarily concerned with winning candidates as much as they are with contributing to candidates sympathetic to their needs and viewpoints. A PAC contribution, whatever the amount, is a demonstration of support. That support is appreciated. A carefully planned budget is an extra guideline for PAC management to gauge actions and contributions. If designed and adhered to, it can provide long-term benefits. **PAC**

For over nine years, Jerry Rapp worked in the government relations office of Bristol-Myers Company. In May 1980 he opened his own consulting business, Jerry Rapp and Associates. Most recently he served as director of the Mid-Atlantic Prelude to Victory Dinner, worked in the Reagan-Bush campaign, and was assistant to the co-chairman of the Presidential Inaugural Committee 1980.

VI. PAC LEGAL QUESTIONS

PAC Activities: In-Kind Contributions and Independent Expenditures

H. Richard Mayberry, Esq.
Law Offices of H. Richard Mayberry, Jr.

IN-KIND CONTRIBUTIONS

The 1980 elections witnessed a surge of activity by political action committees. A number of factors, including clarification of the legal avenues for political activities, the advent of limitations on individual contributions, and a recognition that collective political efforts provide a stronger voice in the political process, combined to produce new directions in organizational government affairs programs.

A growing number of associations, corporations and labor organizations complement their legislative activities with PACs, allowing them to support elected officials both during the legislative sessions and at election time.

PACs typically support candidates by contributing money, the "mother's milk" of politics. Today's candidate for political office, from city council to the presidency, must be prepared to pay a campaign staff, hire pollsters, rent office space, purchase advertising, and so forth. Many candidates rely on PAC money to help pay for these important campaign ingredients.

But most office-seekers need more than money. Some services and skills, such as technical research papers and management expertise, are not readily available or cannot simply be purchased. However, while candidates often lack these resources, many of them are abundant in common interest organizations and can be made available to candidates.

Most PACs evaluate candidates and disburse direct money contributions. But first, they should determine if candidates can be more effectively aided through two other, often neglected, PAC activities: in-kind contributions and independent expenditures, both of which can maximize the use of existing resources and greatly aid candidates.

THE NON-MONETARY OPTIONS

PACs collect voluntary contributions in order to support candidates by making contributions and expenditures. A campaign contribution is "anything of value given to or provided on behalf of a candidate to influence a federal election."[1] A contribution can be either a money gift to the candidate (the typical form of PAC assistance) or it can be goods and services provided to the candidate, known as an "in-kind" contribution. Another type of candidate support is the independent expenditure: a disbursement made to pay for a communication expressly advocating the election or defeat of a clearly identified candidate without the candidate's cooperation.[2]

Supplying resources to candidates in the form of in-kind contributions and independent expenditures promotes a fundamental purpose of many groups: to express their viewpoint through the governmental process.

Many now consider their PACs an essential component of a successful government relations program. They are vehicles for pooling individual contributions to effectively support candidates who understand the importance of issues affecting their members and employees.

Many of the same organizational resources employed in legislative efforts can also be valuable to candidates when they are made available through PACs. Such political programs can also be used to promote active involvement of the group's organization in the governmental process.

USING ORGANIZATIONAL RESOURCES: A CASE STUDY

Here is an entirely fictional scenario of an in-kind PAC contribution:

An association of energy users has a vital concern with energy policy and commits considerable resources to governmental affairs. Recent research by industry experts funded by the association resulted in a white paper universally recognized as an authoritative study.

Congressional staffers on one of the energy committees incorporated some of the best ideas from this study into a bill that would provide increased fuel supplies for users in a manner consistent with national conservation policy and environmental standards. Association government affairs officers communicated their members' support for the bill as it passed the House. The measure was under consideration by the Senate when the session ended for the biennial elections.

Several energy committee members running for reelection and several candidates challenging incumbents strongly supported this legislation. They approached the association's PAC for campaign assistance.

The association PAC saw the opportunity to help elect candidates favoring the legislation and, incidentally, to convey the industry's position to the public. The first impulse was to make a direct money contribution from the PAC to the candidates.

However, PAC officials decided these candidates could be best supported, and the viewpoint of the association best communicated, if the PAC made in-kind contributions and independent expenditures.

One approach was to permit the association's energy issue manager to take a leave of absence, with his regular salary paid by the association's PAC, for a temporary assignment on a candidate's staff. Also, the white paper that led to the proposed legislation was made available to candidates backing the bill. Candidates were also offered the association's energy expertise, to help them develop their energy positions during the campaign.

Such association activity is perfectly lawful. The value of the services and materials would constitute an in-kind contribution, which would have to be paid for by the PAC and would be subject to reporting requirements and a $5,000 per candidate per election ceiling (imposed on federal-level elections.)

Another approach taken by our fictional PAC would be to locate states and districts where a large number of energy users were doing business and place advertisements presenting the voting records of incumbents on the proposed energy bill and related legislation.

These political advertisements were made without the candidates' cooperation or consultation, thereby constituting an independent expenditure.

IN-KIND VS. INDEPENDENT: DISTINCTIONS

In the above case study, providing an issue paper directly to candidates was an in-kind contribution, while the newspaper political advertisements were independent expenditures.

The distinction can be illustrated by the following example:

> A person might purchase billboard advertisements endorsing a candidate. If he does so completely on his own, and not at the request or suggestion of the candidate or his agent's (sic) that would constitute an "independent expenditure on behalf of a candidate ...." The person making the expenditure would have to report it as such.

> However, if the advertisement was placed in cooperation with the candidate's campaign organization, then the amount would constitute a gift by the supporter and an expenditure by the candidate -- just as if there had been a direct contribution enabling the candidate to place the advertisement himself. It would be so reported by both.[3]

To qualify as an independent expenditure, several elements must be present. Unless these strict standards are met, candidate support activities other than direct money contributions are presumed to be in-kind contributions.[4]

The type of contribution has a direct bearing on the total dollar value of contributions that can be provided to a candidate. While contributions are limited by law in federal elections to $1,000 per candidate for each election and to $5,000 per candidate each year for a qualified multi-candidate PAC,[5] the Supreme Court has held that independent expenditures cannot be limited.[6] Consequently, even pending legislation restricting PAC contributions (the so-called Obey-Railsback bill) has no effect on independent expenditures.

IN-KIND CONTRIBUTIONS

Although few PACs have previously taken advantage of this form of candidate support, in-kind contributions have several advantages over cash gifts:

- They exploit existing resources. By using the productivity and skills of the organization's staff, the PAC is in a position to exercise control over how candidates use PAC contributions.

- In-kind contributions lead to a truer and more representative amplification of the group's positions than do direct money contributions, which are readily assimilated into a candidate campaign treasury. Consequently, in-kind contributions bring greater visibility to the organization. Also, it is possible that a staff person who aids a successful candidate will be consulted on the same issues after the election.

- Interest groups are in the business of affecting public perspectives on issues. Using the specialities of their organization, candidates are more likely to accurately reflect their positions and the rationale behind them.

An in-kind contribution is a specific type of contribution defined by existing law. From the perspective of an incorporated association, corporation, or labor oragnization, a contribution includes "any direct or indirect payment ... or any service, or anything of value ... to any candidate in connection with a federal election."[7]

179

The term "anything of value" is all-encompassing, including goods, facilities, equipment, supplies, personnel, or virtually anything[8] else which has more than a minimal value.[9]

Incorporated organizations and labor unions must be able to recognize when anything of value is given to a candidate, because they are prohibited from making a contribution or expenditure in connection with a federal election unless it is paid for from voluntary political contributions collected by a political action committee. While direct money contributions from organizational funds are easily restricted from political uses, it is more difficult to monitor and restrict advice and counsel of employees and the sharing of legislative materials. Management must be careful that no unwitting in-kind contributions are made.

VALUATION AND REPORTING

Generally, all PAC contributions and expenditures must be accounted for[10] and complete records maintained for three years.[11] These records must be available for inspection by the Federal Election Commission and must provide an accurate basis for completing the mandatory periodic reporting to be filed with the FEC.[12]

Each in-kind contribution must be valued at the usual and normal charge attributable for the services or goods, according to the following guidelines for valuation:

Services – In the fictional energy users association example above, an issue manager was released to work on a campaign staff. The association may continue to pay that manager's salary, with the PAC reimbursing the association for the pro rata share attributable to any candidate-related activity. The value of that person's time constitutes an in-kind contribution from the PAC to the candidate and is reportable to the FEC.

The issue manager may work for the candidate in various blocks of time – a day, a week, or several weeks – until the maximum legal limit of $5,000 per election is reached.

In addition to salary, the PAC must also value and report other expenditures – fringe benefits,[13] expenses and any use of association facilities. If the employee is to work for the candidate for several days, then the number of work days in the year (typically 20 per month or 240 per year) must be divided by the salary to determine the value of each day's contribution. If the issue manager's salary is $24,000, the basic reimbursement schedule would be $100 a day.

In fairness to the employee, various fringe benefits should be continued. The value of the fringe benefits is an additional component of the contribution and should be accurately assessed by the association's accounting department. Generally, the value of health and life insurance and pension rights is approximately one-third of the basic salary – $33 a day in the example above. Thus, $133 would be the value of each day's time for the energy user's manager.

Caveat – The above computation is premised on the employee working his or her regular eight-hour day. Assignment to a campaign means more working hours. An argument could be made that hours over eight per day are individual volunteer time and not reimbursable. This may have strength if the issue manager works for a candidate within commuting distance of association headquarters.

However, with a field assignment, a stronger argument runs that, but for electioneering activities, the specialist would not be in the campaign. With field activities, the safer course of action is to value the hourly rate of the issue manager's time and consider each hour a contribution, whether for eight, ten or any other number of hours per day.

Facilities – The issue manager may work for the candidate in the association office, where needed support services are available. The PAC must then assign a value and reimburse the association for use of all such facilities. An hourly value for the facilities may be computed by prorating the cost of offices. If clerical staff is used, their hourly rates must also be computed and reported. All expenses, including space and additional staff, must be allocated to specific candidates in FEC reports.[14]

Goods – Various written materials, including issue papers, opinion polls, and membership lists, of the association may be provided to a candidate and paid for by the PAC. Each would be considered an in-kind contribution. For issue papers that are compiled and/or written by association staff, employee time and expenses in producing the papers must be computed and reported unless they are part of the public domain. For example, if the issue paper was presented as testimony before a congressional committee and became available through a committee report, no value need be assigned it. Otherwise, its value becomes a contribution.

Since issue papers may have multiple uses, their costs, can be prorated according to the number of uses. For example, an issue paper used for both lobbying and electioneering may have cost $200 for production. The in-kind contribution would be half the total cost, $100.

Membership organizations often make their membership lists available to candidates. The ususal and normal charge for these lists would be an in-kind contribution to a candidate.

Many associations conduct member polls, or purchase polls from outside agencies. Polls made available to candidates constitute an in-kind contribution to the candidate and a reportable expenditure by the candidate[15] unless, prior to receipt, results presented to the candidate have been made public without request, authorization, prearrangement or coordination by the candidate-recipient.[16]

Any methods that reasonably reflect the benefit to the candidate may be used to value the poll.[17] For example, the timeliness of the poll affects its value.[18] As with all contributions, adequate records must be maintained, sufficient to support the valuation of the contribution.

RECORDKEEPING AND REPORTING

The PAC must maintain records of all in-kind contributions, including the date, value of contribution and the name and address of each candidate on whose behalf any expenditure was made.[19] It must report this information periodically[20] to the FEC, whenever the expenditure within the reporting period or calendar year exceeds $200.[21]

The candidate must value the in-kind contributions received and consumed on the date received[22] and report them on the appropriate schedule of receipts, identified as "in-kind contributions."[23] The PAC may facilitate the candidate's reporting by sending a form letter giving applicable information (PAC name and address, value of contribution, etc.).

Exceptions -- Although virtually every candidate-related activity by an association constitutes a contribution or expenditure, some latitude for volunteer and intra-organizational political activities exists.

Organization personnel may, without compensation, volunteer their time on behalf of a candidate.[24] Employees cannot be coerced or rewarded for their volunteer activity.[25] Generally, volunteer efforts would be undertaken outside of working hours, before or after working hours, during lunch periods, or during bona fide, although compensable, vacation time or other earned leave time. An employee may engage in volunteer political activity during working hours only if the time taken is made up within a reasonable period.[26]

Employees engaged in volunteer political activity may make "occasional, isolated, or incidental" use of corporate or union facilities and are required to reimburse their employer only to the extent overhead costs are increased.[27] Such activity cannot exceed one hour per week or four hours per month.[28] Greater use of corporate or labor organization facilities is allowed if it is reimbursed within a commercially reasonable time for the normal and usual rental of the facilities.[29]

A corporation or labor organization may also, at its discretion, allow other (nonstaff) persons engaged in volunteer political activity to use copying machines, space and other organizational facilities (such as telephones and typewriters) if the normal and usual rental is charged.[30] If a corporation or labor organization regularly makes meeting rooms available to community organizations it may also make rooms available on a nonpartisan basis to political groups (on the same general terms). This would not constitute an in-kind contribution.[31]

A final, but important, service not considered an in-kind contribution allows an organization to render legal and accounting services for a candidate, provided the lawyer or accountant is a regular employee of the corporation or union and the services are rendered solely to insure the candidate's compliance with the federal election or tax laws.[32] **PAC**

FOOTNOTES

[1]11 C.F.R. sec. 100.7.

[2]11 C.F.R. sec. 109.

[3]"The House and Senate Reports to the Federal Election Campaign Act of 1971, as amended in 1974, provide guidance in differentiating individual expenditures that are contributions and candidate expenditures ... from those treated as independent expenditures subject to the ... ceiling. The House Report speaks of independent expenditures as costs 'incurred without the request or consent of a candidate or his agent.' H. Rep. No. 93-1239, p. 6 (1974). The Senate Report addresses the issue in greater detail." Buckley, at 703, n. 53, quoting S. Rep. No. 93-689, p. 18 (1974).

[4]11 C.F.R. sec. 109.1 (c).

[5]11 C.F.R. sec. 110.

[6]*Buckley v. Valeo*, 424 U.S. 1 (1976).

[7]It is noteworthy that any services or goods provided "in connection with a federal election," regardless of intent to influence the election, are considered as contributions from an association. 11 C.F.R. sec. 114.1 (a) (1). Cf., the general definition, which includes the requirement that the disbursement be "for the purpose of influencing the nomination for election, or election, of any person to federal office" to be considered a contribution. 11 C.F.R. sec. 100.7.

[8]11 C.F.R. sec. 100.7 (a) (1).

[9]Some items, such as recognition that a volunteer is affiliated with an organization, are so difficult to assign a value or have such a small value that a de minimus principle applies and they are not considered a contribution.

[10]11 C.F.R. sec. 102.9.

[11]For an overview of recordkeeping and reporting requirements, see FEC Campaign Guide for Political Committees, Washington, D.C.: GPO, 1978.

[12]11 C.F.R. sec. 104.

[13]11 C.F.R. sec. 114.12 (c) (1).

[14]11 C.F.R. sec. 106.3.

[15]11 C.F.R. sec. 106.4 (b).

[16]11 C.F.R. sec. 106.4 (c).

[17]11 C.F.R. sec. 106.4 (e).

[18]After 16 days, the value would be decreased by 50 percent of the amount allocated, with further decreases after 60 days. 11 C.F.R. sec. 106.4 (f), (g).

[19]11 C.F.R. sec. 102.9.

[20]11 C.F.R. sec. 104.5.

[21]11 C.F.R. sec. 104.3 (b).

[22]Technically, the PAC and the candidate could assign different values to the in-kind contribution. Practically, they do not.

[23]11 C.F.R. sec. 104.13.

[24]11 C.F.R. sec. 100.7 (b).

[25]11 C.F.R. sec. 114.5 (a).

[26]11 C.F.R. sec. 100.7 (a) (3).

[27]11 C.F.R. sec. 114.9 (a).

[28]11 C.F.R. sec. 114.9 (a) (1) (iii).

[29]11 C.F.R. sec. 114.9 (a) (2).

[30]11 C.F.R. sec. 114.9 (d).

[31]11 C.F.R. sec. 114.12 (b).

[32]11 C.F.R. sec. 100.7 (b) (13).

INDEPENDENT EXPENDITURES

Referring once again to the fictional story of the association of energy-users in the previous section, the association purchased political advertising in districts where many energy-users resided. This is another option for influencing the election of favored candidates. Because the PAC purchased the ads without consulting the candidates, it was considered an independent expenditure.

According to one commentator, "the independent expenditure route provides an outlet for political generosity" and "almost invariably includes advertising: television, radio and newspaper spots, brochures and bumper stickers."[1]

An independent expenditure must meet specific criteria. It is a communication purchased to "expressly advocate the election or defeat of a clearly identifiable candidate" and must not be made "with the cooperation or with the prior consent of, or in consultation with, or at the request or suggestion of" a candidate or his agent.[2] Associations, as well as corporations and unions, are prohibited from directly making independent expenditures.[3] They must therefore be made through PACs.

Qualification. Each expenditure must specifically qualify as an independent expenditure, or it will be treated as an in-kind contribution.[4] To qualify, certain elements are required: 1) expression of advocacy, 2) clear candidate identification and 3) lack of candidate (or his agent's) cooperation.

"Advocacy" means a communication containing a message advocating the election or defeat of a candidate, using expressions such as "elect," "vote for," and "defeat."[5] A "clearly identified candidate" means a candidate's name or photograph appears in the communication. The candidate's identity must be apparent by unambiguous reference.[6]

In evaluating distribution of a congressman's voting record on specific issues by an interest group which assessed the "correctness" of each vote in relation to organizational philosophy as independent expenditures, one U.S. Court of Appeals gave a literal meaning to the term "advocacy."[7] "The words *expressly advocating* mean exactly what they say." According to this court, express words encouraging election or defeat are required. Merely publishing voting records (or presumably voting ratings, if this interpretation is carried to a logical conclusion) without a specific candidate endorsement would not be an independent expenditure. Instead, it is public discussion of public issues, which is not regulated by the Federal Election Commission.

Similarly, a political cartoon, without advocacy language, has been considered more of an expression on a public issue than a statement of advocacy for or against the election of the individual depicted in the cartoon.[8]

Because the expenditure must be made independent of a candidate or his agent, the information on which a decision is based to make an independent expenditure must be derived from sources other than the candidate.

For example, a PAC may poll a district to determine sensitive issues and then shape political advertising linking the candidate it is endorsing with the voting public's consensus on that issue.

But, prior to the advertising, any contact with a candidate or his agent might mean loss of "independence." Most organizations making independent expenditures scrupulously avoid any candidate contact, before or after the expenditure, to avoid being vulnerable to charges of collusion and to protect their right to make further independent expenditures.[9]

Even if direct contact is avoided, communications prepared by a candidate, but paid for by a PAC, are not independent expenditures but in-kind contributions.[10] Therefore, contact with an impartial third party to secure materials or information prepared by a candidate is considered coordination with the candidate. In effect, the neutral party has become an agent for the candidate.

Federal election regulations classify anyone in the candidate's campaign organization with authority to make expenditures an agent.[11] But the FEC's interpretation of these regulations has appeared in the past to extend further to any campaign employee, regardless of whether he or she has express expenditure authority.[12] Therefore, any contact, professionally, socially, or otherwise, with campaign staff should be avoided by those making independent expenditures.

A more difficult question arises when a PAC decides to use consultants and vendors, in making candidate-related independent expenditures, who have provided goods or services to the same candidate. Recently, the Federal Election Commission gave guidance on when these consultants and vendors became agents of the candidate and consequently would destroy the independence of any expenditures they were involved with.[13]

- An advertising firm which does work for a candidate is an agent of the candidate.

- A consultant who serves in the capacity of a political consultant, advisor or campaign worker for a candidate is an agent of the candidate.

- A polling firm which undertakes polling activity for a candidate not involving any election advocacy is not an agent.

- A media time-buyer working for a candidate is an agent.

- A direct-mail firm which solicits funds for a candidate not involving any election advocacy is not an agent.

- A list-broker with a candidate is not an agent.

Expenditures to purchase campaign goods and services may initially be independent but become in-kind contributions if shared with the candidate or political committees. For example, the value of the services of a political researcher whose salary is prepaid by an independent expenditure becomes a contribution if the researcher is sent to work for a candidate. Also, the gift of a poll to a candidate which showed certain data relevant to a particular candidate is an in-kind contribution.[14]

An unresolved question is whether a PAC could make independent expenditures on behalf of a candidate after making an in-kind contribution for that candidate. An argument could be made that a PAC that had coordinated its in-kind contributions with a favored candidate is forever an agent of the candidate. However, if the degree of intimacy between the candidate and campaign is limited to a specific transaction, i.e., a single in-kind contribution, it would appear that future expenditures not based on information gained from the candidate should qualify as independent expenditures.

A PAC making independent expenditures, which are unlimited if they meet all the elements previously discussed, may accept up to $5,000 per year from contributors.[15] Consequently, the fundraising potential of an independent expenditure committee is not enhanced in relation to other political committees.[16] If such a political committee solicits contributions for specific candidates with the intent to forward the contributions to the candidate, the committee is not engaged in making independent expenditures, but is acting as a conduit for the candidate.[17]

Notice and Reporting. Each communication constituting an independent expenditure must provide the public with notice of the identity of persons paying for the political advertisement and that the ad is not authorized by any candidate.[18] The disclaimer need not be placed on the front face or page of any such materials.

A PAC must itemize and report each independent expenditure exceeding $250 on FEC Form 3, Schedule E.[19] An independent expenditure of $1,000 or more made within one to twenty days before an election must be reported to the FEC within 24 hours after it is made. The reports must certify (under penalty of perjury) that the expenditure is independent from a candidate, and must provide other information concerning the communication and committee, and its contributor.

Caveat. Independent expenditures have proven a potent means of communicating a political viewpoint in the 1980 election. However, certain "unchartered waters" remain in interaction with potential candidate agents. With the procedural complexities, a PAC making independent expenditures should closely follow the advice of its federal election lawyer.[20] **PAC**

FOOTNOTES

[1]Maxwell Glen, "How to Get Around the Campaign Spending Limits," *National Journal*, June 23, 1979, pp. 1044-1046. (Article title suggests potential for independent spending.) Political advertising, as with campaign buttons, qualifies as independent expenditures if the producing organization is independent of the candidate's organizations. Information Letter to GOP Feminist Caucus (September 10, 1976).

[2]"(A)n expenditure by a person for a communication expressly advocating the election or defeat of a clearly identified candidate which is not made with the cooperation or with the prior consent of, or in consultation with, or at the request or suggestion of, a candidate or any agent or authorized committee of such candidate." 11 C.F.R. sec. 109.1 (a).

[3]The independent expenditure regulation defining person specifically excludes a corporation. 11 C.F.R. sec. 109.1 (b) (1). In light of *First National Bank v. Bellotti*, 98 S.Ct. 1407, 1422, n.26 (1978) striking down a statute prohibiting referendum-related corporate expenditures, the constitutionality of the ban on federal election-related independent expenditures is not totally clear.

[4]11 C.F.R. sec. 109.1 (c).

[5]11 C.F.R. sec. 109.1 (b) (2).

[6]11 C.F.R. sec. 109.1 (b) (3).

[7]*FEC v. Clitrim*, U.S. Court of Appeals for the Second Circuit, No. 79-3014, February 5, 1980, reprinted in Fed. El. Camp. Fin. Guide (CCH) at ¶ 9107.

[8]*FEC v. AFSCME*, U.S. District Court for the District of Columbia, No. 78-2114, May 14, 1979, reprinted in Fed. El. Camp. Fin. Guide (CCH) at ¶ 9078.

[9]11 C.F.R. sec. 109.1 (a)(4)(i); contact is permissible merely to request FEC guidelines on independent expenditures. 11 C.F.R. sec. 109.1 (a)(4)(ii).

[10]11 C.F.R. sec. 109 (d) (1).

[11]11 C.F.R. sec. 109 (b) (5).

[12]See, for example, FEC Campaign Guide for Political Committees, p. 9.

[13]Advisory Opinion 1979-80 (March 12, 1980).

[14]Ibid.

[15]2 U.S.C. sec. 441 a (a) (1) (c). *Mott et al v. FEC*, U.S. District Court for District of Columbia, No. 79-3375, June 30, 1980, reprinted in Fed. El. Camp. Fin. Guide (CCH) at ¶ 9134 (upholding constitutionality of this provision).

[16]Cf. Advisory Opinion 1979-40 (August 17, 1979) and Advisory Opinion 1979-49 (October 5, 1979).

[17]Advisory Opinion 1980-46 (June 25, 1980).

[18]11 C.F.R. sec. 109.3 (referencing sec. 110.11).

[19]Generally, 11 C.F.R. sec. 109.2.

[20]Compliance with the federal election laws can become so complex that one bar association ruled general PAC consultants are only free to impart their general knowledge of federal campaign laws: "When legal problems arise that are sufficiently difficult and complex that the professional judgment of one trained in law is required, a lawyer must be consulted. Anyone else attempting to advise a PAC would be involved in unauthorized practice of law" -- District of Columbia Bar Code of Professional Responsibility, Opinions No. 52 (1978).

H. Richard Mayberry, Jr., a political lawyer in Washington, D.C., advises organizations on how to set up and run political action committees and meet FEC recordkeeping requirements. In addition to providing PAC operations manuals and solicitation materials, Mayberry represents PACs before the FEC and serves as PAC counsel in regards to the legal aspects of organizational political activities.

Mayberry is an adjunct professor at The George Washington University where he is responsible for teaching a full semester seminar on PACs and campaign finance in the graduate program in legislation.

Formerly, Mayberry was with the Office of General Counsel of the Chamber of Commerce of the United States and served as in-house counsel in connection with corporate political matters. He speaks frequently on the topic of PAC formation and operation.

Organization and Administration:
PAC Legal Considerations

William E. Sudow, Esq.
Fried, Frank, Harris, Shriver and Kampelman
with Kenneth J. Vandevelde, Esq.

This chapter is a brief overview of some of the legal considerations relating to the organization and administration of a PAC. The discussion includes sections on the advantages of a PAC, the steps that should be taken to organize a PAC, the relationship between a corporation and its PAC, legal limits relating to PAC fundraising activities, tax considerations and record-keeping and reporting requirements. A discussion of the legal limits relating to methods which a PAC may use to influence an election – direct contributions, in-kind contributions and independent expenditures -- is included in a separate chapter.

One word of caution. Although the basic rules regarding PACs are relatively straightforward, certain sections of the law are complex and some provisions are ambiguous and subject to differing interpretations. Where a legal interpretation of the law is required, it is recommended that a PAC seek the professional judgment of a lawyer.

ADVANTAGES OF A PAC

The existence of nearly 1,200 corporate PACs by Election Day 1980 is the greatest testimony to the advantages of organizing a PAC. This figure contrasts dramatically with the 89 corporate PACs which existed in 1974. Clearly, the word is out: A PAC is well worth the time, money and effort.

The original impetus for creating political action committees was legal. Decades ago, Congress prohibited corporations from making a money contribution to certain candidates for federal office.[1] This basic limitation was strengthened through a series of amendments, including provisions in the Federal Corrupt Practices Act of 1925, the War Labor Disputes Act of 1943, the Labor Management Relations Act in 1947, and the Federal Election Campaign Act of 1971, which broadened the prohibition and made it applicable to both corporations and labor unions. With this evolution, however, came specific authority for a corporation or labor union to use its own resources to set up separate segregated funds which were authorized to solicit voluntary contributions from certain corporate employees or union members.

The significance of PACs was greatly enhanced by the Federal Election Campaign Act Amendments of 1974 which included strict limits on contributions to candidates for federal office. Prior to 1974, an individual could contribute unlimited amounts. Although the 1974 amendments included limits on the amount of contributions a PAC could make, the PAC limit was higher than the limit imposed on individuals. Thus, PACs became an increasingly important source of campaign funds.

The benefits of forming a PAC fall into several general categories:

- Legal
- Financial
- Corporate
- Tactical
- Educational.

The most important advantage of a PAC is that it provides a thoroughly legal -- and legitimate -- way for a corporation to use corporate resources to influence the political process in a way which is conducive to corporate objectives. The Federal Election Campaign Act, as amended, specifically permits a corporation to organize and maintain a political action committee.[2] This includes authority to pay the costs of PAC-sponsored solicitations and fundraising events and to influence all the decisions of its PAC, including the selection of candidates to receive contributions from the PAC.

193

A PAC can have more financial clout in an election than an individual contributor. As indicated above, the 1974 FECA amendments imposed a limit on contributions by individuals of $1,000 per candidate per election.[3] However, if a PAC qualifies as a "multicandidate committee," it may contribute $5,000 to a candidate per election.[4]

A PAC may also make "independent expenditures," i.e., "an expenditure expressly advocating the election or defeat of a clearly identified candidate which is not made with the prior consent of, or in consultation with, or at the request or suggestion of a candidate."[5]

The ability of a PAC to raise funds is enhanced by a provision in the Act which permits an individual to contribute up to $5,000 in "non-earmarked" funds to a PAC in a calendar year.[6] If a contribution is earmarked, i.e., directed through a PAC to a particular candidate, it would be counted against the individual's $1,000 candidate contribution limit. Therefore, a PAC may not accept from any contributor more than $1,000 of earmarked contributions per candidate per election.[7]

It is possible, therefore, for an individual to contribute $1,000 to Candidate X in an election and for a PAC, to which the individual has contributed $5,000, also to contribute $5,000 to Candidate X in the same election.[8]

The PAC can focus and direct political contributions so that they will have a discernible impact on elections which are of the greatest interest to the sponsoring corporation.

The PAC also serves other corporate objectives beyond influencing a given election. It provides a clearly defined focus for the expression of corporate political interests. This can eliminate confusion over who speaks about the corporation's political objectives and who has responsibility for furthering those objectives.

Finally, the PAC can provide a focal point for the financial aspect of a corporation's political activity. Those wishing to contribute know where to send their contributions. Similarly, the existence of a PAC may relieve the pressure on individual corporate executives who may be asked to make personal contributions to a candidate.

By centralizing its political activity in a PAC, the corporation also can realize a number of tactical advantages over less structured methods of political activity. Because the PAC typically is a continuing organization rather than an ad hoc group put together for a single election, it can engage in long-term planning and action. For example, coordination of expenditures through a PAC allows the PAC to target its contributions to those regions or candidates that can put the funds to their most efficacious use. Further, an established PAC is in a position to provide seed money for candidates very early in a campaign, a time when the money often is needed most.

The PAC is an effective way of disseminating information and encouraging informed political participation. Through its PAC, a corporation has a means for presenting its point of view to its employees, the general public, and even its elected representatives, whether in city hall, the statehouse, or Congress. Further, individuals who do not have the time or the interest to participate actively in political affairs can contribute to a PAC, confident that the PAC officers will direct contributions to candidates or causes which the contributors would support.

ORGANIZATION OF A PAC

Organizing a PAC is relatively simple and straightforward. To comply with the Act, a corporation must take certain basic steps to organize and register its PAC. In addition, many corporations elect to create more formal structures to facilitate the administration of their PACs.

The Act requires that a PAC register with the Federal Election Commission within ten days of its establishment.[9] As a result of an amendment to the Act included in the Federal Election Campaign Act Amendments of 1979, a PAC is established when it is organized, regardless of the amount of its financial activity.[10] Events which constitute "establishment" may include the following:

- A vote by a corporation's board of directors to establish a PAC which will participate in federal election campaign activities;

195

- Selection of officers to administer the PAC; and

- Payment of the initial operating expenses of the PAC.[11]

To register, a PAC must file with the Commission a Statement of Organization (FEC Form 1, Appendix A). The form, along with a packet of general information, may be obtained by request from the Commission.

To meet its minimum registration requirements, a PAC must report the following information:[12]

- *Name*. The name, address and type of committee. The Act now requires that the name of a PAC include the name of its "connected organization,"[13] the corporation which "directly or indirectly establishes, administers or financially supports a political committee."[14] The PAC may use a clearly recognized abbreviation or acronym by which the connected organization is commonly known.[15] Where a PAC is sponsored by more than one corporation, its name should reflect the name of the corporation that paid for its establishment and administration.[16]

- *Connected Organization*. The identity of the connected organization.

- *Custodian of Books*. The name, address, and position of the custodian of the books and accounts of the committee. The PAC's treasurer may be designated as the custodian.

- *Treasurer*. The name and address of the treasurer of the committee. The 1979 amendments eliminated the requirement that a PAC have a chairman. However, the Act requires that a PAC have a treasurer and specifically prohibits a PAC from receiving a contribution or making an expenditure if the office of treasurer is vacant.[17] The treasurer is the chief financial officer of a PAC and is

196

required under the Act to use his best efforts to obtain, maintain and submit the information required by the Act.[18]

- *Depository* . The depositories used by the PAC . A PAC must designate one or more depositories and maintain at least one checking account at its depository .[19]

A corporation may elect to incorporate its PAC. The Act specifically provides that an incorporated PAC is permitted to engage in political activities which corporations are otherwise prohibited from undertaking, provided the PAC is "incorporated for liability purposes only ."[20] Incorporation, however, does not completely insulate the treasurer, who remains personally responsible for carrying out his duties under the Act.[21]

A PAC cannot accept a contribution or make an expenditure without a treasurer, and therefore may wish to designate an assistant treasurer who can assume the duties and responsibilities of the treasurer in the event of a temporary or permanent vacancy or in the event the treasurer is unavailable.[22]

A PAC may wish to designate a chairman, who should enjoy the confidence of and have access to the corporation's top management. If the PAC is small, the chairman may also be responsible for the day-to-day activities of the PAC . However, if the PAC is large, it may wish to designate a senior corporate officer to be chairman of the PAC and appoint a vice chairman to handle the daily affairs .

Most PACs are governed by a board of directors, which may be appointed in any manner which the connected corporation wishes. For example, the board may be selected by the chief executive officer of the corporation . Or, the board may be composed of certain corporate officers who serve *ex officio* .

The powers of the board also may be subject to the discretion of the connected corporation . While the corporation may wish to vest the board with policy-making authority regarding the operation of the PAC, it is wise to delegate authority over the day-to-day affairs of the PAC to the PAC's

197

officers, who may be appointed by the board. Delegating authority to PAC officers will enable the PAC to operate quickly without the need to assemble board members.

However appointed, a board supplies a means for integrating key corporate personnel into the management of the PAC. This can:

- Insure that the PAC functions consistently with corporate policy;

- Build support for the PAC within the corporation;

- Facilitate the formulation of a PAC policy which is based on a wide consensus within the corporation rather than on the preferences of a few individuals.

Depending upon its size and budget, a PAC may want to establish standing committees to be responsible for such tasks as:

- Fundraising;

- Determining the type of activities in which it will engage and identifying candidates to receive contributions;

- Monitoring legislation under consideration by Congress or the state legislature;

- Voter education campaigns;

- Voter registration activities.

If the connected corporation is particularly concerned about establishing a PAC program which is compatible with corporate policy, the by-laws may require that particular committees include members of the PAC board of directors or specific corporate officers. This can provide an effective compromise between delegating too much or too little authority to PAC officers and employees.

One important decision that a PAC should make at the time of its formation is whether to become involved in both federal and non-federal elections. A PAC which is active solely with regard to state and local elections is not regulated by the Act. However, one which commingles federal and non-federal funds and activities will be required to conduct its state and local activities in full compliance with the Act. Therefore, if a PAC is active in both areas, it should structure its operation in such a way as to shelter its state and local activities from the limitations and reporting requirements imposed by federal law.

To assist the PAC in this endeavor, the Commission has adopted regulations which allow a PAC to designate separate campaign depositories for its federal and non-federal election campaign funds.[23] Only funds subject to the limitations of the act may be deposited in the federal account, and all contributions or expenditures made by the PAC in connection with a federal election must be made from the federal account. The PAC is required to maintain the federal account in compliance with all recordkeeping and reporting requirements of the Act. Administrative expenses are to be allocated between the federal and non-federal accounts according to the benefit each account derives.

A PAC which is involved in both federal and non-federal elections must satisfy further requirements not otherwise imposed on a PAC engaged exclusively in federal election activities. Specifically, the PAC may deposit in the federal account only those contributions which:

- Are designated for the federal account by the contributor;

- Result from a solicitation which expressly states that the contribution will be used in connection with a federal election; and

- Are made by contributors who are informed that all contributions are subject to the prohibitions of the Act.

Once the basic organizational decisions have been made, a PAC should draft a set of by-laws. Although by-laws are not required under the Act, they offer several advantages, including:

- Forcing the PAC organizers to think through important and basic organizational questions at an early point in the existence of the PAC before problems arise and before PAC resources are tied up in electoral politics;

- Providing guidance to PAC members and employees concerning the types of activities which are compatible with corporate policy and federal law;

- Giving legitimacy and credibility to the PAC in the eyes of potential contributors and noncorporate personnel.

The by-laws should include the following:

- The name of the PAC;

- The purpose of the PAC and a general description of the activities in which it is authorized to engage;

- A description of those who have ultimate control over the PAC's operation, and the manner in which such persons are appointed or chosen;

- A description of all PAC officers and committees, along with the powers and responsibilities of each and a description of how each is appointed;

- A description of the PAC's membership and any requirements for becoming a member;

- The method of amending the by-laws;

- The disposition of assets upon dissolution.

Sample by-laws can be found in Appendix B.

PACS AND CONNECTED CORPORATION RELATIONSHIP

As a general rule ,a corporation is prohibited under the Act from making an "expenditure"or "contribution ," (as these terms are defined in the Act [24])in connection with an election to a federal office.[25] The Act specifically provides, however, that a corporation may engage in the following carefully defined activities relating to federal elections:

- Communications by a corporation to its stockholders and executive or administrative personnel and their families on any subject;[26]

- Nonpartisan registration and get-out-the-vote campaigns by a corporation aimed at its stockholders and executive or administrative personnel and their families;[7]

- The establishment, administration and solicitation of contributions to a separate segregated fund to be utilized for political purposes by a corporation.[28]

With respect to corporations which do organize and maintain separate segregated funds (PACs), the Act includes specific guidelines which strictly prescribe the scope of the PAC's solicitations and assure that participation is purely voluntary . Of course ,the Act's general limitations regarding contributions to political committees would also apply with respect to contributions to a PAC.

A corporation may exercise control over its PAC.[29] Through its key personnel, a corporation may make all the decisions relating to PAC solicitations and the use of funds contributed to its PAC . For example, corporate officials may decide, within the limits imposed by law :

- The recipients of campaign contributions;

- The amount of the contributions;

- The timing of the contributions;

- The nature and timing of PAC fundraising activities;

- The nature of the PAC's other activities, such as congressional lobbying or a voter education campaign.

A corporation may use general treasury monies for the establishment, administration and solicitation of contributions to its PAC.[30] The terms "establishment, administration and solicitation costs" are defined in the regulations as "... the cost of office space, phones, salaries, utilities, supplies, legal and accounting fees, fundraising[31] and other expenses incurred in setting up and running a (PAC) ..."[32] In interpreting these regulations, the Commission ruled recently that a corporation may pay the expenses, including transportation, breakfast and luncheon expenses, incurred in holding meetings to explain the corporate PAC to its executive and administrative personnel.[33] Thus, a corporation is authorized under the Act to absorb most of the significant costs of organizing and maintaining a PAC.[34] And since these costs are not considered contributions or expenditures under the Act, the corporation is not obligated to report them to the Commission.[35]

FUNDRAISING

The lifeblood of a PAC is its ability to raise funds successfully. In soliciting contributions, a PAC must be careful to comply with the specific guidelines in the Act and related regulations regarding the individuals who may be solicited, the manner in which these solicitations may be made and the availability of methods of solicitation to the labor organizations representing the corporation's employees. In addition, those responsible for administering a PAC must be aware of the provisions in the Act relating to the general limitations on political contributions to political committees.

With the exception of the "twice-yearly solicitations," contributions may be solicited only from the stockholders and their families and the executive or administrative personnel and their families of the PAC's connected organization.[36] Executive or administrative personnel are defined as "individuals who are paid on a salary rather than hourly basis and who have policy-making, managerial, professional or supervisory responsibilities."[37]

Solicitations of these individuals may be made at any time and may be made either in writing or orally.

Many corporations have newsletters or other forms of communications which may reach the corporation's hourly employees and the general public ,as well as its stockholders and executive and administrative personnel. This may be a convenient means for reporting on the PAC's activities ; however , the corporation should exercise extreme caution to insure that the communication is not construed as a solicitation. Any solicitation of the public and the corporation's hourly employees (except the "twice yearly solicitations") would be in violation of the Act.

The Commission has carved out a narrow exception to this prohibition in its interpretation of what would be considered a solicitation of the public. This exception was created by the Commission in a 1973 Advisory Opinion when it ruled that a labor organization could publish a solicitation in a magazine , 3 percent of whose readers were nonsolicitable persons (AO 1978-97). The solicitation contained a conspicuous caveat that only union members were being solicited and that contributions from nonmembers would be returned. A more recent Advisory Opinion put an upper limit on the exception by prohibiting a similar solicitation in a magazine , 10 percent of whose readers were nonsolicitable persons (AO 1980-139).

The Commission has provided some guidance through recent advisory opinions regarding the types of communications which would be considered solicitations. In one opinion , the Commission concluded that a proposed article in a corporate newsletter was a solicitation for voluntary contributions because the article described the fundraising activities of the PAC and contained a quote from the chairman of the corporation commending the enthusiasm of the employees who participated in the PAC activities during the previous year.[38] In contrast , the Commission held that a notice which included a report stating the number of contributors , the soliciation authorizations provided to the trade association's PAC and the amount of contributions received and made by the PAC did not constitute a solicitation. In that instance , the Commission found that the notice did not expressly encourage support of the PAC's activities nor did it provide readers with information on how they could contribute to the PAC.[39]

Although a corporation may adhere strictly to these solicitation guidelines, the regulations anticipate that a PAC may accidentally or inadvertently solicit persons other than those it is permitted to solicit. In such a case , the solicitation would not be deemed a violation of the Act , provided the corporation or its PAC used its "best efforts to comply with the limitations regarding the persons it may solicit and the method of solicitation."[40] The regulations also authorize a PAC to retain contributions from persons otherwise permitted to make contributions.[41]

A corporation is also authorized to solicit contributions from all its employees two times each calendar year.[42] These "twice-yearly solicitations" must be in writing and must be made by mail addressed specifically to the employees at their residences. In addition, each such solicitation must assure the recipient that:

- The PAC has established a custodial arrangement in accordance with 11 C F R. sec. 114.6(d);

- The corporation cannot be informed of the persons who do not make contributions; and

- Persons who in a calendar year make a single contribution of $50 or less or multiple contributions aggregating $200 or less may maintain their anonymity by returning their contributions directly to the custodian.[43]

If a corporate PAC undertakes a twice-yearly solicitation, the act requires that the corporation make available to the labor union which represents the corporation's employees or the employees of its subsidiaries, branches, divisions, or affiliates, the method used to solicit these employees. A corporation must notify the labor organization of its intent to solicit and the method it intends to use within a "reasonable time *prior* to the solicitation" to allow the labor organization an opportunity to make its own solicitations.[44]

Fundamental to the concept of PACs is the principle that contributions to a PAC must be voluntary and may not be secured by force, job discrimination or financial reprisals.[45] To insure that contributions are voluntary, a person soliciting contributions must inform the person being solicited of:

- The political purpose of the PAC; and

- The person's right to refuse to so contribute without any reprisal.[46]

If the solicitation is in writing, it must include these written assurances.

The regulations do permit a corporation or its connected PAC to suggest an appropriate amount to be contributed, provided the person soliciting the contribution informs the persons being solicited that such guidelines are merely suggestions and that the individual is free to contribute more or less than the guideline without reprisal.[48]

A corporation must make available to a labor organization representing its employees the methods it uses to solicit voluntary contributions from its stockholders and executive or administrative personnel and their families. The methods must be available on the written request of the labor organization and at a cost sufficient only to reimburse the corporation for the expenses incurred in making the method available.[49]

The regulations include three specific examples of solicitation "methods" which may be made available to a labor organization:

- Payroll deduction plans, check-off systems, or other plans which deduct contributions from the dividend or payroll checks of stockholders or executive or adminis-trative personnel;[50]

- Computers used for addressing envelopes or labels used for solicitation; and

- Corporate facilities such as a company dining room or cafeteria, used for meetings.[51]

GENERAL CONTRIBUTION LIMITATIONS

A PAC also must comply with the basic limits in the Act on contributions received by political committees.

A person may not contribute more than $5,000 to a PAC within a calendar year.[52] The amount a person may contribute may be limited further if it is earmarked for a specific candidate. In such a case, the individual's aggregate contributions to the candidate, whether made directly to the candidate or indirectly through the PAC, cannot exceed $1,000 per election.[53] An individual may not make contributions to federal candidates or to political committees supporting federal candidates aggregating more than $25,000 in any calendar year. For purposes of this limitation, contributions made to a candidate in a year other than when the election is held shall be deemed to have been made in the year in which the election is held.[54]

It is unlawful for a foreign national to make, either directly or indirectly, and for any person to solicit, accept or receive from a foreign national, any contribution in connection with any election to any political office. A foreign national is defined as a "foreign principal" as that term is defined by section 611(b) of Title 22 United States Code (except it shall not include a citizen of the United States) and persons who are not citizens of the United States and who have been admitted for permanent residence as that term is defined by section 1101(a)(2) of Title 8 of the United States Code.[55]

No person may make a contribution in cash which exceeds $100 with respect to an election to federal office.[56]

It is unlawful for a PAC knowingly to accept a contribution made by one person in the name of another person.[57]

TAX CONSEQUENCES

Taxation of political organizations is a recent phenomenon. For many years, the Internal Revenue Service (IRS) took the position that political contributions were not income to the recipient and were not deductible by the contributor.[58]

However, in 1974, the IRS ruled that political organizations are not exempt from income taxation and are required to file annual tax returns.[59] The following year, Congress responded by enacting sec. 527 of the Internal Revenue Code[60] which established the current rules governing the taxation of political organizations . Under sec . 527, a PAC qualifies for a limited tax-exempt status as long as it is organized and operated primarily for the purpose of receiving contributions and making expenditures within the meaning of the Act.[61] A PAC still may engage in other activities, such as supporting legislation ,without losing its tax -exempt status ,as long as these activities do not alter the PAC's "primary purpose ."[62]

Assuming a PAC meets the "primary purpose" test, the IRS excludes from taxation all so -called "exempt function income ," which includes the following :[63]

- A contribution of money or other property to the PAC;

- Membership dues or fees;

- Proceeds from a political fundraising event which are not received in the ordinary course of any trade or business (Note that the IRS has ruled that proceeds from the sale of art reproductions were not exempt function income where the sales occurred over a period of months and the proceeds were used to support the political organization itself rather than for contributions to candidates ,*Rev . Ruling* 80-103); and

- Proceeds from the sale of political campaign materials , as long as the sale was not in the ordinary course of any trade or business .

To qualify for a tax exemption , the income listed above must be segregated from all other income received by the PAC and used exclusively to influence the nomination or election of candidates for federal , state or local office .[64] Failure to segregate these funds will result in their being taxed ,even though used for exempt purposes .[65]

Section 527 also permits a PAC to deduct from taxable income amounts spent to produce taxable income .[66] Thus, expenditures made to produce the "exempt function "income listed above are not deductible ,while expenditures made to produce taxable income are deductible .

The PAC is required to file its tax return two and half months after the close of the taxable year[67] and is required to use Form 1120-POL. (See Appendix C.) A PAC with taxable income, such as interest earned on its accounts, will be taxed as if it were a corporation, with certain exceptions:[68]

- The PAC is allowed to claim an automatic deduction of $100;

- The PAC may not claim a net operating loss deduction;

- The PAC may not claim the benefit of the graduated corporate tax rate;

- The PAC may not claim certain special deductions normally allowed to regular corporations, such as the dividends received deduction. '

Finallly, a PAC which is preparing to dissolve may avoid paying a tax on unexpended funds by:

- Returning the funds to known contributors;[69]

- Contributing the funds to another PAC;[70]

- Contributing the funds to an exempt public charity; or[71]

- Contributing the funds to the general fund of the federal, state, or local governments.[72]

A tax credit is allowed for contributions of cash from individuals to a PAC provided that the PAC is organized and operated for the *exclusive* purpose of influencing the nomination or election of candidates to federal, state or local political office.[73] A PAC which wishes to engage in other activities, such as general educational or legislative activities, may preserve the tax deduction for its contributors by establishing a separate campaign committee. This separate campaign committee should meet the exclusive purpose test mentioned above, and its activities and funds should be segregated from those of the PAC which established it. Further, contributions should be made directly to this campaign committee and not channeled through the PAC.[74]

The IRS Code entitles the taxpayer to a tax credit for an amount equal to half of all political contributions made during the taxable year, provided the recipient PAC satisfies the "exclusive purpose test." The maximum credit allowed is $50 per year, or $100 in the case of a joint return.

To assist a contributor in claiming a tax credit, a PAC should include in its acknowledgement of the contribution a verification to the contributor that the contribution was placed in a fund which is used for the exclusive purpose of influencing the nomination or election of candidates to federal, state or local office.

Contributions of property are not eligible for the tax credit.[75] A taxpayer who contributes appreciated property to a PAC will be taxed as if he or she had sold the property.[76] No loss is allowed for a taxpayer who contributes depreciated property to a PAC.[77]

Recent legislation confirms that no federal gift tax is imposed on contributions of money or property to a PAC.[78]

As explained elsewhere, the Act permits corporations to use corporate funds to establish and administer a PAC and to finance PAC fundraising activities. The Treasury Regulations appear to prohibit a corporation from deducting any of these expenses from its taxable income,[79] although the IRS has not answered this question definitively.

RECORDKEEPING AND REPORTING REQUIREMENTS

The Act requires a PAC to maintain certain records internally, and to file regular reports with federal and state governments. Fortunately, the recent trend has been toward simplifying these requirments.[80]

Nevertheless, these requirements remain detailed and complicated. The description below necessarily can be nothing more than a broad outline containing only the most basic requirements. A PAC is well advised to seek professional legal and accounting assistance prior to establishing its record-keeping and reporting mechanisms.

The treasurer of the PAC is required to keep an account, using any reasonable accounting procedure, of all contributions received by the PAC.[81] This account must include:

- The name and address of anyone who contributes more than $50 to the PAC;

- The name, address and identification of any person who contributes more than $200 in a calendar year, or of any political committee contributing any amount;

- The date of receipt and the amount of the contributions.

The treasurer must keep a similar account of all PAC disbursements, made by or on behalf of the PAC.[82] The account must include:

- The name and address of every person to whom any disbursement is made;

- The date, amount and purpose of all disbursements;

- The office sought by the candidate on whose behalf the disbursement was made, where applicable;

- A receipt or invoice to the payee or a cancelled check to the payee for each transaction in excess of $200. For a credit card transaction, the documentation must include a monthly billing statement or customer receipt.

Records required by the Act must be kept for three years after the report to which such records relate is filed.[83]

A recent amendment to the Act provides that the treasurer or his authorized agent will be deemed to be in compliance with the recordkeeping requirements of the Act if he uses his "best efforts" to obtain, maintain, and submit a record and if he retains a record of his efforts.[84] Where the treasurer is required to have a receipt, invoice or cancelled check, the treasurer's best efforts must include at least one written effort per transaction to obtain such documents.[85]

PACs are required to file periodic reports on FEC Form 3X.[86] (See Appendix D.) If the PAC supports or opposes candidates for election only to the U.S. Senate or only to the U.S. House of Representatives, the reports must be filed with the Secretary of the Senate or the Clerk of the House of Representatives, respectively.[87] All other PACs must file their reports with the Commission.[88]

Commission regulations permit the PAC to choose betwen either of two reporting schedules.[89] One of the schedules bases reports on the timing of the elections. During an election year, a PAC using this schedule must file the following reports.[90]

- Quarterly reports due on January 31, April 15, July 15, and October 15, covering the preceding calendar quarter which ends on the thirtieth;

- Pre-election reports due 12 days prior to any primary or general election (or sent by certified or registered mail 15 days prior to the election) in which the PAC made contributions or expenditures not previously reported;

- Post-general election reports, due 30 days after any general election;

- Note that a quarterly report need not be filed for any quarter in which a pre-election report was due during the period between the fifth and fifteenth days following the close of the calendar quarter.

A PAC which is operating on the first schedule must file during a non-election year the following reports:[91]

- Semi-annual reports due on July 31 and January 31 covering the six months that end on the thirty-first of the preceding month.

The second schedule which a PAC may choose for filing purposes requires that monthly reports be filed no later than 20 days after the end of each month.[92] However, in any year in which a regularly scheduled general election

211

is held ,the PAC is required to file a pre-election report ,a post-general election report (both as described above) and a year-end report due on January 31 of the following year .[93] These reports are to be filed in lieu of the November and December monthly reports .

A PAC is entitled to switch reporting schedules once per calendar year by notifying the Commission of its intention at the time it files a report due under its current reporting schedule .[94]

The Commission also has established a special reporting requirement for large independent expenditures made very late in the campaign . Any independent expenditure aggregating $1,000 or more made fewer than 20 days prior to an election, but more than 24 hours before 12:01 of election day , must be reported within 24 hours of when the expenditure is made .[95]

Reports filed by a PAC will be considered in compliance with the Act if the treasurer or his authorized agent has used his ' best efforts " to obtain , maintain, and submit the required information .[96] These best efforts must include at least one effort per solicitation documented in writing to learn the identification of each person contributing more than $200 in a calendar year to the PAC .[97] This effort should consist of a clear request to the contributor for the contributor 's name ,mailing address ,occupation and employer ,and should inform the contributor that such information is required by law .

In addition to any reports which must be filed with a state under state campaign finance laws ,the PAC is required by the Act to file reports with state governments concerning federal election expenditures in the following circum-stances :

- Reports of independent expenditures made in support of or in opposition to any person seeking nomination or election to the office of Vice-President or President must be filed with the state in which the expenditures were made , and the state in which the PAC has its head-quarters ;[98]

- Whenever a PAC makes expenditures on behalf of a candidate for Congress , all periodic reports which normally must be filed with the Commission and which

212

disclose expenditures on behalf of congressional candidates must be filed with the state in which the congressional candidate sought office;[99]

- A PAC making contributions in connection with a
Presidential election and required to file a report by the
act must file a copy of the report in the states in which the
PAC and the recipient campaign committee have their
headquarters.[100] **PAC**

FOOTNOTES

[1]Act of 1907, 34 Stat. 864.
[2]2 U.S.C. sec. 441b(b)(2)(C).
[3]2 U.S.C. sec.441a(a)(1)(A).
[4]Sec. 441a(a)(2). If a PAC does not qualify as a multi-candidate committee, it
may not contribute more than $1,000 to a candidate per election. A
multi-candidate committee is defined in the act as a committee which (i)
has been registered under the act for at least six months; (ii) has received
contributions from more than 50 persons; and (iii) has made contributions
to five or more candidates for federal office. 2 U.S.C. sec.441a(a)(4).
[5]11 C F R. sec.109.1(a).
[6]2 U.S.C. sec.441a(a)(2)(C).
[7]2 U.S.C. sec.441a(a)(1)(A); 2 U.S.C. sec.441a(a)(8).
[8]Individual contributions are also subject to a provision in the act which
prohibits an individual from making contributions to federal candidates as
well as to political committees which support federal candidates which
aggregate more than $25,000 per calendar year. 2 U.S.C. sec.441a(a)(3).
[9]2 U.S.C. sec.433(a).
[10]2 U.S.C. sec.432(4)(B).
[11]11 C F R. sec.102.1(c).
[12]2 U.S.C. sec.433.
[13]2 U.S.C. sec.432(e)(5).
[14]2 sec.431(7).
[15]11 C F R. sec.102.14(c); AO's 1980-10, 23 and 86.
[16]AO 1980-98.
[17]2 U.S.C. sec.432(a).

[18] 2 U.S.C. sec.432(h)(2)(i).

[19] 2 U.S.C. sec.432(h)(1).

[20] 11 C.F.R. sec.114.12(a).

[21] Id.

[22] 11 C.F.R. sec.102.7(a).

[23] 11 C.F.R. sec.102.5.

[24] Expenditure and contribution are defined broadly in the act to include not only payments, distributions, loans, etc., but also "anything of value, made ...for the purpose of influencing any election for federal office." The definitions except certain specific activities, including volunteer services, certain unreimbursed travel and subsistence expenses incidental to volunteer activity and certain legal and accounting services rendered to insure compliance with the federal election laws. 2 U.S.C. sec.431(8) and (9); 11 C F R. sec.100.7 and sec.100.8. In AO 1980-137, the Commission ruled that computer services given to a senate campaign committee to insure that the committee was in compliance with the Act did not constitute expenditures or contributions, although the corporation was required to report its costs incurred.

[25] 2 U.S.C. sec 441b(a).

[26] If such communications expressly advocate the election or defeat of a clearly identified candidate, the costs relating to such communication which exceed $2,000 for any election must be reported to the FEC in accordance with the act. 2 U S C. sec.431(9)(13)(iii).

[27] This provision has been held by the Commission to authorize a corporation to make contributions to a non-profit organization established to conduct voter registration drives. AO 1980-92.

[28] 2 U S C. sec.441(b)(2). Any payments made or obligations incurred in connection with these activities is specifically excepted from the definitions of "contribution" and "expenditure." 2 U S C. sec.431(8)(B)(vi) and (9)(B)(v).

[29] 11 C F R. sec.114.5(d).

[30] 2 U S C. sec.441b(b)2(C); 11 C F R. sec.114.1(a)(2)(iii).

[31] A discussion of certain methods for fundraising is included below.

[32] 11 C F R. sec.114.1(b).

[33] AO 1980-50.

[34] "A corporation may not use the establishment, administration, and solicitation procedures as a means of exchanging treasury monies for voluntary contributions." 11 C.F.R. sec.114.5(b). The regulations also suggest

214

that where a corporation uses "raffles or entertainment to raise funds "it is a reasonable practice for the PAC to reimburse the corporation for costs which exceed one-third of the money contributed. 11 C.F.R. sec. 114.5(b)(2).

[35] 11C F R.sec.114.5(e). The one limited exception is a requirement to report certain expenses relating to legal and accounting services rendered to the PAC. 11 C.F.R. sec.114.5(e)(2)(ii).

[36] 2U.S.C.sec.441b(b)(4)(A)(i). In addition, a corporate PAC is authorized to solicit the executive or administrative personnel and their families of the corporation's subsidiaries, branches, divisions, affiliates and their families, 11 C.F.R. sec. 114.5(g)(1); and the shareholders of the corporation that is the parent of the corporation which established the PAC. AO 1978-75.

[37] 11C F R.sec.114.1(c). The term does not include professionals represented by a labor organization or salaried foremen or other salaried lower level supervisors with direct supervision over hourly employees. 11 C.F.R. sec.114.1(c)(2).

[38] AO 1979-13.

[39] AO 1979-66. See also AO's 1978-17 and 1978-83, and AO 1980-65 in which the Commission concluded that a trade association solicitation authorization form included in a magazine it distributed to members of the association was not a solicitation, but a prior solicitation authorization required under 2 U.S.C.sec.44 1b(b)(4)(D).

[40] 11 C F R.sec.114.5(h).

[41] 11 C F R. sec.114.5(j).

[42] 11 C F R. sec.114.6. Challenges to the restrictions on the solicitation of a corporation's employees brought by a corporation and trade association were recently dismissed on the grounds that they were not ripe for decision. *Martin Tractor v .Federal Election Commission* (D.C.Cir. 1980); *National Chamber Alliance for Politics v. Federal Election Commission*, ___ U.S. ___ (1980).

[43] 11C F R.sec.114.6(c). Contributions which aggregate more than $200 in a calendar year must be reported to the Commission. See "Recordkeeping and Reporting Requirements."

[44] 11 C F R.sec.114(e).

[45] 2 U.S.C.sec.441b(b)(3)(A).

[46] 2 U.S.C.sec.441b(b)(e)(B)&(C).

[47] 11 C F R.sec.114.5(a)(5).

215

[48] 11 C F.R. sec.114.5(a)(2).

[49] 2 U.S.C. sec.441b(b).

[50] Although payroll deduction plans may be used, a so-called reverse check-off contribution plan where an amount is automatically deducted from a person's dividends or payroll checks has been found to be coercive *per se* and, therefore, unlawful under the Act. *Federal Election Commission v. National Education Association*, 475 F.Supp. 1102 (D.D.C. 1978).

[51] 11 C F R. sec.114.5(k).

[52] 2 U.S.C. sec.441a(a)(1)(C).

[53] 2 U.S.C. sec.441a(a)(1)(A) and sec.441a(a)(8).

[54] 2 U.S.C. sec.441a(a)(3).

[55] 2 U.S.C. sec.441e.

[56] 2 U.S.C. sec.441g.

[57] 2 U.S.C. sec.441f.

[58] T. 3276, 1939-1 C.B. 108; Treas. Reg. sec.1.162-201(c)(1) (1965); Rev. Ruling 71-449, 1971-2 C.B. 77. Several recent law review articles contain excellent descriptions of the tax consequences of political campaign finance activity. See, e g., Schoenblum, From De Facto to Statutory Exemption: An Analysis of the Evolution of Legislative Policy Regarding The Federal Taxation of Campaign Finance, 65 Va. L R. 513 (1979); Comment, Federal Taxation of Political Campaign Organizations, 49 Miss.L F. 911 (1978); Comment, Tax Subsidies for Political Participation, 31 Tax Lawyer 461 (1978).

[59] Rev. Ruling 74-21; 1974-C.B. 14.

[60] Act of January 3, 1975; P.L. No. 93-625; 88 Stat. 2108.

[61] 26 U.S.C. sec.527(e)(1).

[62] (1974) U.S.C.A.N. 7504.

[63] 26 U.S.C. sec.527(c)(3).

[64] Id.

[65] (1974) U.S.C.A.N. 7504.

[66] 26 U.S.C. sec.527(c)(1)(B).

[67] 26 U.S.C. sec.6072(b).

[68] 26 U.S.C. sec.527(a); 26 U.S.C. sec.527(b); 26 U.S.C. sec.527(c).

[69] Rev. Ruling 74-22; 1974-1 C.B. 16.

[70] 26 U.S.C. sec.527(d)(i).

[71] 26 U.S.C. sec.527(d)(2).

[72] 26 U.S.C. sec.527(d)(3).

[73] 26 U.S.C. sec.41.

[74] Treas. Reg. 1.41-1(a).
[75] 26 U.S.C. sec.41(c)(1).
[76] 26 U.S.C. sec.84.
[77] (1974) U.S.C.A.N. 7509.
[78] 26 U.S.C. sec.2501(a)(5).
[79] Treas. Reg. 1. 162-20(c); See also 26 U.S.C. sec.162(e)(2)(A).
[80] See Federal Election Campaign Act Amendment of 1979, Senate Report No. 96-319; House Report 96-422.
[81] 2 U.S.C. sec.432(c); 11 C.F R. 102.9(a).
[82] 2 U.S.C. sec.432(c); 11 C.F R. sec. 102.9(b).
[83] 2 U.S.C. sec.432(c); 11 C.F.R. sec.102.9(c).
[84] 2 U.S.C. sec.432(c); 11 C.F.R. sec.102.9(d).
[85] Id.
[86] 11 C.F.R. sec.104.2(e)(3).
[87] 2 U.S.C. sec.432(g); 11 C.F.R. sec105.1; 11 C.F R.sec.105.2.
[88] 2 U.S.C. sec.432(g)(4); 11 C.F.R. sec.105.3; 11 C.F R. 105.4.
[89] 11 C.F.R. sec.104.5(c).
[90] 11 C.F.R. sec.104.5(c)(1).
[91] 11 C.F.R. sec.104.5(c)(2).
[92] 11 C.F.R. sec.104.5(c)(3)(i).
[93] 11 C.F.R. sec.104.5(c)(3)(ii).
[94] 11 C.F.R. sec.104.5(c).
[95] 2 U.S.C. sec.434(i), 11 C.F.R. sec.104.4.
[96] 2 U.S.C. sec 434(i), 11 C.F.R. sec 104.7(a).
[97] 11 C.F.R. sec.104.7(b).
[98] 2 U.S.C. sec.439(a)(2); 11 C.F.R. sec.108.2.
[99] 2 U.S.C. sec.439(a)(2); 11 C.F R. sec.108.2.
[100] 2 U.S.C. sec.439(a)(2); 11 C.F.R. sec 108.4.

William E. Sudow has been associated since 1975 with the Washington, D.C./New York firm of Fried, Frank, Harris, Shriver and Kampelman. His legal work includes: general corporate, banking, and election law; international trade and licensing arrangements; real estate development; and legislative work with the U.S. Congress.

Prior to associating with the firm, Sudow served as special assistant to Rep. John Brademas (D-Ind.), Assistant Majority Whip, U.S. House of Representatives. His responsibilities with Brademas included work on congressional leadership matters and major substantive assistance on significant pieces of legislation involving both domestic and foreign affairs. He also assisted Brademas by drafting major portions of the 1974 amendments to the Federal Election Campaign Act. As a senior member of the House Administration Committee, Brademas played a major role in consideration of the Act.

Kenneth J. Vandevelde is an associate with Fried, Frank, Harris, Shriver and Kampelman. A *cum laude* graudate of Harvard Law School, Vandevelde specializes in election law, Indian law and general litigation.

VII.   DEALING WITH THE FEC

The Federal Election Commission:
A Guide for Corporate Counsel

Jan W. Baran, Esq.
Baker and Hostetler

An understanding of the Federal Election Commission (FEC or Commission) is essential to one who counsels political action committees (PACs), corporations, or trade associations that undertake political activity. Counsel will discover that the substantive law is often arcane, the activity is politically and publicly controversial, and the FEC is still relatively young and periodically unpredictable. There exists a potential for public embarrassment of a client in addition to the normal legal dangers and consequences of a federal election law violation.

Contact with the agency is virtually inevitable. Reports must be filed, committees are subject to audit, and protective advisory opinions can only be obtained from the FEC. The purpose of this article is to guide counsel and committee officials on how to approach the FEC and its staff. The dynamics and decision-making process of the Commission is not altogether ascertainable from the language of the Federal Election Campaign Act as amended (FECA),[1] or the regulations.[2] After five years of existence, the FEC, like any other governmental organization, has settled into a mode of operation that is in part a result of practice rather than statutory edict. This article discusses common agency practice as well as enacted law and promulgated rules of procedure. The discussion below focuses on the Commission and its staff's organization, the processing of reports filed under FECA, and the administrative procedures relating to audits, investigations, and the issuance of advisory opinions.

THE FEC AND ITS STAFF

Historical Background

A major goal of the "post-Watergate" campaign financing reform movement was the creation of an independent agency with the responsibility and power to enforce and administer federal election laws.[3] This goal was realized in the enactment of the Federal Election Campaign Act Amendments of 1974 which established the FEC.[4] The FEC was heralded as an agency which "will assure judicious expeditious enforcement of the law, while reversing the long history of nonenforcement."[5] Congress intended to devise a "comprehensive system of civil enforcement"[6] over which the FEC would have primary jurisdiction.[7] Although the 1974 Amendments were effective January 1, 1975,[8] the first commissioners were not selected and confirmed until April. One reason for the delay was the unique and ponderous appointment process by which members were confirmed and which ultimately was found unconstitutional by the Supreme Court in *Buckley v. Valeo*.[9]

Prior to the creation of the FEC, the enforcement of FECA was left to the United States Department of Justice which was assisted by "supervisory officers," meaning the Clerk of the United States House of Representatives, the Secretary of the Senate, and the Comptroller General of the United States.[10] Rather than replacing these institutions, the FEC supplemented their activities with respect to administration of the election laws. Although the Commission has exclusive civil jurisdiction,[11] the Department of Justice still retains its customary authority to prosecute criminal violations of FECA.[12] Except for the Comptroller General, the supervisory officers are still active in administering FECA. The Clerk and Secretary are *ex officio* nonvoting members of the Commission.[13] Furthermore, some reports required by FECA must be filed originally with the Clerk and Secretary.[14] Many of the powers granted to the FEC, however, were new. Conspicuous among these powers was the power to issue advisory opinions.[15]

Perhaps the most controversial act taken by the FEC during its first year of existence involved the issuance of an advisory opinion relating to PAC activity. Advisory Opinion 1975-23 (SUNPAC)[16] is viewed as a watershed in the development of corporate sponsored PACs.[17] It constitutes the first detailed administrative clarification of the lawful operation of a PAC . The controversial aspect of the opinion was the conclusion that a corporation may solicit all employees ,in addition to stockholders ,for voluntary contributions .[18] Congressional reaction to this holding led directly to that portion of the 1976 Amendments which altered and expanded on present day section 441b .[19] Furthermore , the advisory opinion process itself became suspect and the FEC was accused of changing substantive law through the use of these opinions .[20]

After the FEC was declared unconstitutionally constituted by the Court in *Buckley v .Valeo* ,Congress made wholesale changes in the Act and refused to simply reconstitute the Commission as suggested by President Ford .[21] Many elements of the 1976 Amendments were designed to hold the FEC publicly accountable for exercising "an outrageous abuse of power "in issuing the SUNPAC decision .[22] Consequently , restrictions were placed on the Commission 's ability to issue advisory opinions ,[23] informal opinions were prohibited ,[24] the substantive law of PACs was enlarged,[25] and the congressional veto [26]was refined to permit either House to reject any discrete portion of proposed FEC regulations.[27] The 1976 Amendments also recodified FECA's criminal provisions and transferred them from Title 18 to Title 2.[28] Simultaneously, the FEC 's enforcement role was increased , although special emphasis was placed on informal resolution of violations of FECA .[29]

Congressional interest in the FEC had not dissipated by the time the 1979 Amendments [30] were enacted . Congress continued to refine the Commission 's powers through the systematic repeal of provisions which granted discretion to the Agency . The FEC 's powers to formulate general policy ,[31] grant limited reporting waivers ,[32] and require data other than that specifically required by FECA on reports [33] and registration statements [34]were eliminated . The Commission is now required to submit all its forms to Congress in the same fashion as regulations ,subject to a veto by a majority of either House .[35] The Commission must issue advisory opinions within sixty days .[36] Finally , the FEC 's discretion in conducting audits is considerably curtailed .[37]

The Commissioners

The Commission is composed of eight members — six voting commissioners and two nonvoting *ex officio* commissioners.[38] The latter two members are the Clerk of the House of Representatives and the Secretary of the Senate,[39] who fulfill their duties at the FEC through respective deputies. These deputies, like their principals, are employees of Congress, but they maintain offices at the Commission. The *ex officio* members, through their deputies, actively participate in the affairs of the Agency. The deputies attend all formal FEC functions, including hearings and meetings. In particular, they are present at both open and closed Commission meetings and participate in the discussion of all advisory opinions, investigations, and personnel matters.

The voting commissioners are appointed for staggered six year terms.[40] No more than three of these members may be affiliated with the same political party,[41] and all must be full-time commissioners.[42] The Chairman and Vice Chairman are elected by the voting members from among themselves. A commissioner may be Chairman only once during his or her term; the tenure for a Chairman is one year.[43] The Chairman and the Vice Chairman must be affiliated with different political parties.[44] Commissioners may not delegate their votes and all decisions must be made by a majority vote of the members.[45] An absolute majority of four votes is required before the FEC may proceed in a civil suit, issue an advisory opinion, issue a regulation or conduct an investigation.[46]

The Commission is granted exclusive jurisdiction with respect to civil enforcement of FECA and is charged with the general responsibility of administering and seeking compliance with FECA.[47] The FEC is vested with investigative powers including the power to issue subpoenas and orders and the power to initiate civil actions.[48] It also may issue rules and regulations, forms, and advisory opinions.[49]

The Staff

Each commissioner has a small personal staff comprised of an executive assistant and a secretary. Consequently the Commission relies heavily on its general staff. The FECA provides for two staff positions, the Staff Director and the General Counsel, both of whom are appointed by the Commission.[50] In recent years the size of the total staff has numbered approximately 250 persons. Technically, the entire general staff reports to the Staff Director who, with the approval of the Commission, hires all personnel.[51] In practice, the

General Counsel supervises and manages his own staff which comprises roughly one -third of the general staff. The Office of General Counsel is organized by legal function, including advisory opinions, legislation and regulation, enforcement (administrative), and litigation. Association with members of the legal staff is likely to be limited to formal statutory proceedings such as investigations, rulemaking, and advisory opinions.

Informal contact with nonlegal staff is far more likely. The nonlegal staff is organized by operational divisions --Public Information Division, Reports Analysis Division, Audit Division, Administration Division, Data Services Division, and Public Records Division. An individual subject to FECA, or counsel, conceivably could come into contact with each of these divisions, with the exception of the Data Services and Administration Divisions.

The Public Information Division contains the Press Office and provides services to the general public. Free publications, including forms, copies of the statute and regulations, and the Commission's monthly newsletter, *The FEC Record*, are available. Nonlegal staff is trained to answer basic questions about the law and the Commission over the telephone. This service is provided nationwide through the use of a toll-free "hot line." Answers obtained by informal means are not binding on the Commission and offer no legal protection.[52] The service is helpful, however, if used for general informational purposes.

The Reports Analysis Division is responsible for the processing and analysis of all reports and statements filed with the FEC.[53] The reports are available to the public both in hard copy and microfilm form at the Public Records Division. Any report can be reproduced at cost. Finally, the Audit Division conducts the FEC's audits.[54]

PROCESSING OF REPORTS

FECA requires various individuals and political committees to file statements[55] and reports[56] which must disclose the organization and financial activity of the reporting entity. Reports from PACs are filed directly with the FEC.[57] These documents are received and processed by the Commission's Reports Analysis Division (RAD) which is supervised by an Assistant Staff

Director . RAD is organized into two branches ,the Candidate Branch and the Non -Candidate Branch . Each branch is further subdivided into sections . The name of each branch and section reflects the type of filer whose reports are processed ,reviewed ,and analyzed by that portion of the staff . Consequently , the Candidate Branch ,through the Presidential and Congressional Sections , processes documents from candidates and their authorized committees . The Non -Candidate Branch ,through the Party and Non -Party Sections ,handles reports and statements from political committees other than candidates and their committees . PAC reports are within the responsibility of the Non -Party Section of the Non -Candidate Branch .

Each section is composed of a Section Chief and several reports analysts . The Non -Party Section contains approximately one -dozen reports analysts who must review the documents of the more than 2,000 political committees that are not affiliated with a political party or candidate . The reports analyst is customarily an individual who is a recent college graduate , not an attorney or an accountant ,and the first link in a chain of events which may ultimately result in a formal enforcement proceeding .

The duties of a reports analyst are largely mechanical and clerical . The analyst 's first duty is to verify that all required reports have in fact been filed by the committee . When a report is initially received ,the reports analyst will undertake a preliminary review of the document to ascertain its technical sufficiency . He will check for any mathematical errors or omitted information . The report is then coded for subsequent data entry into the FEC 's computer . Virtually all aggregate totals from the summary pages of the report (FEC Form 3x)will be entered as will most data relating to large individual contributors . All contributions made by PACs to candidates and committees are coded and entered into the computer . The staff utilizes this data to monitor compliance with statutory limits on contributions and to prepare statistical studies on campaign financing . Computer printouts are also used by the press and the public and may be obtained from the Public Records Division .

The reports analyst has one very significant enforcement responsibility : to send written inquiries to a reporting committee regarding any perceived inaccuracies ,deficiencies or statutory violations that appear on a report . The majority of these inquiries are entitled Requests for Additional Information (RFAIs). RFAIs are form letters signed by the Staff Director that expressly refer to the individual reports analysts who initiated the inquiry . An RFAI is not a formal Commission investigation ,and is not prompted by a Commission vote . It does request a response from the committee ,either an explanation or an amendment to a report . RFAIs may be resolved informally and a treasurer who receives such a letter should contact the named reports analyst directly .[58]

If a committee is able and willing to provide the requested information , the matter should be immediately resolved . The reports analyst will not confirm in writing that the committee's response satisfactorily answers the inquiry , but he will provide such assurances orally . The overwhelming majority of RFAIs are concluded in this manner .[59] If the committee ignores or refuses to respond to the RFAI ,or if the committee's response is deemed either inadequate or a confirmation of the presence of a violation ,the entire matter may be referred to the Office of General Counsel for possible enforcement action .[60] The potential for such a referral makes it imperative that a committee's treasurer and counsel promptly and fully respond to an RFAI ,if doing so does not otherwise incur additional risk .

RFAIs and any responses are always a part of the public record . This reinforces the overall view that such inquiries relate to nonsubstantive reporting irregularities and deficiencies . A different procedure is used by RAD for what may be characterized as substantive violations of FECA . For example ,corporate or union contributions ,and contributions in excess of the applicable limits are viewed as substantive violations . If such a receipt is disclosed in a report ,the reports analyst will initiate a Surface Violation Letter (SVL). An SVL is not part of the public record , because there is a high probability that the inquiry will lead directly to a formal investigation . If the committee can provide an explanation for the apparent violation , the matter may not be referred to the Office of General Counsel . The committee also may be able to take remedial steps to rectify the problem . For example , the committee may refund any improper contribution . In either event ,the FEC still could commence formal proceedings upon the recommendation of the General Counsel to whom the matter may be referred by the reports analyst . Remedial action will not guarantee that no further action will be taken , but formal proceedings are much less likely . If circumstances reflect a knowing and willful violation of the FECA ,the Commission may institute enforcement proceedings regardless of the committee's remedial efforts .

227

In general, RFAIs and SVLs can be resolved informally, but must be approached with the understanding that they may be a harbinger of subsequent enforcement proceedings.

AUDITS

The FEC may conduct audits of any political committee.[61] The Commission must give priority to audits of committees that receive federal funds pursuant to the public financing provisions of FECA.[62] Prior to the 1979 Amendments, the Commission utilized its general auditing powers to conduct audits of committees which were selected at random,[63] and of committees, including PACs, whose financial activity exceeded certain arbitrary dollar amounts.[64] The legal basis for these types of random and arbitrary audits, however, has been eliminated.[65] Presently, audits may be conducted after the Commission establishes thresholds for substantial compliance with FECA, and thereafter specifically finds, by a vote of at least four commissioners, that a particular committee has failed to meet the threshold requirements.[66] The ensuing audit must commence within thirty days of the vote.[67]

The audit process[68] begins with written notification to the treasurer of the committee to be audited. A time and place for the audit will be proposed in the notice. The FEC has been flexible in granting extensions of time, particularly if a delay is necessary in order to assemble all of the committee's records. The audit is normally conducted at the committee's offices. The FEC will use facilities at a local federal office building, however, if the audit would cause a physical inconvenience or dislocation to the committee. At the appointed time and place for the start of the audit, the FEC auditors will conduct an entrance conference with the committee's treasurer and any other committee personnel whom the treasurer may wish to be present, such as counsel. At the conference, the lead auditor will explain the basis for the audit and the general procedures that will be used. The treasurer will be requested to certify the location and existence of all depositories that have been used by the committee during the period subject to audit. The lead auditor will also request that the treasurer or other knowledgeable person explain the committee's bookkeeping system.

The actual audit is conducted in a manner designed to verify the accuracy of the committee's reports and to determine the committee's compliance with FECA. Therefore, in addition to verifying and reconciling the committee's bank statements, the auditors will attempt to substantiate the committee's reports with the committee's records. This is done on a sampling basis whenever possible. Sample itemized expenditures will be traced back to invoices, cancelled checks, and any other records.[69] The auditors will also request samples of solicitation materials used by the committee. In the case of PACs, the auditors will check for the presence of statutorily required notices.[70] If the PAC is connected to a trade association, the auditors will review and verify the mandatory prior approval statements from corporate members.[71]

At the conclusion of the field work, the auditors will hold an exit conference with the treasurer. The treasurer will be informed of the preliminary audit findings. In the event that inaccuracies or discrepancies are discovered, the treasurer will be told of any remedial action that can be taken, such as filing amendments to reports or registration statements. The findings are presented orally and there is no mechanism that affords the committee an opportunity to contest the auditors' findings before a written audit report is presented by the staff to the Commission. The auditors may refer apparent violations of FECA to the General Counsel who may recommend to the FEC that a formal investigation be conducted pursuant to FECA's enforcement provisions.[72]

After the auditors have completed their field work and the committee has taken any suggested remedial action, the auditors will prepare an audit report. The report will include one of three basic auditor statements. If the reports accurately reflect the committee's activity and if the committee is in compliance with FECA in all material respects, the auditors will state an unqualified opinion to that effect. If the audit reveals certain discrepancies, a qualified opinion will be included in the audit report and the reporting discrepancies and deficiencies will be noted in detail. The third type of auditor's statement concludes that the audit has revealed that the committee's reports do not reflect the committee's financial activity and /or the committee has not complied with FECA. The auditor's report is circulated to the commissioners for their review. A copy is not provided to the committee. If all comissioners agree to the findings in the report, the report is deemed final and released to the committee and the public. If any commissioner objects to the audit findings, the report will be placed on the next Commission meeting agenda for discussion. Unless the Commission votes to consider the report in closed executive session, the report will be considered in open session, at which time it will be made a public document.[73] The report is not considered final until approved by at least four commissioners.

Although an audit may result in an enforcement proceeding or an audit report adverse to the committee, neither FECA nor FEC procedures afford the committee an opportunity to contest an auditor's findings during the audit process. Therefore, it is important that counsel monitor the audit and be present at both the entrance and exit conferences. The auditor's preliminary findings as articulated during the exit conference should be closely scrutinized and discussed with the auditors. If counsel disputes a specific finding, there is limited recourse in preventing such a finding from appearing in the audit report. The most direct and immediate action is to resolve the matter informally with the auditors. If such discussions are unsuccessful, however, the only remaining recourse available to counsel is to appeal in writing directly to the Commission.

INVESTIGATIONS

In General

The FEC, through its General Counsel, investigates possible violations of FECA.[74] The agency is charged with seeking compliance through informal methods of conference, conciliation and persuasion.[75] The Commission maintains that the investigative process is nonadjudicative in that the FEC does not make specific findings of fact or conclusions of law.[76] In the event that the FEC and a respondent are unable to resolve a matter through conciliation, the FEC may seek judicial enforcement in federal district court where the matter will be adjudicated as a civil case.[77]

Despite FECA's emphasis on informal resolution of violations, liability for criminal prosecution, including imprisonment of up to one year, is provided.[78] The FEC may refer a knowing and willful violation to the Attorney General of the United States.[79] The Attorney General, independent of the Commission, may initiate a criminal prosecution.[80]

230

The fact that an FEC civil enforcement proceeding may evolve into or be conducted concurrently with a criminal prosecution for the identical violation will profoundly affect the manner in which counsel represents a respondent at the Commission. In some aspects counsel will be faced with a Hobson's choice. On the one hand, FECA encourages informal resolution of disputed violations between the FEC and a respondent. Often times a formal conciliation agreement will be highly desirable and advantageous to a respondent. Such an agreement constitutes a complete bar to any further civil action on the matter [81] and, perhaps more importantly, must be taken into account by a court in any criminal proceeding in weighing the seriousness of the violation and the appropriateness of any penalty [82]. Therefore, a conciliation agreement in which the FEC specifically notes the absence of any knowing and willful violation [83] would seriously undermine any criminal proceeding in which intent must be proved in order to establish a criminal violation.

On the other hand, FECA's emphasis on informal settlement of a violation can subject a respondent to great risks. A conciliation agreement is not guaranteed under FECA. Any statements submitted by respondent to the FEC during administrative proceedings may constitute admissions which either the FEC or the Department of Justice may attempt to introduce as evidence in either a civil or criminal proceeding. Although statements may be barred on the grounds that they constitute offers of settlement in the course of conciliation negotiations,[84] such an exclusionary rule has not been explicitly established in any court to date. In light of these tactical considerations, counsel for a respondent must initially evaluate his client's total potential liability and on a case-by-case basis determine which approach would be most advantageous to the client. There are substantial risks inherent in either refusing to conciliate with the FEC or in being too forthcoming.

Commencement of Enforcement Proceedings

The FEC designates its section 437g investigations as Matters Under Review (MURs). Each MUR is assigned a number by the Office of General Counsel at the time a file is opened on the matter. MURs are initiated in one of two ways. Most commonly, a division of the FEC, such as the Reports Analysis Division or the Audit Division, will refer an apparent violation to the

Office of General Counsel.[85] The General Counsel will make a determination as to whether the matter should be brought before the Commission with a recommendation that it find reason to believe that a violation of FECA has occurred.[86] The Commission may accept or reject the recommendation, but in either event the respondent is not notified that proceedings have commenced until after a Commission finding.

Proceedings may also be initiated on the basis of a complaint.[87] The complaint may be filed by any person and must be in writing, signed, sworn, and notarized.[88] The FEC also requests that a complaint contain a clear and concise recitation of the facts that the complainant believes constitute a violation of the FECA, copies of any relevant supporting documentation, and /or suggested sources who may substantiate or provide the pertinent facts.[89] If a complaint satisfies the technical statutory requirements, the FEC is required to notify and send a copy of the complaint to the respondent within five days.[90]   Unlike a respondent in an internally generated matter, a respondent subject to a complaint is provided an opportunity to challenge the investigation before the FEC considers whether a violation has occurred. Such a respondent may submit, within fifteen days from receipt of a copy of the complaint, a letter or memorandum setting forth factual and legal reasons why the Commission should take no action and dismiss the complaint.[91]   The Commission may dismiss the complaint at any time, but it may not find reason to believe that respondent has violated FECA until the fifteen-day period has expired or until it has considered a timely filed submission.[92]

A respondent may retain counsel to make the submission on his behalf and otherwise to represent him during an investigation. The respondent must advise the Commission in writing that he will be represented by counsel [93] and must authorize counsel to receive all notifications and pleadings, including subpoenas and orders.[94] The respondent retains control over the confidentiality of the investigation. Without the respondent's written consent, no aspect of the Commission's investigation may be made public by any person, including Commission members and employees.[95]

Reason to Believe Finding

The first decision by the Commission regarding a MUR is whether to dismiss the matter or whether to find there is reason to believe that a violation by respondent has occurred . In arriving at a decision ,the Commission must consider any submission of the respondent in reply to a complaint.[96] In all cases the FEC will consider the General Counsel's report and his recommenda - tions . The report ,which is not available to the respondent ,[97] will contain a description of the facts and a legal argument in support of the General Counsel's recommendation . The Commission will consider and discuss the report ,which will have been circulated to them ,at an executive meeting . The meeting is closed to the public . The General Counsel and the staff attorney who is assigned the MUR will present the case to the commissioners . Neither the respondent nor respondent's counsel may be present or make an oral presentation to the Commission at any time . The Commission has never conducted a hearing in conjunction with an investigation .

A vote of four commissioners is required to find reason to believe that respondent violated FECA.[98] Thereafter, respondent or counsel will be notified by a letter ,signed by either the Chairman or Vice Chairman ,that sets forth the specific violation and the factual basis for the FEC's finding.[99] The Commission will then proceed to gather information concerning the MUR.[100] The FEC may issue written interrogatories, orders and subpoenas, and conduct depositions.[101]

Probable Cause to Believe Finding and Conciliation

At such time as the FEC concludes that it has sufficient facts relating to the MUR ,it must next make its second major determination . As in the reason - to believe stage the process is initiated by the General Counsel . On the basis of the investigation that has been conducted , the General Counsel must prepare a brief that will include an exposition of the factual and legal issues of the case and a recommendation as to whether the Commission should find probable cause to believe that respondent has violated FECA.[102] The General Counsel must send a copy of his brief to the respondent or his counsel.[103] Within fifteen days of receipt, respondent's brief may be filed with the Commission Secretary.[104] The General Counsel may then review the respondent's brief and advise the Commission as to whether he intends to proceed with the recommendation.[105] FECA requires the affirmative vote of four commissioners for a finding of probable cause to believe.[106] The respondent is notified of such a finding by the General Counsel, and the Commission is thereafter bound to attempt to correct or prevent the violation through conciliation efforts for a period of at least thirty days, but no more than ninety days.[107]

The statutory time limitations for conciliation have prompted the FEC to encourage respondents to initiate negotiations prior to a finding of probable cause to believe. If respondent indicates in writing his desire to commence negotiations toward a conciliation agreement, such negotiations may be commenced, and any subsequent agreement may be ratified by the Commission when it finds probable cause to believe.[108] A conciliation agreement is not final until it is approved by four commissioners and signed by the respondent and the General Counsel.[109]

FECA does not specify the form or content of a conciliation agreement The FEC, however, usually requires two provisions. First, the FEC through its legal staff, normally insists on a penalty, the amount of which is negotiable.[110] Second, the FEC ordinarily demands a clause in which the respondent acknowledges that his acts have contravened a provision of FECA. In return for this admission, the FEC will often agree to a provision stating that the violation was not knowing or willful. The remainder of the agreement will incorporate statements of fact, general conditions of the agreement and respondent's acknowledgement of Commission jurisdiction over him and the subject matter of the MUR. The agreement, once approved by four commissioners, bars the Commission from proceeding further against the respondent with respect to the matters that are the subject of the agreement.[111]

Civil Actions

If the respondent and the FEC fail to agree upon a conciliation agreement during the statutory conciliation period, the Commission may institute a civil action against the respondent in a United States district court in a district in which the respondent is found, resides, or transacts business.[112] Such action must be approved by a vote of four commissioners.[113] The FEC may seek and the court may grant injunctive relief and/or civil penalties.[114] Either party may appeal the judgment of the district court to the appropriate court of appeals, and, thereafter, to the United States Supreme Court upon a writ of certiorari.[115] FECA requires each court to advance the action on the docket ahead of all other matters, except similar suits, and suits challenging the constitutionality of the Act pursuant to section 310[116] of FECA.[117]

Complainant's Rights

After a complainant has filed a complaint, he may not participate in the investigation. He will not be apprised of any FEC action except termination or dismissal of the MUR.[118] FECA, however, does provide a complainant with the right to institute a private cause of action against the FEC, if the Commission has failed to act upon the complaint within 120 days after it is filed, or if the Commission has dismissed the complaint.[119] In the case of a dismissed complaint, the complainant must file suit within sixty days after dismissal.[120] If the court declares that the FEC's inaction or dismissal was contrary to law, the court may direct the Commission to take action specified by the court within thirty days.[121] If the Commission fails to conform with the court's declaration within the designated time, the complainant may institute a private civil action against the respondent and seek judicial enforcement of FECA for the violation involved in the original complaint.[122]

ADVISORY OPINIONS

The FEC may render advisory opinions regarding the application of any provision of FECA or FEC regulations to a specific fact situation.[123] Any person may obtain an advisory opinion by filing a written request setting forth the specific transactions or activity regarding which the person is seeking an opinion.[124] Requests that seek a Commission ruling concerning the activities of third parties do not qualify for advisory opinions.[125] The activity described in the request must be activity that the requesting party plans to undertake or is presently undertaking and intends to undertake in the future.[126] Upon receipt of the request, the General Counsel will make an initial determination as to whether the request qualifies as an advisory opinion request and whether sufficient facts have been provided regarding the specific activity or transac- tion.[127] If the request is deemed incomplete, the General Counsel will notify the requestor within ten days of receipt and specify the deficiencies in the request.[128]

The Commission must issue an advisory opinion within sixty days after it has received a complete written request.[129] The request must be made public by the FEC and interested parties may submit written comments within ten days thereafter.[130] A vote of four commissioners is required for approval of any advisory opinion.[131] If four commissioners fail to agree on an advisory opinion within the sixty-day time limit, a letter to that effect will be sent to the requestor.[132] Any person who receives an unsatisfactory or unfavorable advisory opinion may within thirty days submit a written request for reconsideration.[133] The FEC will consider the request only upon the motion of a member who voted with the majority that originally approved the advisory opinion.[134] If four commissioners vote for such a motion, the original advisory opinion is vacated.[135]

An advisory opinion issued pursuant to these procedures is the only opinion of an advisory nature that may be issued by the Commission or its staff.[136] An advisory opinion affords a requesting party and others similarly situated broad protection from subsequent enforcement or prosecution. The requesting party may rely upon the opinion, as may any other person involved in any activity which is materially indistinguishable from the activity with respect to which an advisory opinion is rendered.[137] Furthermore, any such person who acts in good faith in accordance with the term of the advisory opinion may not be subjected to any of FECA's sanctions as a result of such reliance.[138]

CONCLUSION

Congress has been accused of intentionally establishing a weak FEC.[139] Critics point out that no one is in charge; there is no permanent chairman and no administrative leadership.[140] In order to achieve partisan balance, Congress has produced an agency that must make decisions by committee, if at all. Consequently, policy direction often is not clearly perceived or understood by the staff.[141] Counsel who practice before the FEC must be prepared to cope with this institutional problem. Direct access to the Commission is limited. Counsel will not always know when staff may be acting without clear policy direction. This danger exists in the investigative process, particularly during conciliation negotiations. At all times counsel must bear in mind that final approval rests with at least four commissioners and not with the legal staff.

Therefore, it is important to ascertain the precise mandate under which the staff is negotiating. If FEC policy is uncertain, it should be clarified through the staff. In the case of advisory opinions, which often flesh out FEC policy, counsel should be prepared for the possibility that difficult questions may not receive a consensus response. With an even number of commissioners, tie votes will occur, occasionally along partisan lines.

Counsel must at times represent a client's interest at the FEC without the benefit of public rules of procedure. This is true with respect to audits and reports analysis. In both cases a staff decision may result in enforcement proceedings. The FEC, however, has not to date set forth audit or reports analysis procedures for use by counsel and the public. Until such procedures are provided, counsel must depend on the FEC staff and on their reputed willingness to be cooperative and helpful to those who are subject to FECA.

PAC

FOOTNOTES

[1] 2 U S.C. sec. 431-455 (1976 & Supp. III 1979) (originally enacted as Federal Election Campaign Act of 1971, Pub. L. No. 92-225, sec. 301, 86 Stat. 11, *as amended by* Federal Election Campaign Act Amendments of 1974, Pub. L. No. 93-433, sec. 201, 88 Stat. 1272; Federal Election Campaign Act Amendments of 1976, Pub. L. No. 94-283, sec. 101, 90 Stat. 475; and Federal Election Campaign Act Amendments of 1979, Pub. L. No. 96-187, sec. 101, 93 Stat. 1339).

[2] 11 C.F.R. sec. 100-115 (1980).

[3] *Federal Election Campaign Act of 1973: Hearings on S. 372 Before the Subcomm. on Communications of the Senate Comm. on Commerce*, 93d Cong., 1st Sess. 63 (1973) (statement of John W. Gardner, Chairman, Common Cause).

[4] Federal Election Campaign Act Amendments of 1974, Pub. L. No. 93-443, sec. 208, 88 Stat. 1279 (current version at 2 U.S.C. sec. 437c (Supp. III 1979)).

[5] 120 Cong. Rec. 35135 (1974) (remarks of Rep. Frenzel).

[6] *Id.* at 35134 (remarks of Rep. Hays).

[7]Federal Election Campaign Act Amendments of 1974, Pub. L. No. 93-443, sec. 310(b), 88 Stat. 1281 (current version at 2 U.S.C. sec. 437c(b)(1) (Supp. III 1979)).

[8]Id. sec. 410(b), 88 Stat. 1304.

[9]424 U.S. 1, 109, 119-43 (1976). The 1974 Amendments provided that two commissioners were to be appointed by the President, two by the President pro tempore of the Senate and two by the Speaker of the House of Representatives. Federal Election Campaign Act Amendments of 1974, Pub. L. No. 93-443, sec. 310, 88 Stat. 1280-82 (current version at 2 U S.C. sec. 437c (Supp. III 1979)). The latter four selections had to be made upon the recommendations of the respective majority and minority leaders. Id. All six nominees had to be confirmed by a majority of both houses of Congress. Id. In Buckley, the Court held that most of the powers of the FEC could be exercised only by "Officers of the United States" who were nominated by the President and confirmed by the Senate in accordance with art. II, sec. 2, cl. 2, of the Constitution. Buckley v. Valeo, 424 U.S. at 140. Since the manner in which the majority of the original commissioners were appointed was not in conformity with the Constitution, the FEC was barred from exercising its powers, subject to a limited stay of the Court's judgment, until properly constituted. Id. at 141-43.

[10]Federal Election Campaign Act of 1971, Pub. L. No. 92-225, sec. 301, 309, 86 Stat. 12, 18 (repealed 1974).

[11]2 U.S.C. sec. 437c(b)(1) (Supp. III 1979).

[12]See text & note 80 infra.

[13]2 U.S.C. sec. 437c(a)(1) (Supp. III 1979). See text & note 39 infra.

[14]See text & note 57 infra.

[15]2 U.S.C. sec. 437d(a)(7) (Supp. III 1979).

[16]Advisory Opinion 1975-23, 40 Fed. Reg. 56,584, Fed. Elec. Camp. Fin. Guide (CCH) ¶ 5151 (Nov. 24, 1975).

[17]See Note, Corporate Political Action Committees: Effect of the Federal Election Campaign Act Amendments of 1976, 26 Cath. U L. Rev. 756, 762-66 (1977).

[18]40 Fed. Reg. at 56,585, Fed. Elec. Camp. Fin. Guide (CCH) ¶ 5151 (Nov. 24, 1975); see 40 Fed. Reg. at 56, 586 (dissenting opinion of Commissioners Harris and Tiernan). In a discussion of former 18 U S.C. sec. 610 (Supp. II 1972) (repealed 1976) (current version at 2 U S.C. sec. 441b (1976 & Supp. III 1979)), the Court in Buckley v. Valeo appears to have

repudiated the position of the SUNPAC dissenters and ratified the position of the majority . The Court noted that corporate and union treasury funds could be used 'to solicit contributions from employees . stockholders and union members." See *Buckley v. Valeo*, 424 U.S. 1, 28 n. 31 (1976). But see H.R. Rep. No. 917, 94th Cong., 2d Sess. 6-7 (1976).

[19] 2 U.S.C . sec . 441b (1976 & Supp . III 1979). *See* 122 Cong . Rec . 8570-72 (1976) (remarks of Rep . Brademas); *id* . at 8576 (remarks of Rep . Thompson);*id* . at H 3782 (daily ed . Mar . 30, 1976) (remarks of Rep . Brademas). The 1976 Amendments substantially amended former 18 U .S .C .sec . 610 (current version at 2U S .C .sec . 44 1b (1976 &Supp .III 1979))by restricting the manner in which and the number of times that a corporation may solicit nonexecutive employees for voluntary contribu- tions to the corporation 's PAC ;prohibiting corporations and their PACs from soliciting the general public ;broadening the class subject to section 44 1b to include trade associations ,membership organizations ,coopera- tives and corporations without capital stock ;requiring trade associations to obtain specific written approval from a member corporation prior to soliciting any executive within that corporation ;and creating a qualified right for labor organizations to demand from a corporation in which its members are employed the use at cost of the payroll deduction for purposes of collecting member contributions to the union 's PAC .Federal Election Campaign Act Amendments of 1976, Pub . L . No . 94-283, sec . 321, 90Stat . 490-92 (current version at 2U S .C .sec . 442b (1976 & Supp . III 1979)).

[20] 122 Cong. Rec. 8866, 8882-84 (1976) (remarks of Reps. Gaydos and Maguire). One proposal ,subsequently discarded during consideration of the 1976 Amendments , was a requirement that advisory opinions be reduced to regulations within 30 days and submitted to Congress for a potential veto by either chamber. H.R. 12,406, 94th Cong., 2d Sess., 122 Cong . Rec . 9112 (1976).

[21] See President's Message to Congress Transmitting a Draft of Proposed Legislation to Establish the Offices of Members of the Federal Election Commission (Feb . 16, 1976). In *Buckley* ,the Court gave Congress 30 days to pass remedial legislation ,in the absence of which the FEC would not be authorized to function . 424 U S . at 142-43.

[22] 122 Cong. Rec. 8571 (1976) (remarks of Rep . Brademas).

[23]2 U.S.C. sec. 437f (1976) (amended 1979) (advisory opinion must concern 'the application of a general rule of law "already contained in FECA or in FEC regulations).

[24]*Id*.

[25]*Id*. sec. 441b (1976 & Supp. III 1979); *see* text & note 19 *supra*.

[26]2 U.S.C. sec. 438(c)(2) (1976) (current version at *id*. sec. 438(d)(2) (Supp. III 1979)).

[27]*Id*. sec. 438(c)(5) (1976) (new definition of "rule or regulation") (current version at *id*. sec. 438(d)(4) (Supp. III 1979)).

[28]Federal Election Campaign Act Amendments of 1976, Pub. L. No. 94-283, sec. 105, 201, 90 Stat. 481, 496.

[29]*See* 2 U.S.C. sec. 437g(a)(5)(A) (1976) (amended 1979).

[30]Federal Election Campaign Act Amendments of 1979, Pub. L. No. 96-187, sec. 101, 93 Stat. 1339.

[31]2 U.S.C. sec. 437d(a)(9) (1976) (repealed 1979).

[32]*Id*. sec. 436(b) (repealed 1979).

[33]*Id*. sec. 434(b)(14) (repealed 1979).

[34]*Id*. sec. 433(b)(11) (repealed 1979).

[35]*Id*. sec. 438(d) (Supp. III 1979).

[36]*Id*. sec. 437f.

[37]*See id*. sec. 438(b).

[38]*Id*. sec. 437c(a)(1).

[39]*Id*.

[40]*Id*. sec. 437c(a)(2)(A).

[41]*Id*. sec. 437c(a)(1).

[42]*Id*. sec. 437c(a)(3).

[43]*Id*. sec. 437c(a)(5).

[44]*Id*.

[45]*Id*. sec. 437c(c).

[46]*Id*.

[47]*Id*. sec. 437c(b)(1).

[48]*Id*. sec. 437d.

[49]*Id*.

[50]*Id*. sec. 437c(f).

[51]*Id*.

[52]*See* 2 U.S.C. sec. 437f(b) (Supp. III 1979); text & note 136 *infra*. The Commission has successfully sought a conciliation agreement against a respondent in an enforcement proceeding, see text and notes 102-11

infra ,notwithstanding that the respondent had acted in reliance upon the written opinion of an FEC attorney . FEC ,Campaign Practices Rep ., May 29, 1978,at 13 (quoting the General Counsel's Report in MUR 413 (In re Gun Owners of America), the respondents "could rely on Commission advice only if it were delivered in an advisory opinion ").

[53]*See* text & notes 55-60 *infra* .

[54]*See* text & notes 61-73 *infra* .

[55]2 U.S.C. sec. 433 (Supp. III 1979).

[56]*Id.* sec. 434.

[57]*Id.* sec. 432(g)(4); 11 C.F.R. sec. 105.4 (1980). Reports by candidates for the House and their principal campaign committees are filed with the Clerk of the House of Representatives . 11 C F R .sec . 105.1 (1980). Reports by candidates for the Senate and their principal campaign committees are filed with the Secretary of the Senate . *Id* .sec . 105.2. In this respect the Clerk and the Secretary act as custodians for the FEC , and are required to forward to the Commission copies of all statements and reports within 48 hours .

[58]A treasurer should confer with counsel before responding to an RFAI in order to determine whether the inquiry may relate to an apparent violation of the Act . Any response may be used subsequently by FEC lawyers as an admission of a violation . Counsel normally should not deal with the reports analyst ,however ,in order to avoid creating the impression that a serious substantive violation has been uncovered .

[59]*See generally* (1978) FEC Ann .Rep . 17.

[60]2 U.S.C. sec. 437g (Supp .III 1979);*see* text & notes 74-122 *infra* .

[61]2 U.S.C. sec. 438(b) (Supp. III 1979).

[62]*Id .;see* I.R.C. sec. 9007, 9008(g), 9038.

[63]FEC Record, Sept. 1977, at 6.

[64]FEC Record, Feb. 1979, at 5. Historically the FEC has not had the time or resources necessary to audit substantial numbers of nonparty political committees . In 1977,only 10 of 1,389 registered nonparty committees were audited . (1977)FEC Ann .Rep . 68, 71. In 1978 the Commission audited 53 of 1,903 registered nonparty committees . (1978)FEC Ann . Rep . 89, 101.

[65]*See* 2 U.S C . sec. 438(a)(8) (Supp .III 1979).

[66]*Id* .sec. 438(b). The FEC may also authorize and conduct audits and field investigations in the course of enforcement proceedings . *Id* . sec . 437g (a)(2); 11 C F R .sec . 104.16(c) (1980).

[67]2 U.S.C. sec. 438(b) (Supp. III 1979).

[68]There are no published rules of procedure regarding audits. In 1977 the FEC announced "procedures for conducting audits." FEC Record, May 1977, at 3. But the announcement merely described the following "seven-step auditing process" which had been approved by the Commission on April 7, 1977: 1) A detailed pre -audit review at the FEC of all reports and statements filed by the party, 2) An "Entrance Conference" between the auditors and the candidate or committee to explain the purpose of the audit, outline its procedures, obtain necessary documents, records and statements, and answer any questions about the audit process, 3) A field review to verify the candidate or committee's records, 4) An "Exit Conference" between auditors and the candidate or committee to discuss the results of the audit, subsequent audit procedure, and possible suggestions for improved recordkeeping and reporting, 5) A staff report to the Commission on the audit results, 6) Commission review of the report to decide what action, if any, to take with respect to these results, and 7) Publication of all completed audits. *Id*.

[69]Reported itemized contributions will be verified by using bank deposit slips and any documentation provided to the committee by the contributor such as payroll deduction authorization cards or direct mail cards.

[70]*See* 2 U.S.C. sec. 441b(a)(3)(B), (C), 441d (1976 & Supp. III 1979); 11 C.F.R. sec. 110.11 (1980).

[71]*See* 2 U.S.C. sec. 441b(a)(4)(D) (1976 & Supp. III 1979); 11 C.F.R. sec. 114.8(d) (1980).

[72]2 U.S.C. sec. 437g (Supp. III 1979).

[73]FEC Record, Sept. 1979, at 5.

[74]2 U.S.C. sec. 437g (Supp. III 1979); 11 C.F.R. sec. 111 (1980).

[75]2 U.S.C. sec. 437g(a)(4)(A)(i) (Supp. III 1979).

[76]Commission attorneys have argued in federal district court that the FEC "does not adjudicate, hold trials, determine civil or criminal liability, issue orders, indict or impose any legal sanctions on its own." Memorandum of Points and Authorities in Support of Motion to Dismiss at 15, National Right to Work Comm. v .FEC, No. 77-786-A (E D.Va., filed Oct. 20, 1977).

[77]2 U.S.C. sec. 437g(a)(6) (Supp. III 1979).

[78]*Id*. sec. 437g(d).

[79]*Id*. sec. 437g(a)(5)(C).

[80]*See,e g.,* United States v. Operating Engineers Locai 701, Fed. Elec. Camp. Fin. Guide (CCH) ¶ 9095 (9th Cir. Oct. 1, 1979), *cert. denied,* 48 U.S.L.W. 3536 (Feb. 9, 1980); United States v. Tonry, 433 F. Supp. 620, 623 (E D. La. 1977); United States v. Jackson, 433 F. Supp. 239, 241 (W D.N.Y. 1977),*aff'd,* 586 F. 2d 832 (2d Cir .),*cert. denied,* 440 U.S. 913 (1978). The FEC and the Department of Justice have signed and publicly issued a Memorandum of Understanding regarding their respective jurisdiction over enforcement of FECA. 43 Fed. Reg. 5,441 (1978).

[81]2 U.S.C. sec. 437g(a)(4)(A)(i) (Supp. III 1979).

[82]*Id.* sec. 437g(d)(3).

[83]See text & notes 110-11 *infra.*

[84]*See* Fed. R. Evid. 404.

[85]*See* text & notes 58-60, 72 *supra.*

[86]2 U.S.C. sec. 437g(a)(2) (Supp. III 1979); 11 C.F.R. sec. 111.3, 111.8 (1980). Investigations may also be commenced after a matter has been referred to the FEC by an agency of the United States or by a state. 11 C F R. sec. 111.8 (1980).

[87]2 U.S.C. sec. 437g(a)(1) (Supp. III 1979); 11 C.F.R. sec. 111.3 (1980).

[88]2 U.S.C. sec. 437g(a)(1) (Supp. III 1979); 11 C.F R. sec. 111.4 (1980). Statements made in a complaint are subject to statutes governing perjury. 11 C F R. sec. 111.4 (1980).

[89]11 C.F.R. sec. 111.4 (1980).

[90]2 U.S.C. sec. 437g(a)(1) (Supp. III 1979); 11 C.F.R. sec. 111.5(a) (1980). A technically deficient complaint is returned to the complainant without further action. A copy of the faulty complaint is also sent to any person identified therein as a respondent. 11 C F R. sec. 111.5(b) (1980).

[91]2 U.S.C. sec. 437g(a)(1) (Supp. III 1979); 11 C.F R. sec. 111.6(a) (1980). The computation of time is based on the Federal Rules of Civil Procedure. 11 C F R. sec. 111.2 (1980).

[92]2 U.S.C. sec. 437g(a)(1) (Supp. III 1979); 11 C.F R. sec. 111.6(b) (1980).

[93]11 C.F.R. sec. 111.23 (1980). The respondent must provide the Commission with the attorney's name, address and telephone number. *Id.*

[94]*Id.* sec. 111.13(b).

[95]2 U.S.C. sec. 437g(a)(12) (Supp. III 1979); 11 C.F.R. sec. 111.21 (1980). No person may make public any FEC notification or investigation. 11 C.F R. sec. 111.21 (1980). Violators may be prosecuted and penalized up to $2000,or up to $5000 in the case of a knowing and willful violation.

Id . A complainant may be barred from publicly disseminating copies of a complaint that he has filed with the FEC . 2 U S .C .sec . 437g (a)(12) (Supp .III 1979);*see* 11 C .F R .sec . 111.21 (1980);*see also* Common Cause v .FEC ,Fed .Elec .Camp .Fin .Guide (CCH) ¶ 9089 (D D .C . Aug. 10, 1979).

[96] 2 U .S.C .sec . 437g(a)(1) (Supp .III 1979); 11 C .F .R .sec . 111.6(b)(1980).

[97] At the conclusion of an investigation , all reports by the General Counsel are made public along with most other documents relating to a specific MUR . Closed MUR files are not indexed or reported ,but they are available from the Public Records Division . *See* 11 C F R .sec . 111.20 (1980).

[98] 2 U .S.C . sec . 437g(a)(2) (Supp. III 1979); 11 C.F .R . sec . 111.9 (1980).

[99] 2 U .S.C . sec . 437g(a)(2) (Supp. III 1979); 11 C .F .R . sec . 111.9 (1980).

[100] 11 C .F .R . sec . 111.10 (1980).

[101] *Id* . sec . 111.11-.15.

[102] 2 U .S.C . sec . 437g(a)(3) (Supp. III 1979); 11 C.F .R .sec . 111.16 (1980).

[103] 2 U .S.C . sec . 437g(a)(3) (Supp. III 1979); 11 C.F .R .sec . 111.16 (1980).

[104] 2 U .S.C . sec . 437g(a)(3) (Supp. III 1979); 11 C.F .R .sec . 111.16 (1980).

[105] 11 C .F .R . sec . 111.16(d) (1980). FEC regulations do not prescribe any procedures in the event that the General Counsel decides not to proceed with his original recommendation . The spirit of the statute , however , appears to require that he submit to respondent any revised brief or recommendations in order to preserve the respondent 's right to submit a brief on respondent 's behalf .

[106] 2 U .S.C . sec . 437g(a)(4)(A)(i) (Supp. III 1979); 11 C .F .R . sec . 111.17 (1980). The Commission is not required to adopt the General Counsel 's recommendation ,whether he proposes a finding of probable cause or no probable cause . Furthermore ,the Commission may fail to attain a four - vote majority for either course of action . A majority may agree simply to take no further action . 11 C F R .sec . 111.17(b) (1980).

[107] 2 U .S.C .sec . 437g(a)(4)(A)(i) (Supp .III 1979). The conciliation period is shorter if the probable cause to believe finding occurs during the 45-day period immediately preceding any election . *Id* . sec . 437g (a)(4)(A)(ii).

[108] 11 C .F .R .sec . 111.18(d)(1980). The use of this conciliation procedure not only insulates the parties from FECA 's time limitations ,it also obviates the need for the filing of briefs .

[109] *Id* . sec . 111.18(b).

[110] *See* 2 U .S.C . sec . 437g(a)(5)(A), (B) (Supp .III 1979) (penalty provisions applicable to conciliation agreements). The Commission will often commence negotiations by suggesting a penalty equal to the dollar

amount of the contribution or expenditure involved in the violation . The amount will be higher for knowing and willful violations .

[111]*Id*. sec. 437g(a)(4)(A)(i). The FEC may seek judicial enforcement of a conciliation agreement if respondent violates any of its terms . *Id* . sec. 437g(a)(5)(D).

[112]*Id*. sec. 437g(a)(6)(A). FEC regulations permit a respondent to enter into a conciliation agreement even after civil suit has been filed . 11C F R .sec. 111.19(c) (1980).

[113]2 U .S .C. sec. 437g(a)(6)(A) (Supp. III 1979); 11 C.F.R. sec. 111.19(b) (1980).

[114]2 U .S .C. sec. 437g(a)(6)(A)-(C) (Supp. III 1979);*see* AFL-CIO v .FEC, No. 78-1937 (D.C. Cir. April 1, 1979).

[115]2 U .S .C. sec. 437g(a)(9) (Supp. III 1979).

[116]*Id*. sec. 437h (1976) (amended 1979).

[117]*Id*. sec. 437g(a)(10) (Supp. III 1979); *id*. sec. 437h (1976 & Supp. III 1979).

[118]11 C.F.R. sec. 111.9(b), 111.17(b), 111.18(e) (1980).

[119]2 U .S .C. sec. 437g(a)(8)(A) (Supp. III 1979). The FEC and not the respondent is the proper defendant initially in a complainant's suit . *See* Common Cause v .FEC , 82 F R D . 59, 60 (D D C . 1979);text &note 122*infra* . No other private cause of action may be asserted on the basis of a violation of the Act . *See* Cort v .Ash , 422U S . 66, 74-77 (1975).

[120]2 U .S .C. sec. 437g(a)(8)(B) (Supp. III 1979).

[121]*Id*. sec. 437g(a)(8)(C).

[122]*Id* .;*see* National Right to Work Comm .v .Thomson , Fed .Elec .Camp .Fin . Guide (CCH) ¶ 9042 (D .D .C .Aug. 31, 1977). *See generally* Hampton v . FEC ,No. 77-1546 (D .C . Cir .July 21, 1978); Walther v . FEC , 47 U .S .L .W. 2698 (D .D .C .Apr. 17, 1979); Walther v . Baucus , Fed .Elec . Camp . Fin. Guide (CCH) ¶ 9077 (D. Mont. Mar. 16, 1979).

[123]2 U .S .C. sec. 437d(a)(7) (Supp. III 1979).

[124]*Id*. sec. 437f(a)(1); 11 C.F.R.sec. 112.1(b)(1980). FECA includes within the definition of "person" an individual ,partnership ,committee ,associa - tion ,corporation ,labor organization or any other organization or group of persons . 2U S C .sec. 431(11) (Supp .III 1979); 11C F R .sec. 100.10 (1980). Therefore, either a corporation or a PAC may request an advisory opinion . Prior to the enactment of the 1979 Amendments , corporations did not have standing to request an advisory opinion . 2

U.S.C. sec. 437f (1976) (amended 1979); *see* FEC Response to Advisory Opinion Request 1978-62, Fed. Elec. Camp. Fin. Guide (CCH) ¶6085 (July 19, 1979).

[125] 11 C.F.R. sec. 112.1(b) (1980). Questions regarding the conduct of third parties may be the subject of an administrative complaint. 2U.S.C.sec. 437g(a)(1) (Supp. III 1979). See text & notes 87-90, 118-22*supra*.

[126] 11 C.F.R. sec. 112.1(b) (1980). A hypothetical question does not qualify as an advisory opinion request. *Id*. The Commission has yet to distinguish a hypothetical question from a question relating to activity that the requesting party intends to undertake in the future. A requestor must clearly assert his intention to undertake specific activity in order to avoid having the question characterized as hypothetical. There are no sanctions if the requestor fails to undertake the activity after an advisory opinion is rendered.

[127] *Id*. sec. 112.1(d).

[128] *Id*.

[129] 2 U.S.C. sec. 437f(a)(1) (Supp. III 1979). The period is shortened to 20 days if the request is made on behalf of a candidate or his authorized committee within 60days preceeding an election. *Id*.sec. 437f(a)(2); 11 C.F.R. sec. 112.4(b) (1980).

[130] 2 U.S.C.sec. 437f(d)(Supp.III 1979); 11 C.F.R.sec. 112.2,.3 (1980);*see* National Conservative Political Action Comm. v. FEC, No. 78-1543 (D.C. Cir. March 11, 1980); text & note 135 *infra*.

[131] 2 U.S.C. sec. 437c(c) (Supp. III 1979); 11 C.F.R. sec. 112.4(a) (1980).

[132] 11 C.F.R. sec. 112.4(a) (1980).

[133] *Id*. sec. 112.6(a).

[134] *Id*.

[135] *Id*. sec. 112.6(d). FECA does not provide for judicial review of FEC advisory opinions. A court of appeals has concluded, however, that a plaintiff has standing to challenge an advisory opinion granted to a third party on the basis that the defendant FEC failed to follow statutory and promulgated administrative procedures in issuing the opinion. National Conservative Political Action Comm .v .FEC ,No . 78-1543,slip op .at 7 (D.C .Cir .March 11, 1980). The court further held that the plaintiff must exhaust administrative remedies provided in 2U.S.C.sec. 437g before a court may assert jurisdiction over a suit against the recipient of the advisory opinion. *Id* .at 5-6,n .8;National Conservative Political Action

Comm .v .FEC ,Fed .Elec .Camp .Fin .Guide (CCH) ¶ 9057 (D D C . Apr . 28, 1978);see text &notes 118-22*supra* . The court did not address the circumstances under which the recipient of an advisory opinion could obtain standing ,and a court could assert jurisdiction ,with respect to a substantive challenge to an advisory opinion .

[136] 2 U .S .C . sec . 437f(b) (Supp . III 1979); 11 C .F .R . sec . 112.4(f) (1980).

[137] 2 U .S .C . sec . 437f(c)(1) (Supp . III 1979); 11 C .F .R .sec . 112.5(a)(1980).

[138] 2 U .S .C . sec . 437f(c)(2) (Supp . III 1979); 11 C .F .R .sec . 112.5(b)(1980).

[139] Institute of Politics, John F . Kennedy School of Government , Harvard University ,An Analysis of the Impact of the Federal Election Campaign Act , 1972-78,at 16 (prepared for the House Comm .on Administration).

[140] *Id* .

[141] *Id* . This criticism accompanied a recommendation that Congress amend FECA by providing for a presidentially appointed Chairman who would have administrative powers . *See generally Reform Spawned Agency Stirs Discontent* , 38 Cong .Q .Weekly Rep . 1019, 1025 (1980).

The author gratefully acknowledges the assistance of
Jeffrey S . Holik , Esq ., in the preparation of this article .

Jan W. Baran is with the Washington, D.C. office of the law firm Baker and Hostetler.

A graduate of Vanderbilt University Law School, Baran joined Baker & Hostetler in July 1979 after serving as the executive assistant to the past chairman of the Federal Election Commission, the Honorable Joan D. Aikens.

Baran is a regular lecturer on the subjects of campaign financing laws and regulation of corporate and trade association political activity.

VIII. PAC FINANCING
          AND ACCOUNTING

Federal Campaign Finance "Reform"

Alexander W. Keema
General Partner, KV Associates

During most of the last decade, I had the opportunity to observe at close hand and participate in the evolution of campaign finance "reform" at the federal level. During those years, my profession involved the process of policy development and administration of federal election laws and regulations, first under the General Accounting Office and later under the Federal Election Commission. The following are some personal observations on the evolution of the Campaign Finance Law, how it has worked in practice and my own view of how a more effective campaign finance "reform" might be achieved.

THE 1971 ACT

The Federal Election Campaign Act of 1971 was the culmination of a long-term election reform movement backed by "public interest" lobbies, the principal one being Common Cause. It accomplished three basic goals:

1. *Full disclosure of campaign finance activities.* The 1971 Act provided for full disclosure of all financial activity, and itemization of transactions in excess of $100.

2. *Limitations on how much a candidate could spend in his own campaign out of his personal funds, and the funds of his immediate family.* These provisions (limiting presidential candidates to $50,000, Senate candi-

dates to $35,000 and House candidates to $25,000) grew out of the notoriety received by a number of wealthy candidates running for federal office in 1970 and in earlier years, who financed their campaigns largely from personal wealth. Reformers argued that wealthy individuals should not be allowed to "buy" their way into office simply because they happened to be wealthy. The limitation provisions were designed to provide more equal opportunity to candidates who did not have personal wealth.

3. *Limitations on the total amount a candidate could spend on media advertising.* These provisions (limiting media spending to 10¢ per eligible voter) grew out of criticism, common at the time, of the impact of media advertising, particularly television, on the electoral process. The reformers argued that candidates were being "packaged" for sale to the public through slick media campaigns created by Madison Avenue. The 1968 Nixon campaign was a frequently cited example. (The media limitations were thrown out by the courts as unconstitutional, prior to the passage of the 1974 amendments.)

Responsibility for administration of the 1971 law was split among the General Accounting Office (GAO), the Office of the Secretary of the Senate and the Office of the Clerk of the House of Representatives. The GAO, a relatively non-political audit and investigative arm of the Congress, was given responsibility for presidential campaigns as well as for party and political action committees that supported presidential candidates. Not surprisingly, the Senate and House decided to oversee themselves.

The new law was vigorously enforced by the GAO which involved that agency early-on in the investigation of financial abuses related to the Watergate scandal. The GAO later conducted more than 400 audits of political committees, including every major presidential candidate committee, every state party committee, the national committees of both major parties and several minor parties, as well as most larger PACs and many local party organizations. The Senate, belatedly, borrowed a few GAO auditors to review the 1972 Senate campaigns under the guidance of the secretary's office. Administration of the law in the House amounted basically to receiving and filing disclosure reports.

THE 1974 AMENDMENTS

The 1974 Amendments to the Federal Election Campaign Act, heavily influenced by the Watergate scandals, created the Federal Election Commission. The Commission was created to unify and standardize administration of law and was thought, by some, to be the answer to a perception of lax enforcement by the Senate and House with respect to their own members. The Commission was to be composed of six members, ostensibly one Democrat and one Republican each to be appointed by the President, the Senate and the House respectively. This appointment scheme was a constitutional first, later to be rejected by the Supreme Court.

However, in addition to creating the Federal Election Commission, several fundamental changes were made to the law, altering its basic purpose and operation. The principal changes were:

1) *Imposition of contribution limits.* As most observers of current events will remember, the 1974 amendments to the campaign finance law were passed in the wake of the Watergate scandals. The Watergate Committee revealed not only that the Nixon administration had been involved in unlawful acts, but also that huge campaign contributions had flowed into the Nixon campaign coffers from both personal and illegal corporate sources.

Many of these contributions were made with an implied promise of a "quid pro quo," in the form of favorable government action on behalf of the contributors. However, it was little noted in the press at the time that the great majority of large contributions, and virtually all of the illegal contributions, were made prior to April 7, 1972, the effective date of the 1971 Act. Some $20 million was raised by the Nixon campaign prior to April 7, and none of it was subject to disclosure, or to audit by the General Accounting Office. Its ultimate disclosure more than a year later was the result of subpoenas issued by the Senate Watergate Committee, and a civil suit filed by Common Cause.

Having personally audited several of the legitimate Nixon Re-Election Committees (post-April 7 transactions only), I find it inconceivable that the pre-April 7 fundraising methods would ever have been used by those responsible in the Nixon campaign had they known that the sources of these contributions and the amounts raised would ultimately be disclosed to the public, and to law enforcement agencies. After April 7, the financial records of the Nixon campaign were handled primarily by large public accounting firms, and were, for the most part, flawless.

Nevertheless, disclosures of financial abuses uncovered in the 1972 campaign provided ample justification for the contribution limits imposed by the 1974 amendments. ($1,000 per individual for each election, and $5,000 per qualified multi-candidate committee.) Reformers reasoned that large contributions made to candidates by wealthy individuals and groups representing particular economic interests bought, if not any specific "quid pro quo," at least access to the candidate, and therefore influence on the candidate's thinking. The limitations were designed to curb such influence.

2. *Spending limitations.* With the 1971 media limitations ruled unconstitutional, there remained no effective curb on campaign spending by federal candidates. So, in the name of "reform," Congress imposed, in the 1974 amendments, limits on total campaign spending by federal candidates. Many believed, at the time, that this provision primarily served the interests of incumbents, since incumbents have built-in advantages such as the "frank," a high level of name recognition, etc. Others opposed expenditure limits on the grounds that political campaigns, on the whole, are actually under-financed rather than over-financed. Dr. Herbert Alexander, Director of the Citizens' Research Foundation, and author of several books on campaign financing, has often expressed this view.

3. *Public financing.* With total spending limits in place, reformers in Congress realized that, with tight contribution limits imposed on political fundraising, it would be extremely difficult for presidential candidates to raise sufficient funds to conduct a nationwide primary campaign for nomination, or to run a nationwide general election campaign. The answer to this problem was to be found in public financing of presidential campaigns.

The primary election process presented an obvious problem since virtually anyone can declare himself a presidential candidate in the primaries. The solution was found in the "threshold concept," requiring the raising of $5,000 in each of 20 states in amounts of $250 or less in order to qualify for federal matching funds. Fifteen candidates running for nomination by the two major parties met the threshold in 1976 and received matching funds totaling

254

about $24 million. An additional $43.6 million in straight grants was distributed to the major party presidential nominees for the general election and $4.1 million was paid to the two major parties to finance their national nominating conventions. In the 1980 elections, $30.6 million in primary matching funds was distributed to ten presidential candidates, with $62.0 million for the general election and $8.8 million for the conventions.

BUCKLEY V. VALEO AND THE 1976 AMENDMENTS

It was no great surprise to bureaucrats at the Federal Election Commission when the Supreme Court ruled on January 30, 1976, in "Buckley v. Valeo," that the appointment scheme devised by Congress for the Commission was unconstitutional. This ruling effectively suspended the official activities of the Commission until, several months later, it was reconstituted as an executive agency under the 1976 amendments.

However, aside from its direct impact upon the Federal Election Commission itself, the Supreme Court decision also had a major effect upon the character of campaign financing in Senate and House races as well. The principal changes were:

Elimination of spending limits while retaining contribution limits. Total spending limits in federal election campaigns were ruled unconstitutional. Nevertheless, the elimination of spending limits did not, in most cases, result in increased total spending in Senate and House races during 1976. The greatest curb in total spending turned out to be the inability of candidates to raise funds under the tight contribution limits upheld by the Supreme Court ruling. In fact, total spending in Senate and House races appeared to be significantly less in 1976 than in prior presidential election years.

Elimination of the limits imposed upon candidates' use of their personal funds. This provision was also found to be unconstitutional by the Supreme Court. The Court's ruling brought campaign finance "reform" to precisely the opposite result from that intended in the original 1971 Act. The 1971 Act was designed to prevent wealthy candidates from "buying" their way into office at the expense of their less wealthy opponents. Under present law, a millionaire candidate is free to spend unlimited amounts from his own pocket, while his "unwealthy" opponent is limited to what he can raise in $1,000 (or $5,000) contributions.

Thus, the wealthy candidate has a far greater advantage than he did prior to 1971 "reform." The so-called "fat cats" can no longer provide major financing for less "fat" candidates.

THE FEDERAL ELECTION COMMISSION

As in most attempts to substitute the judgment of well-meaning legislators for the operation of a free market, the result of election finance "reform" has been the creation of a cumbersome government bureaucracy to administer a set of complex legal requirements and regulations. Direct costs to the taxpayers for the Federal Election Commission are budgeted at $9.2 million for this fiscal year. Additional costs to political committees of complying with the law are probably several times that amount.

Post-election audits of presidential campaigns have proven to be interminable affairs, with continuous haggling between campaign staffs and the Commission's staff regarding the "legitimacy" of particular receipts and expenditures and the supporting records required. The final audit report on the Carter primary campaign of 1976 was not completed and released by the Commission until April 1979. The inordinate time and expense required for such audits results from the cumbersome nature of the matching funds concept as applied to political campaigns. Matching funds audits are extremely complex with a great deal of room for differences of opinion between the auditors and the auditees.

THE FUTURE OF ELECTION REFORM?

It has been noted in the press, and many observers agree, that the 1976 and 1980 elections entailed significantly less political spending than elections in prior years. Much has been made of the lack of local citizen involvement, the lack of bumper stickers and posters and the lack of local fundraising and spending. The turn-out of registered voters in presidential elections continues its downward trend approaching only 50 percent of those eligible to vote.

I submit that the subdued nature of recent political campaigns can be attributed to the contribution limits, and the expenditure limits imposed on presidential campaigns receiving federal funds. Federal candidates, with the exception of those who have used their personal wealth, generally have had less money to spend. Local groups have stayed out of the political process for fear of making illegal "contributions-in-kind." At the same time party structures have been weakened through the application of a single contribution limit to all party committees in the same state, while the power of special interest group PACs has been enhanced through their ability to make unlimited "independent expenditures" on behalf of candidates they favor, or against candidates they oppose.

The cure most commonly proposed for these ills is to provide federal matching funds for Senate and House campaigns in general elections, and possibly in the primaries as well.

While public financing of presidential campaigns can be viewed as reasonably workable, if not totally successful, the extension of this concept to House and Senate campaigns in the form of matching funds would increase the administrative burdens both for the Federal Election Commission and for the candidates themselves, to an extent few realize. It is difficult to calculate the number of bureaucrats necessary to maintain adequate control over the certification of matching funds to perhaps 1,000 federal candidates, or to conduct post-election audits of all such campaigns within a reasonable time after the election.

In any case, a major increase in the size and complexity of the administrative machinery would be inevitable under any extension of the matching funds concept beyond the presidential level. Some FEC commissioners, while officially neutral, find this concept attractive in terms of expanding their bureaucratic empire. So it goes.

AN ALTERNATE APPROACH TO FINANCING ELECTIONS

With the ascendancy of Republicans to power in Washington, the concept of matching funds for Senate and House campaigns has become, effectively, a dead issue. The Republican minority in Congress has opposed

257

the concept all along, defeating more than one attempt by the Carter White House and the Democratic majority to enact it over the past four years.

Perhaps the time has now arrived when serious consideration can be given to a proposal which I believe would resolve the major problems behind the orgy of campaign finance "reform" we have seen over the last decade. It is my belief that we can, by a simple change in the tax code:

1. Significantly expand citizen participation in the political process;
2. Substantially increase available funding for the political process at all levels;
3. Substantially reduce the costs of fundraising for political campaigns;
4. Significantly increase the financial resources of regular party organizations;
5. Significantly curb the financial power of special economic and other interest groups to affect the political process; and
6. Reduce the advantage now enjoyed by wealthy candidates who finance their campaigns from personal funds.

These goals can be achieved, in my view, through adoption by the Congress of a simple change to the Internal Revenue Code. Title 26, Section 41 of the Code now provides for a tax credit of up to $50 for political contributions by individuals. The tax credit is allowable for one-half of total contributions, requiring $100 in contributions to qualify for the $50 credit.

Curiously, contributions by individuals to PACs qualify for tax credits in the same way as contributions made directly to political parties or candidates. The law makes no distinction between subsidizing PACs and subsidizing candidates. The taxpayers pick up half of the cost in both cases.

I believe that the current allowable tax credit should be increased to 100 percent for contributions of up to $50 made directly by individuals to political candidates and official party committees. Contributions to PACs should not qualify for these tax credits. In conjunction with this tax change, the Congress should repeal direct federal financing of presidential campaigns.

258

HOW WOULD IT WORK?

A 100 percent tax credit for political contributions would create a "citizen-controlled" form of public financing benefiting the electoral process at all levels of government. Each taxpayer would be provided with a personal "franchise" to distribute a maximum of $50 in public funds to the candidate(s) or party(ies) of his choice during each calendar year. Citizens could be encouraged to exercise this franchise through public service advertising, just as they are now routinely encouraged to exercise their franchise to vote.

The existence of a public financing franchise would increase substantially the total amount of funding available to candidates, their committees and political parties as well as expand citizen participation in the political process itself. With an estimated 130 million taxpayers in the United States, a participation rate of only 10 percent would inject up to $650 million into the political process, all in individual contributions of $50 or less.

Given this franchise, citizen interest and involvement in the political process could be expected to increase, for the same reason that a person's interest in a football game increases as a result of a wager placed on the outcome of the game. In political terms, this means more citizen interest in candidates and political issues. The existence of a public financing franchise, available to all taxpayers, would also reduce the fundraising costs to political campaigns, as "spontaneous" contributions flow to those candidates who generate citizen support through news reports of their positions on vital issues.

Elimination of contributions to PACs from eligibility would restrict public financing in the political process to candidates and regular party committees. This modification would make it more difficult for political action committees to raise contributions, since such contributions would represent totally private funds. Under the present 50 percent tax credit system, half of all $100 contributions made to special interest political action committees actually represent public funds. Under a 100 percent tax credit, restricted to candidates and regular party organizations, an increasing proportion of campaign financing could be generated in small amounts, directly from private citizens, while the financial impact of special interest groups on the political process would be correspondingly reduced.

With the introduction of a citizen's public financing franchise, the present form of public financing and the complex administrative machinery necessary to implement it would become unnecessary. The present "matching funds" concept is designed to provide the greatest amount of public funding to those candidates who generate the widest public support, as evidenced by the largest number of small contributions received. A 100 percent tax credit system would reach precisely this same result in a far more direct way, without the necessity of the Federal Election Commission acting as an intermediary. The role of the Commission would be reduced to administraton and enforcement of the disclosure and limitation provisions of the law, a complex task in itself.

UNKNOWN FACTORS

The principal unknown in the 100 percent tax credit approach is the degree to which it would stimulate small political contributions by the public. Some knowledgeable observers would undoubtedly argue that such a tax credit for political contributions would not appreciably increase the number of individual contributors beyond the 8 percent to 9 percent who now contribute something under the present tax structure. However, this argument ignores the substantive distinction between a 50 percent and a 100 percent tax credit. Under a 50 percent credit the contributor makes a real sacrifice in his own consumption of goods and services in order to support the candidate, party or PAC of his choice. Under a 100 percent tax credit, the sacrifice in consumption is only temporary, since the full amount contributed will be deducted from the contributor's tax bill (or added to his tax refund) in the following year.

The other side of the public participation argument is that so many people might take advantage of their opportunity to make a political contribution using federal tax money that the political process would become over-financed, leading to waste and mismanagement in political campaigns. However, neither argument is supported at this point by much reliable statistical data.

Necessary statistics to support a political decision on a 100 percent tax credit might be gathered through a nationwide poll of the voting age, tax-paying public. Such a poll could ascertain, among other things, the percentage of people who made political contributions in 1976, 1978 and 1980, as compared to the percentage of people who say they would have made a contribution subject to a 100 percent tax credit.

Results of such a poll, assuming the responses are reliable, could be used as the basis for the key policy decisions. If, for example, 20 percent of those responding said they would contribute to political parties and candidates if the 100 percent tax credit were available, and a determination was made that $800 million in public funds should be provided to support the political process, then the maximum allowable tax credit should be $31.

If, on the other hand, 40 percent of those surveyed said they would contribute under a 100 percent tax credit, and the same $800 million in public funding was desired, then the maximum allowable tax credit should be only $15 or $16 per individual.

In either case, the essential ingredients for public policy purposes are:

1. A determination of how much public funding is needed in the political process; and
2. An accurate estimate of the rate of public participation in financing the political process through a 100 percent tax credit mechanism.

The extent of public financing necessary is, in turn, largely dependent upon the statutory contribution limits. If the limitations on contributions by political action committees and individuals ($5,000 and $1,000 respectively) were reduced, then the total requirement for public funding through the 100 percent tax credit mechanism would be correspondingly increased, necessitating a higher maximum allowable credit per individual. In any case, the maximum amount allowed as a tax credit provides a readily adjustable mechanism to control overall public financing of the political process. The decision as to which political parties and candidates receive public financing, and the actual distribution of it, are left to the discretion of the public. Minor party candidates would have equal access to public funding to the extent they could generate public support.

Finally, for a 100 percent tax credit to stimulate a significant increase in the total number of small contributors, the public would have to made aware of it. This could be accomplished through a public information campaign, financed by Congress, as part of a "real" election reform package.

By putting a fixed amount of financial/political clout into the hands of every taxpayer, the Congress might actually succeed in reawakening the political awareness and concern of individual citizens throughout the nation. Each individual would face the annual Hobson's choice of either contributing to a candidate or political party, or of contributing to the IRS. **PAC**

Alexander W. Keema is a general partner as well as a founding partner of KV Associates, a Washington, D.C. consulting firm specializing in federal government procurement and business/government relations. Keema came to Washington in 1971 to accept a job as a management analyst with the General Accounting Office (GAO), the congressional watchdog agency. In early 1972, he became the first professional to staff GAO's then infant Office of Federal Elections. There, he began what would become a long professional career at the core of the federal election reform movement. He worked with the nuts and bolts of the FEC in 1978. At the FEC, he played a major role in developing the reporting forms and regulations which now govern campaign disclosure, contribution and spending limits, and the procedures used in administration of the Presidential Matching Funds Progarm.

After leaving the FEC, Keema spent two years with the Office of Federal Procurement Policy within the Office of Management and Budget where he worked on regulatory reform in federal government procurement. Keema is well-known today for his consulting on government procurement and federal election campaign finance.

PAC Accounting Guidelines

James Nesbitt
Partner, Coopers & Lybrand

It is imperative for managements of organizations sponsoring or contemplating political action committees to know the laws and regulations governing a PAC's operations, particularly in today's volatile political climate – with special interests from every band of the spectrum crying for attention. Any fumbling in the financial record-keeping and reporting requirements can endanger the PAC's future fundraising efforts, thereby preventing it from contributing money to candidates for federal office* whose views the sponsoring organization endorses.

Since corporations, associations and unions sponsoring PACs should consult with both their CPAs and their attorneys to be certain they are in compliance with the Federal Election Campaign Act (FECA), it is comforting to realize that legal and accounting services fees paid for setting up, administering and soliciting contributions to a PAC are not considered political contributions or expenditures. The IRS is currently developing regulations that may affect the tax deductibility of those expenses.

The treasuryship function is undoubtedly the keystone of the PAC. Existing law requires each PAC to have a treasurer to accept contributions and make expenditures. This treasurer is personally responsible for the timeliness, accuracy and completeness of organizational statements, accounting records and related reports filed with the FEC.

---

*PACs can also be formed to support state and local candidates. Before doing so, however, they should consult state and local laws and regulations.

Many organizations, wishing to divorce themselves entirely from the PAC operation, can by law hand over virtually the entire treasuryship function to a CPA firm. The accounting firm then receives all contributions directly, records them and performs all the necessary accounting and financial reporting for PACs. However, PACs are not yet required by law to be audited. And if the sponsoring organization wants an audit of its PAC, it would have to be performed by an accounting firm other than the one carrying out the treasuryship function.

COMPLEX, DETAILED REQUIREMENTS

The principal financial reporting and compliance provisions controlling PACs are embodied in the Federal Election Campaign Act and its various amendments, the latest being PL 96-187, enacted at the beginning of 1980. These amendments made numerous changes in PAC financial reporting requirements.

REPORTING

Once the decision is made to establish a PAC, it should register with the FEC. Present laws require a registration statement (FEC Form 1, Statement of Organization for a Political Committee) to be filed within 10 days after the organization date. Any amendments must be filed within 10 days after certain information in the original registration has been modified.

In addition, any PAC that has filed a Form 1 must also file periodic reports (FEC Form 3 and related supplementary schedules) disclosing information about the PAC's contributions and expenditures. Those reports must be filed with the House of Representatives, the Senate or the FEC and certain states, depending where Form 1 was filed and the location of the PAC-supported candidates.

Form 3 reports must be filed quarterly. Since quarterly reporting rules are especially burdensome in an election year, many PAC treasurers find it easier to comply by reporting monthly. A PAC may request permission from the FEC to file Form 3 reports monthly, rather than quarterly.

CONTRIBUTIONS

By definition, contributions to a PAC include any direct or indirect payments, distributions, loans, advances, services, gifts of money or anything of value to influence a federal election. PACs may receive and make contributions.

PAC accounting records must comply with numerous legal restrictions. The records should be sufficiently detailed so that the treasurer can prepare the required FEC reports and determine that all contributions the PAC accepts are legal. The contribution file (necessary to comple Form 3) should contain:

- Each donor's name, address, occupation and principal place of employment,

- Amount and date of every contribution and

- Aggregate amount of contributions made by each individual, for both the current FEC reporting period and the year to date.

Any person giving over $200 to a PAC in a calendar year must be identified by name in Form 3, along with the amount.

PACs may not accept more than $5,000 from one person in a calendar year. As contributions are received and processed, individual contribution records should be reviewed to be sure that the limit has not been exceeded. The FECA also prohibits individuals from donating more than an aggregate amount of $25,000 to PACs or political candidates in a calendar year.

Many PACs send receipts to each donor, acknowledging the contribution. Usually in the form of a thank-you letter, the receipt is sufficient to document any income tax benefits the donor might claim.

"EARMARKED" CONTRIBUTIONS

PACs may accept an "earmarked" contribution, which is money donors have specified that the PAC donate to a particular candidate or campaign committee. When a PAC receives an earmarked contribution, it informs the candidate promptly. Furthermore, it must hand over the money within a specific time and identify the source.

"IN-KIND" CONTRIBUTIONS

In-kind contributions require the treasurer's closest scrutiny. These noncash donations include services and property and, like cash contributions, must be assigned a value and reported to the FEC. As in-kind contributions also come under the $5,000 lid, treasurers must value them very carefully. Donated property (e.g., stocks and bonds) is valued at the fair market value (FMV) at the date of gift. When a PAC receives donated services (unpaid volunteers are generally excluded from this category, however), the FMV of the services is based upon the hourly rate (salary plus applicable fringe benefits) of the persons giving the services. These are reported as both a receipt and an expenditure.

When a PAC sells property received as an in-kind contribution, it must report on Form 3 the proceeds of the sale as a cash contribution. If the proceeds top $200, the identification, occupation and business address of both the property's donor and buyer must also be reported.

PROHIBITED CONTRIBUTIONS

Included among the types of contributions PAC treasurers may not accept are donations:

- From national banks,

- From government contractors,

- From foreign nationals without a permanent U.S. residence,

- From persons making contributions in the name of another person,

- From corporations organized under federal law,

- In-cash or currency from a person whose cash contributions exceed $100,

- From donors who have overspent their contribution levels, and

- From anonymous donors who give more than $50.

INTERNAL ACCOUNTING CONTROLS

A good system of internal accounting controls strengthens the overall effectiveness of the organizational structure and insures that contributions will be properly accounted for. For security purposes, procedures should be designed so that duties are segregated. For example, people performing cash-receipt functions should not perform or be responsible for cash disbursements. The person who prepares bank deposits should not record cash receipts or prepare the monthly bank reconciliations.

Other basic internal control procedures should include:

- Immediate restrictive endorsement of all checks upon receipt,

- Photocopying of all checks on receipt,

- Development of daily control totals of all contributions for subsequent comparison to the cash-receipt records, and

- Monthly reconciliation of bank accounts and a detailed review by a responsible official.

A PAC should promptly deposit all contributions it accepts in a bank account established for the PAC's sole use. Under no conditions should PAC contributions be deposited in the sponsoring organization's bank account. Many PACs use either a lock-box or a post-office box arrangement to maintain tight internal accounting controls over the deposit function. If a lock-box is not used, procedures should be developed so that all cash and checks received are deposited on the day of receipt.

EXPENDITURES/FORMS OF PACS

An expenditure is a contribution of anything of value given for influencing a federal election (in the context of this article). While the law prohibits corporations from making expenditures for political purposes, a PAC may make certain kinds.

For FECA contribution-limit purposes, PACs are classified as either "multicandidate" or "registered." A multicandidate PAC is defined as one that has: 1) registered with the FEC for at least six months, 2) received contributions from more than 50 donors and 3) made contributions to five or more candidates for federal elective offices. A multicandidate PAC may donate up to $5,000 annually to a candidate for any election (primary and general elections are counted separately for this limitation), and up to $15,000 a year to one national political party committee.

A "registered" PAC does not meet the defined requirements for a multicandidate PAC, but it has registered with the FEC. Registered PACs are restricted to a ceiling of $1,000 per single candidate per election. Registered PACs may contribute no more than $20,000 in a calendar year to one national political party committee.

No political action committee can spend a penny without authorization from its treasurer or an alternate.

ACCOUNTING PROCEDURES

Accounting procedures for PACs should be so designed that expenditures can be quickly and accurately reported. All except petty cash disbursements must be made by checks drawn on the PAC's bank account. A disbursement file should be set up and maintained, containing the following minimal information for each outlay:

- Name and address of individual to whom the money is given,

- Date and amount,

- Candidate's name and address if payment is made to a candidate,

- Office for which the candidate is running, and

- Other details of the expenditure.

When expenditures to a specific recipient for the current FEC reporting period or year to date go over $200, the particulars must be reported on Form 3.

Appropriate internal accounting control procedures should be installed for disbursements, including:

- Proper written approval by authorized persons for all disbursements, including contributions to political candidates;

- Reconciliation of total expenditures to the PAC's cash-disbursement records for each FEC reporting period and the year to date; and

- Regular reviews of the cash-disbursement records to make sure that all of them are properly reported to the FEC.

FEDERAL TAX TREATMENT

The Internal Revenue Code exempts from payment of federal income tax organizations primarily set up to accept contributions and spend money intended to influence the selection, nomination, election or appointment of candidates for federal, state or local public office. The income a PAC receives in pursuing qualified political activities is exempt-function income and is therefore not taxable if its use is considered associated with that function.

Other types of income, however, like interest, dividends, realized gains on sales of securities or unrelated business income, are considered taxable, at corporate rates. If a political action committee has long-term capital gains, the income tax would be calculated by taking the 28 percent alternative corporate tax rate.

If a PAC has taxable income of more than $100 in one year, it must file a tax return on Form 1120-POL. PACs need not make estimated tax returns, are not subject to the minimum tax rules and may not claim the investment tax credit.

The Code allows people contributing to PACs to claim a tax credit of 50 percent of the amount given, up to a maximum of $50 per individual return or $100 on a joint return. To qualify for tax purposes, the contribution must be used by the PAC for, among other things, furthering the nomination or election of candidates to public office. There are numerous constraints on PAC activities so that contributions can continue to qualify for the credit. Usually, contributions to a PAC participating in general, political, educational or legislative activities do not qualify.

WHAT LIES AHEAD

As more and more companies, associations and unions recognize the worth of political action committees and what can be accomplished through them, their number will undoubtedly mushroom. A basic -- and very important -- ingredient for viable PACs is a detailed, well-kept and accurate financial record. Without it, allegations of wrong-doing could be levelled at both PAC and sponsoring organization, which, at the least, might hamper future fundraising efforts. PACs are a legitimate entity that organizations, through their employees, members and officers, can properly take advantage of in exercising their citizenship rights. **PAC**

James C. Nesbitt is a general practice partner in the Washington, D.C. office of Coopers & Lybrand. Nesbitt directs, on a national basis, the financial services his firm provides to political committees and is also responsible for providing a variety of financial services to a number of political action committee clients.

A frequent speaker at technical seminars sponsored by Coopers & Lybrand, Nesbitt is also heavily involved in the firm's quality control program. He holds CPA certificates from the Commonwealth of Massachusetts and the District of Columbia, and is a member of the American and District of Columbia Institutes of CPAs.

IX. PAC COMMUNICATIONS

Communications and Political Action Committees

A. John Adams
John Adams and Associates, Inc.

A recent informal survey of PAC communications indicated as much variety as in company PACs themselves -- ranging from almost zero to PACs with full-time field organizers and professional journalists turning out highly-professional products.

At the zero end are those PACs which are limited to a small number of top executives of a company. At the other are companies which have developed their PAC activity into full-blown civic action programs, with frequent regional meetings and several-day annual meetings in Washington, where representatives from all plants and divisions of the company have an opportunity to meet with and question leading congressmen and White House staffers.

What makes the difference, usually, is the attitude and commitment of the company CEO and the company's traditional management style. Some take pride in being laid back; others in being aggressive. Not suprisingly, perhaps, the major oil companies have taken a pioneering role in PAC development. Today, Atlantic Richfield's Citizen Action Program is a model which many other large companies are emulating. One of the secrets of its success, according to ARCO executives, is that no employee of the company is excluded from participating. It is open to union and non-union employees alike, but the program's sophisticated newsletter and other regular communications are sent only to PAC members.

In the still relatively new art form of PAC communications, certain items are becoming standard, such as a solicitation letter from the CEO, a more detailed follow-up letter from the senior officer of the PAC and a regular form of reporting on PAC developments to members, either as a typed letter or a printed newsletter.

There the similarities tend to end. Some companies have a glossy brochure explaining the PAC and its purpose; others just a few typewritten pages. Some have highly professional videotape and slide presentations; others rely largely on word-of-mouth. Some communicate regularly on PAC matters with major shareholders; others have no communication with shareholders. It should be noted that some companies which had high hopes of bringing shareholders into their PAC work have been disappointed by the results, with the cost of solicitation often far exceeding the total of contributions received. Others report that slide and tape presentations have not been as effective as hoped and are no longer used.

Overall, with the exception of a score of companies with highly developed programs, PAC communications can be generally described as haphazard. This is surprising considering the general level of communications expertise most companies have at their command. Since effective communication -- in one form or another -- is the obvious key to increased PAC membership, it is also worth noting that most corporations have still done little more than scratch the surface of their membership potential.

A typical Fortune 500 PAC is probably receiving contributions from only about five percent of its salaried employees at most, and the vast majority of these contributions amount to less than $100 a year. Since these are mostly payroll deductions, this means that most of the managers and executives who have signed up are contributing less than $2 a week. Depending on the size of the company, of course, this can still amount to a sizable political fund at the end of two years. But, as these figures indicate, there is enormous potential for growth.

Company executives who have spent a good deal of time soliciting for their PACs explain that many of their colleagues remain suspicious. The PAC organizer of a four-year-old fund explained: "In a meeting of maybe 40 potential contributors, you'll find half a dozen or so who are completely in agreement and pre-sold on the idea. With these, you don't need much communication. They're well-informed and enthusiastic.

"Among the others, however, you find many who feel that somehow a PAC is 'not right' -- that the company shouldn't be doing this kind of thing. They don't like the idea of others deciding which candidates should receive their money. And, on the whole, their political views are probably more liberal than those of their bosses. If we want to grow, these are the people we have to convince."

How to convince them is the communications challenge facing many company PACs today. These employees must be convinced that:

- Top management of the company *wants* them to join.

- Money given to PACs *can* make a difference, and this difference, by helping industry, will indirectly help them.

- Congressional candidates actually *need* these contributions, as campaign costs have soared.

- If PACs representing people in their districts do not help, they are more dependent on contributions – and influence -- from outside groups.

- They can have faith in the members of the PAC committee deciding which candidates to support.

All of the above can be summed up in a word: *credibility.* Some companies unquestionably have greater credibility with their employees than others. If there is a tradition of trust, then the communication job is easier. If there is little trust, then the PAC will have to work a good deal harder for every new member. But even the company which deservedly enjoys high employee loyalty needs to communicate with the great majority of its eligible employees in ways which are especially meaningful to those employees.

This may mean taking a different approach from that used to garner the core of senior management people who make up the typical PAC membership. Already, a number of PAC organizers, frustrated by the difficulty of expanding their membership, have tended to give up, believing that the additional contributions to be gained may not merit the considerable extra effort required to gain them.

Some employees, of course, will never be convinced. For many of the others, person-to-person communication is probably the only kind that will work. But for those who *can* be won over, the effort is well worth making. To reach them, a number of critical areas in the PAC's organization and approach should be examined.

First, the word communication should be interpreted in its broadest sense. It is not enough to send out material or show a tape. PACs should aim at *involving* eligible employees. There are many ways of doing this, from opinion feedback to congressional briefings. One oil company has set up a series of "area committees" which organize local events, including backyard barbecues, to which candidates for public office are invited.

These area committees have their activities reported in their own quarterly newsletter, in addition to the PAC's regular monthly newsletter on political developments. They generate enthusiasm at all employee levels because they provide very obvious learning and personal growth opportunities. "Some of our most enthusiastic members are not management people at all," the PAC organizer reported.

Second, CEOs and other senior officers of the company can demonstrate their interest and involvement more noticeably. The reason they do not, in many cases, is probably that the PAC has never asked them to. Indeed, the PAC's communication to top management is often totally neglected in this regard. This applies, too, to its communication with heads of departments. The company's public relations and industrial relations people, for example, could probably be far more helpful if included as part of the PAC planning team.

Third, in many cases the PAC's communications need to be "de-Washingtonized." Many of them are written by Washington-based executives, who often speak a quite different language from the rest of the company.

Communications should be directly related to the concerns of employees and written in terms familiar to them. Why should they care whether the Davis-Bacon Act is repealed? There is a way of telling them, but not in the usual Washington phraseology. Indeed, PAC communications offer a new and exciting forum for explaining company concerns to employees which simply has not existed before. Some companies have seized this opportunity, but most have not.

Fourth, there is a clear assumption in many corporate PAC publications that all employees are on the same wavelength; that is, they are at least moderately conservative in their views, are against environmentalists and other woolly-minded "do gooders," are against government regulation and "interference" in private business, and are pro-nuclear energy, anti-consumer groups, anti-labor and so on.

This assumption comes through again and again in the description of political developments. In describing candidates that its PAC is supporting, for instance, a company may assume it is significant enough to say that the opponent is "liberal" or "anti-business." The fact is that employees are not all on this wavelength, and find this kind of assumption insulting. They could become valuable members of the company PAC if the PAC's communications were more objective and more professionally written.

Fifth, most PACs — even the best organized of them — do not have a system for periodically changing the members of the committee deciding who receives the money. Most of these "steering" or contributions committees have remained unchanged since the PAC was formed. Most of them are small and the choices are really determined by the head of the company's Washington office.

If PACs are to attract more of a cross-section of the company, then all contributing employees should be eligible for a period of service on the steering committee. Biannual elections could be held for this purpose. This would make membership more attractive. It would provide a valuable learning experience. And it would remove the suspicion, perfectly justified at present, that contributions are decided by a tightly-controlled management clique.

These are just some of the steps that might be taken to increase PAC membership and support. Is the effort worth making? Yes, and here is why.

PACs *are* effective – more so, probably, than anyone thought likely just three short years ago. And their effectiveness has gone beyond just getting better people elected to Congress. They have done that, but they have also made Congress work harder. They have forced closer attention to key economic and energy issues which impact our industries and the people who work in them. They have done all this, almost coincidentally, through a form of synergism which has developed from the increased political awareness they have created. Few congressional offices today are as highly tuned to the subtleties of the legislative process as the Washington offices of our major corporations.

So far, so good. American business has been doing some legitimate catching-up with respect to influencing the political process. Short of a national disaster in the next two years, the Republicans will almost certainly sweep the House of Representatives in 1982, giving us the most business-oriented national government in modern times.

But here's the red flag: All of these happy developments for business have not been lost on labor, consumer and environment groups whose level of sophistication in influencing the media and public opinion remains awesome. They are *superb* communicators. They have the power to make the pendulum swing against business far faster than most of us would care to contemplate.

All the more reason, therefore, for business PACs to use the next two years to dramatically strengthen their membership – to make them more representative of the company as a whole. Liberals in the company should feel as comfortable and enthusiastic about contributing through their PAC as do conservatives. The current lack of broad support among eligible employees in virtually every major corporation is the Achilles heel of the whole PAC system. It presents a perfect target for attacks by anti-business groups and the liberal press, who can portray corporate PACs as representing nothing but a handy disguise for the same old corporate givers the Federal Election Campaign laws were supposed to protect us against. It provides a convenient justification for imposing the restrictions on PAC contributions which already are being called for.

280

To bring in the tens of thousands of additional eligible contributors, PAC communications need a major overhaul. In most companies, the whole area of communication has been neglected. It has been way down on the list of PAC priorities. For the immediate future, it should probably be the *number one* priority.

Each company has its own special needs, related to size, location, type of workforce, areas of business and management style. I will not attempt, therefore, to lay out a specific program. Rather, I would like to encourage all those involved with corporate PACs to start planning now for a major membership drive during the next two years, and to begin by asking: How can PAC membership be made more meaningful to the *average* eligible employee of our company? To really boost membership, this is the person you have to reach.

And I ask you to think big. By that, I do not mean huge amounts of money. But thing big conceptually. Your PAC has enormous potential to provide employees with a significant educational experience. It can provide opportunities to meet and question the nation's policy-makers, understand why your company has a vital interest in specific issues and follow the maneuvering which leads to the development of public policy. Your employees' views can be canvassed on key issues. You can bring PAC members to Washington for special events, and you can arrange for congressional hearings to be held in their own community. In place of the occasional lifeless PAC notice on the bulletin board, you can arrange for true employee participation – generating a feeling of real, tangible benefit from becoming a PAC member.

It will take more time, certainly. It will mean a larger PAC budget, no question. But few managements will haggle over a bigger budget if you can show them a well-planned, thoroughly integrated membership program geared to developing a healthy PAC consciousness throughout the company. If the PAC can be seen as a useful path to a better informed, more aware and participatory employee population, then the benefits to the company will be obvious to all.

The alternative should also receive serious consideration. If PACs continue along their present course, which in most companies means inadequate communication with eligible employees and unrepresentative membership and decision-making on contributions by a small, static, management

281

group, then you are merely inviting growing skepticism among employees and heightened attacks by critics. The present effectiveness of PACs can be undermined just as speedily as it grew so that, if legislation does not eventually kill them, the company's own management may decide to.

Improved communication with employees, therefore, is really the PAC's life insurance. The longer you wait to begin, the more it will cost. **PAC**

A .John Adams is president of John Adams Associates Inc., a Washington public affairs consulting firm which advises on PAC communi - cations . He was director of public affairs of the U S . Price Commission , 1972-73.

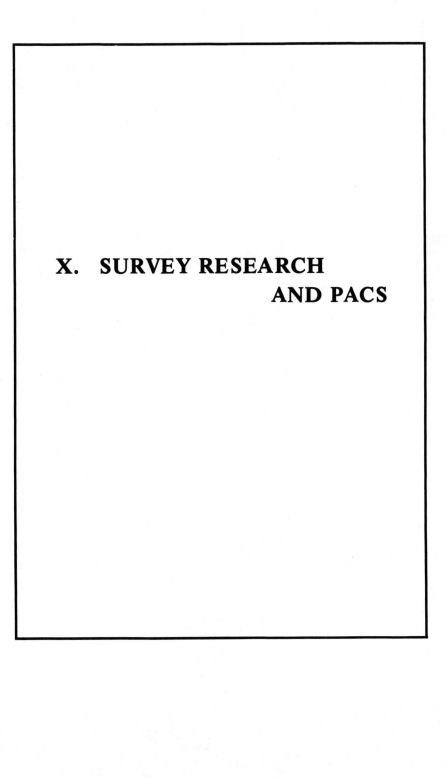

X. SURVEY RESEARCH
AND PACS

Value of Survey Research to PACs

Harry W. O'Neill

President, Opinion Research Corporation

Contributing $121.9 to candidates for federal office between January 1979 and November 1980 were 1,245 business and 625 association political action committees. This is an impressive and growing voice for business in the political process -- and there is every indication that it will continue and become stronger. The continued success of PACs, however (barring unfavorable legislation), depends on the continued receptivity of current contributors to their PACs and the ability of PACs to attract additional contributors.

Hence, it is important for PAC administrators to be sure their PAC is regarded as effective and as delivering the benefits promised. To do so requires a systematic effort, as business PAC members (and potential members) are not a homogeneous group of like-minded people, but are a demographically and attitudinally diverse group of employees, retirees and stockholders. Survey research provides the most reliable approach to obtaining members' collective point of view.

It is necessary to research the views of both current PAC members and those who have not yet contributed. Among current PAC members, the survey should seek answers to the following questions:

- Are you satisfied with the choice of candidates supported?

- Was your point of view on which candidates to support adequately solicited?

- How effective do you think your PAC's support was to the campaigns of the selected candidates?

- Were the issues of concern to you adequately represented by the supported candidates?

- What issues are you most concerned about?

- Do you feel your PAC membership gives you more political influence than if you acted on your own?

- Because of your PAC membership, do you feel more personally involved in the political process?

- As a result of PAC participation, are you better informed about politics?

- As a result of PAC participation, are you better informed about economics?

- Did your family feel more involved in the political process because of your PAC involvement?

- Do you think PACs are a positive influence in the democratic process?

- What criticism, if any, have you heard about business PACs?

- Do you plan to remain a contributor to your PAC? If not, why?

Each segment of potential PAC members -- employees, retirees, stockholders -- needs to be surveyed separately to ascertain why that segment is not contributing and to gain information useful to future solicitation. Here the survey should seek answers to these questions:

- Are you aware of your corporate PAC? If aware, what was your source of information? What is the purpose of your corporate PAC, as you understand it?

- Were you solicited to participate? If no, would you participate? If yes, what form of participation is most comfortable for you?

- What criticisms, if any, have you heard about business PACs?

Another possible area of survey research relative to PACs is among the recipients or potential recipients of PAC contributions. The most obvious identifiable group is the Congress. A study of the congressional view of business PACs might better be underwritten by a group of PACs rather than any one business PAC, as the information sought bears on the entire PAC concept, not on the functioning of an individual PAC. Opinion would be sought regarding such issues as the influence of business PACs in the political process, contributions to incumbent vs. challengers, contribution limitations, the benefit of PACs for the sponsoring company and for the participating members.

Most recently, PACs have begun to use survey research to make more accurate decisions on whom to support in federal, state and local elections. Survey research findings can illuminate sensitive issues and vulnerable candidates. They can give a PAC an idea of what the voting public *wants*. This information has been particularly useful to the larger PACs, such as the National Conservative Political Action Committee (NCPAC), which can make large contributions but want to do so wisely. Survey research helps these PACs to make informed decisions.

The beauty of survey research is that it tells people what other people are thinking. It provides a quantified and easy-to-understand picture of what the public has to say. With the coming of age of business political action committees, it is time for business to tune in to American public opinion. We need to look at business PACs objectively, through the eyes of participants and beneficiaries, not only to make them more effective, but to obtain information that might be useful in warding off attempts to curtail their scope and influence.

PAC

Harry W. O'Neill is president and director of Opinion Research Corporation in Princeton, New Jersey.

A member of Opinion Research Corporation, a subsidiary of Arthur D. Little, Inc., since 1962, O'Neill's principal research activities have been in the fields of politics, public policy issues, community relations, public relations, financial relations and corporate communications. He has, for example, conducted major studies in the areas of air and water pollution, business ethics, police-community relations, community services, and has been involved in the direction of the public opinion research for numerous political campaigns including several presidential campaigns.

XI. CHALLENGERS VS. INCUMBENTS

Challengers vs. Incumbents:
New Winning Strategies

John T. Dolan
National Chairman, National Conservative PAC

The 1980 elections amounted to a watershed success for conservative political action committees. Not only did they help orchestrate the removal of a liberal incumbent president, but they also succeeded in toppling ten incumbent Democratic senators and severely calling into question the records of several other liberal politicians.

As the smoke clears following the November 4 elections, certain political realities present themselves to the American public. The National Conservative Political Action Committee (NCPAC) has monitored those changing political factors for several years, and through sophisticated methodology, innovation and commitment, NCPAC had a noted impact on the outcome of the 1980 elections.

NCPAC is often classified as an "ideological PAC." Totally dedicated to promoting conservative candidates and causes, NCPAC is not affiliated with any one particular corporation, association or political party. It was founded in 1975, and operates with a small, flexible staff that expands temporarily as needs dictate. NCPAC publishes one newsletter quarterly, *NCPAC Report*. Policy decisions are generally made by the national chairman, advised by the National Conservative Policy Advisory Council (an integral part of NCPAC), the general staff and other select consultants.

NCPAC solicits public and private donations and sponsors regional training seminars for conservative candidates and their staffs. Though these are all contributing factors, NCPAC's success is primarily due to four specific factors: methodology, the use of independent expenditures, the candidates endorsed and the solid base of conservative support groups.

NCPAC attributes most of its success to the use of modern research methods such as public opinion surveys. The results of such survey research provide NCPAC with two benefits. First, the survey results are valuable in and of themselves as indicators of public moods (referred to by some as "hot buttons"). Once public sentiments on key issues are identified, NCPAC can make well-informed judgments on which issues to target in a political campaign. This methodology was used across the board in the 1980 senatorial elections, in which NCPAC highlighted such things as Sen. Frank Church's liberal defense voting record to an Idaho public increasingly uncertain about America's status as a world power. NCPAC used the same technique to focus on President Carter's disappointing record and to determine aspects of that record to which the American public was most sensitive. Targeted issue-oriented campaigns are cost-effective.

The second benefit of NCPAC's survey research methodology is its status as an in-kind contribution. Although survey research is a costly undertaking, one general survey could identify issues ("hot buttons") valuable to several different political candidates. Thus the cost of a poll could be divided to meet the $5,000 per candidate in-kind contribution limitation. Furthermore, the FEC has ruled that, over time, the value of survey research declines. So, conceivably, results of a poll taken one month could be used three months later, devalued, and conform to the $5,000 limitation.

It is this use of survey research that helped NCPAC to identify issues most likely to topple an incumbent politician in 1980. Public sensitivities were cultivated to the advantage of conservative challengers in an efficient, cost-effective way. Hence the unprecedented wave of challenger victories. Sophisticated methods have served conservatives well.

Because of NCPAC's nature as an ideology PAC, however, in-kind contribution limits to specific candidates need not often be taken into consideration: NCPAC supports conservative candidates, and we generally do so without directly consulting those candidates. This leads to NCPAC's second success factor: independent expenditures.

An independent expenditure is an expenditure by a PAC for "communications expressly advocating the election or defeat of a clearly identified candidate" without consulting that candidate, according to the FEC. The bulk of NCPAC's expenditures are independent of candidate consultation, allowing for unrestricted spending to affect political outcomes.

Though NCPAC used independent expenditures to its advantage in the 1976 and 1978 elections, 1980 marked a massive increase in this type of spending. NCPAC estimates total independent expenditures in the six Senate races it targeted in 1980 to be $1.2 million plus an additional $2 million for its independent campaign on behalf of Ronald Reagan. By 1982, the committee plans to look at 21 Senate races as well as some House campaigns for independent expenditure. It anticipates a tally of over $2 million in independent expenditures.

Most of the independent expenditure funding has gone towards media campaigns. NCPAC opted again for modern, sophisticated methods and used television, radio and the press to expose the poor records of those incumbents we sought to replace. In Idaho we developed the "Anyone But Church (ABC) Project" and in Indiana, the "If Bayh Wins, You Lose Project." In Iowa we initiated a project to elect Republican Charles Grassley called "The Committee for Another Responsible Senator" and in Missouri, the "Missouri Citizens to Defeat Tom Eagleton Committee."

On a national scale, NCPAC funneled much of its funding into a "Ronald Reagan Victory Fund" which provided for numerous television ads that asked the question: "Jimmy Carter: We trusted him once; can we really afford to trust him again?"

All of these projects were carried out independent of any candidate or candidate's committee. Therefore, there was no spending ceiling on these efforts. These efforts had an enormous effect on the defeat of the incumbent.

NCPAC is committed to supporting conservative challenger candidates, and it has had unprecedented success in getting challengers into office. This is due in part to the methodology and independent expenditures already

293

mentioned. But it is also due to the nature of the candidates themselves – both challengers and incumbents – and to the firm support of conservatives in general. NCPAC contributes heavily to key conservative challengers' campaigns in order to counter the nearly overwhelming "favorables" of the incumbents.

The Americans for Democratic Action, a group I infrequently quote, has estimated that up to 60 percent of a congressman's budget goes towards keeping him in office. That is taxpayers' money spent every year. That 60 percent is used to mail newsletters to constituents, to make public appearances and, in general, to sell the politician for another term. In states like California this amounts to over one million dollars on political expenditures per year! Largely because of this, and the free favorable media attention incumbents get because of their office, they usually have enormously high favorable-to-unfavorable-ratings. No one focuses on their faults, which are usually apparent in their records, until very late in a campaign.

The challenger receives none of these gratuities. A challenger who is under-funded and cannot convince the public that he is the better candidate loses his credibility entirely. He is frequently on the defensive. A challenger seeking to win through destroying his opponent's credibility erodes his own credibility eventually as well.

Challengers almost never start campaigns early enough. George Gallup estimates that up to 60 percent of the voters decide who they will vote for prior to election day, but that is when many challengers often begin and end their campaigns. A challenger who is well-funded, starts early, and seeks to change the public's perception of the incumbent by highlighting issues, maintains his credibility and overcomes the incumbent's advantages.

Most PACs will go out on a limb for a challenger, but it is of the utmost importance to be able to determine the electibility of that candidate.

A few rules on deciding which challengers should be supported:

First, be wary of a candidate who says "everything is going great except for the money." This translates to "I have a miserable overall campaign because I can't raise any money." NCPAC will teach candidates and campaigns how to raise money. We will almost never give cash to a candidate who has not proven he is credible enough to raise it on his own.

Money is almost without exception the critical factor in the success of a challenger. Let's face it: It's tough to knock off an incumbent. In 1980, 92 percent of all incumbent house members were elected. Only in cases where the challenger outspent the incumbent or was at least competitive, did the incumbent lose. PACs can be helpful to challengers by giving or raising money early, but only after a challenger proves he is credible.

Second, make sure the candidate has a burning desire to be elected. I am shocked by the number of candidates who get into a race, and do it poorly because they decide they simply did not like it. I have always thought that there is something wrong with a person who likes to get up at 5 a.m. to shake hands at a factory gate, but that is the type of mentality it usually takes.

Third, make sure the candidate is in the right place. A candidate may be in 100 percent agreement on your issues and be attractive, articulate and well-funded, but if he is a Republican in Harlem, he does not stand a chance. Careful analysis of polling data and past election returns tell us how winable the seat is.

Fourth, determine that the challenger has competent management and/or consultants, or at least a campaign strategy that has been partially implemented. Campaigns are very unsophisticated affairs. Without a professional to guide them, and at least a fairly clear idea of where to go and how to get there, many campaigns die because of inertia.

Fifth, find out how committed he is to your issues. Get him committed in writing. And, ask if he is willing *to lead* your fight in Congress. The recent classes of freshmen have shown how effective a committed new member of Congress can be; make sure he is on your side.

The political trend now in America is towards conservatism, as evidenced by the 1980 election results. But hardly all conservatives who ran were elected. Though NCPAC supports conservative candidates, the rate of success or failure ultimately depends on the support of the voters. For this reason, NCPAC selects candidates with extreme care. Challengers are chosen on their merits as conservatives and are aided if they stand a good chance of winning. Their electibility (for the most part a product of voters' perceptions of them and the incumbent) can be increased by using issues to adjust public perception.

Through careful analysis, thorough survey research, realistic goals, monitoring and strong support, the National Conservative Political Action Committee has increased its influence and honed its techniques. Other PACs can learn from NCPAC's experiences -- as they probably already have – and become increasingly effective in the political arena. **PAC**

John T. Dolan currently serves as chairman of the National Conservative Political Action Committee (NCPAC), which he co-founded in 1975. He also directs the Conservatives Against Liberal Legislation, the National Conservative Research and Education Foundation and the Washington Legal Foundation.

Dolan is a graduate of Georgetown University and of the Georgetown University Law Center. At Georgetown, he served as District of Columbia chairman of Young Republicans and as leader of the campus College Republicans.

Dolan worked at the Committee to Reelect the President in 1972 and at National Political Consultants in 1973 and 1974. In addition to his other activities, Dolan serves on the boards of the Committee for Responsible Youth Politics, the Conservative National Committee and Americans for Nuclear Energy.

XII.   STATES' PERSPECTIVE

States Provide Broad Support

J.E.B. Carney
Executive Director, Grand Old Party PAC

The results of the 1980 elections clearly show the value of concentrating campaign funding and techniques at the local level. The continued growth and development of campaign support for state legislative races has produced changes in what is one of the critical areas of national party building.

Shifting fortunes of the Republican Party over the last ten years serve as an example: In the early 1970s the Republican Party's presence in the states deteriorated from control of 42 chambers with 22 governors in 1971 to a low of 17 chambers and 12 governors in 1976. In only two states were both chambers of the legislature and the state House controlled by the Party.

In 1977, the Republican Party adopted an extensive plan that focused on rebuilding its strength in the legislatures. By 1978 the Republican National Committee's Local Elections Division and by 1979 GOPAC, an independent committee established by Governor Pierre S. du Pont of Delaware, were both concentrating separate efforts on assisting the growth of the party by supporting legislative candidates. GOPAC was specifically designed to help Republican challengers campaigning against Democratic incumbents. These two nationwide organizations, in addition to state and local organizations, had aided a thousand legislative candidates by 1980. They helped to produce a nationwide gain of close to 600 seats and Republican control of thirty-five legislative chambers and 23 governorships.

The formula is basic: Bolster the organization within a state, and not only will there be a greater opportunity for success within that state, but also the national composite strength will improve during federal elections.

This approach is important because of the trickle-up effect success will have on future elections. As recently as 1978, 75 percent of the members of Congress had served in the state legislatures, or held local office. In 1980, better than 2,000 new members were elected to legislative chambers, a turnover of approximately 30 percent. The dynamics of this new blood in the system at the state level will have an impact beyond just a few election cycles. A great number of these freshmen state legislators will probably be active in the political process for the next forty years.

There is another reason for the political interest in the state legislatures: The impact of redistricting in 1981-1983 will set the political tone for the balance of this decade as it has every ten years. Organizations with PACs should be aware of the importance this has on the House and state balances and realize that they can have an impact.

Though the campaign and ethics laws differ from state to state, it is possible to be simultaneously active and in compliance in many states without undue complication. Improved techniques and increased information are making it easier.

As a result, a unique opportunity now exists for PACs to be involved in this process during the next two years, affecting not only the balance of the U.S. House of Representatives, but that of the state legislatures as well. Because state regulations and statutes can have a greater impact than federal activity in similar areas, the redistricting of legislative districts should be of profound interest to organizations with PACs who may be affected by new legislation.

Party control of legislatures is shifting at a rapid rate, the change being accelerated by improved campaign techniques in strategy, communication and management. As legislatures expand their areas of responsibility, the attention to state legislative races will undoubtedly become a principal focus of PAC activity. **PAC**

J.E.B. Carney is currently executive director of GOPAC, a national political organization which supports Republican state legislative candidates. Carney was previously director of political resources for the Republican National Committee from April 1977to April 1979 --a division which worked with PACs and single interest groups . Prior to the Committee ,he spent three months on staff with the President Ford Committee in 1976after completing his work with a congressional campaign in Virginia's 7th District.

Impact of State Government
on PAC Political Strategies

Stevenson T. Walker
Director of Government Relations Service,
Public Affairs Council

A so-called checklist for corporate PACs recently issued this advice: "Give to federal candidates only. Don't worry about state races. If all goes well in Washington, the states will take care of themselves."

The only answer to such naivete is a simple "Baloney!"

The 50 state governments of this country collectively implement more new laws and regulations than does the central government in Washington. And it is going to be more true in the coming decade.

Consider the following facts:

- Over 500,000 people are elected to public office in some 80,000 jurisdictions (50 states and approximately 3,000 counties, 19,000 cities, 17,000 townships, 15,000 school districts, and 26,000 special districts.) Each of these governmental units can tax and regulate to one degree or another.

- The 50 state legislatures consider up to 200,000 bills every two years ... about 60,000 of which relate to business.

- The number of state regulatory agencies has grown from about 300 to over 2,500 in the past two decades.

- In the major industrial states, service in the legislature is virtually a full-time job. The citizen/legislator has just about gone with the wind.

- The average age of state legislators is late 30s; it used to be early 50s. Hundreds of members are in their 20s; in many cases, it is their first job out of college!

These facts quickly tell us that state (and local) governments are active, outspoken and proposal-minded.

Consider these recent developments:

- The 1970s produced "professional societies" for almost every state and local official. The larger ones include the National Conference of State Legislatures, National Governors Association, National Association of Counties, U.S. Conference of Mayors and League of Cities. All are well-staffed with creative people. Their gatherings afford their members the opportunity to exchange ideas — often in the form of legislative proposals. Their publications number in the dozens and connect individual governors, legislators, county commissioners and mayors to an information network with considerable impact.

- Corporate governance issues are being taken up by the states. Proposals requiring companies to give months of advance notice before layoffs and plant closings have surfaced in more than 30 states. Much will be seen of these and other such proposals in 1981 and beyond.

- Revenues for state and local government contain a message: Voters have said "no" to residential property tax increases and may force lawmakers to say "yes" to industrial/commercial property tax increases.

- The infrastructures of major cities (sewers, subways, bridges, roads) so important to commerce are crumbling. Who pays for the rebuilding? Hundreds of state and local pension funds are unfunded or underfunded. State and local employees (most of whom are among the most dedicated workers in this country) seek better pay and deserve secure retirements. Who bails out the poorly managed and broke pension fund?

- Activist citizens have the power to put issues on the ballot in more than 20 states. Almost every industry can be affected: nuclear, container, tobacco, utility, mining, petroleum, *ad infinitum*. Signing petitions has become a national pastime.

These facts and developments are cited for one reason: to establish the rationale for the need of state and local contributions by political action committees.

Here are some thoughts on the subject:

- Check the campaign finance laws in the states where your PAC may contribute. Many conform with the federal law although the contribution limits may differ. Others require the company to report the administrative expense related to that individual state PAC. Several prohibit the use of corporate funds for PAC administration. The Secretary of State's office handles registrations and reports in most states while others have separate election commissoins. (Don't be intimidated by the legal details. Some gray areas persist, but generally the laws are not complex.)

- Over 30 states allow direct corporate contributions to candidates. Examine this alternative. In several states, it is a way of life.

- Many states have statewide business PACs. Pennsylvanians for Effective Government and United for California are but two examples. You may want to support such committees in addition to or in lieu of your own contributions.

- Fundraising for your corporate PAC is easier if you make contributions beyond the federal level. Many employees have a greater interest in gubernatorial, state legislative and mayoral races than they do in the race for the U.S. Senate.

- Corporate PACs contributed an estimated $6 million to state and local candidates in 1979-80. One of the larger PACs raised over $300,000; some 52 percent of its contributions were non-federal. Another company sponsors PACs in a dozen states. Local employees run on the solicitation efforts, and a high degree of autonomy exists in the PAC's operation. (The company provides supervision on legal matters but not on contributions policy.) Over 2,000 employees are participating. That is what it is all about.

Over the past six to eight years, business has begun to realize the role of state and local government in our federal system. During this period, over 1,500 state relations jobs have been created by about 300 companies. Being a good advocate requires a working knowledge of the legislative process. It also requires being involved in the electoral process. In other words, providing information and facts to legislators is the foremost function of a lobbyist; providing support to candidates is an important supplement. **PAC**

Stevenson T. Walker is director of government relations services for the Public Affairs Council, a professional organization of corporate public affairs officers located in Washington.

His work includes organizing and managing some twelve conferences each year in an effort to train corporate representatives on a variety of public issues and programs. Additionally, he directs the Council's clearinghouse on political action committees and campaign finance legislation as well as following state and federal lobbying laws.

Walker is a native of Montgomery, Alabama, where he served for five years as executive assistant to former House Speaker and Governor Albert Brewer. He worked for six years for Standard Oil of Indiana in several positions within the company's public and government affairs department.

XIII. PAC OPPOSITION

PAC Power: An Abuse of Power

David Cohen
President, Common Cause

I.

In 1980, Ronald Reagan defeated President Carter. In 1976, Jimmy Carter defeated President Ford. With these two elections, an old political myth that incumbent presidents have all the political advantage has been laid to rest.

A fundamental revolution in American politics has occurred for another reason. We have now experienced our second presidential campaign year under a public financing system. With all the focus on winners and losers, it is important to recognize the improvements and welcome changes that come from presidential public financing.

A public financing system that matches small private contributions fosters political competition.

In both 1976 and 1980, substantial challenges were mounted against incumbent presidents from within their own parties. In 1976, Ronald Reagan raised important issues in his challenges to President Ford; in 1980, public financing enabled Senator Kennedy to raise issues that otherwise might have been ignored. Just as public financing enabled Representative Udall to challenge Carter all the way, so public financing helped George Bush and John Anderson to continue their races against Republican front-runner Ronald Reagan.

Public financing enables large numbers of citizens to join in funding the campaigns, a role that used to be the province of a small number of wealthy individuals.

Not only does the matching system encourage candidates to seek large numbers of small private contributions during the primary campaign, but millions of citizens make a contribution by designating one dollar of their income tax for the presidential election campaign fund. Since 1976 an average of 37 million individuals each year have checked the campaign fund box on their tax form. Contrast this with the 1972 presidential election in which a small group of 153 large contributors gave more than $20 million to President Nixon's reelection effort.

Public financing helps candidates by:

- Reducing the time and energy they must spend on raising money;

- Eliminating their need to rely on large private contributions;

- Freeing them from dependence on a few large contributors;

- Increasing their ability to compete by providing an additional source of funds;

- Letting them obtain the financial resources to communicate with the voters.

This fundamental and quiet revolution has restored public confidence in the integrity of our presidential election system. While legitimate criticism is heard about our grueling presidential primary process, there are no longer suspicions that a few wealthy individuals or droves of political action committees have purchased special influence with the White House. There is

310

no longer the fear that corporations or labor unions are funneling illegal funds to the campaign of a presidential candidate, in return for the implicit promise of future favors.

There is an acceptance that the rules have been followed and not abused. It is, on its face, plainly healthy for a democracy to have clean campaign financing. Besides, given the results of the 1976 and 1980 elections, who can seriously say that presidential public financing is an incumbent protection act?

II.

The same good health rating cannot be given to congressional races. Congress has refused to consider or establish a similar clean system for its campaigns. It has resulted in a daily increase and enormous growth in the number of interest group PACs which are giving increasing amounts of money to House and Senate races. As a result of this double standard, incumbents enjoy a substantial advantage over their challengers. Senators and representatives are more responsive to the interests of the groups which finance their campaigns than to the needs of their constituents or of the nation as a whole.

Cleanly financed elections are not something to be sought just for aesthetic reasons. The present method of financing congressional campaigns is poisoning our entire political process. The key is not the election itself but what happens afterwards, when the interests that have provided the financing claim the favors to which they believe their largesse has entitled them.

Our nation has become a "special interest state." The special interests represent economic, occupational and regional power. And they are not bashful about using that power. They form political action committees to funnel campaign contributions to elected office holders, giving them special access and enabling them to influence actions in Congress. The power they gain fuels inflation, squeezes subsidies out of tight budgets, and continues a tax system based on narrow favors rather than on equity.

As a result, our representative government is rapidly becoming a government of the PACs, by the PACs and for the PACs.

No wonder people believe that politicians are increasingly out for themselves at the expense of the public and its citizens. Money talks loudly in the Congress. Today, Congress, as an institution, is simply auctioning itself off to a steady stream of bidders. This destructive system cripples political parties, undermines political leadership, weakens political competition and fosters a politics of favoritism and selfishness. It is a system that benefits special interests and buries solutions to our most pressing public problems — inflation, energy and health care. It rubs out our chance to build a fair society.

The growth in number and influence of PACs has been phenomenal. At the end of 1974, there were 516 such committees; in 1980, there were 2,389 at last count. And the number of PACs sponsored by corporations grew even faster, from 89 at year's end in 1974 to 1,127 in 1980.

New committees are forming all the time. And the amount of money they pour into campaigns continues to grow by leaps and bounds. In 1974, $12.5 million went to House and Senate races. In 1978, the amount had already reached $35 million. Conservative estimates for 1980 suggest the figure will approach $60 million. It is an understatement to say that we have only seen the beginning of PAC participation in campaigns. For example, the real estate lobby which increased its giving in four years from $245,000 to over $1.1 million, expects substantial future growth -- especially since only eight percent of the 700,000 National Association of Realtors members had actually given by 1976. Imagine how much money they will have when 20, 30 or even 80 percent of those who are eligible kick into the fund.

This is campaign giving with a purpose. More than half of all PACs have Washington-based lobbying representatives. Behind their contributions are the lobbyists who seek favorable government expenditures, tax benefits and protective regulations. These demands fuel inflation.

Knowing that money talks in Congress, individual special interests are vastly increasing the amount of their contributions.

- In 1974 the National Automobile Dealers Association contributed a modest $14,200 to congressional campaigns, but in 1978 the group's campaign contributions climbed to just under a million dollars -- a 6,000 percent increase.

312

- The real estate lobby knows a "for sale" sign when it sees one. In the election of 1978, the real estate lobby's largesse to congressional candidates topped $1.1 million, up from only $245,000 in 1974. In a three-week period alone between October 1 and October 23, 1978, the group handed out $500,000 in campaign contributions.

- Four labor union PACs are also examples of the enormous growth that has taken place in the amount of PAC contributions between 1974 and 1978. The Communications Workers of America tripled its campaign contributions to congressional candidates in the period, from $140,328 in 1974 to $474,633 in 1978. The Carpenters Union PAC doubled the amount of its contributions from $158,600 in 1974 to $306,202 in 1978. The Marine Engineers Beneficial Association District 2 PAC gave $212,425 in 1978, up from only $49,750 in 1974; and the Hotel and Restaurant Employees' Union contributions jumped from $52,568 in 1974 to $184,028 in 1978. Six of the top ten PACs in terms of total contributions are affiliated with labor unions.

The growth of PACs is no accident. Their principal reason for giving to congressional candidates is not because they are civic-minded. As Justin Dart, Chairman of Dart Industries, has said, dialogue with politicians "is a fine thing, but with a little money they hear you better." Mr. Dart represents one of the largest corporate PACs.

Every day, political money affects congressional decisions -- on dairy price supports, on regulation of the banking industry, on labor legislation, on energy pricing policy. As a result, the present system of financing congressional campaigns through PAC contributions is a costly one for the American taxpayer and consumer. It leads to increased -- often unjustified -- government subsidies, to unfair tax treatment and to regulations that protect narrow economic interests. It rewards those special interest contributors with millions of dollars in favorable economic benefits at the expense of the consumer.

313

The interrelationship between organized lobbying and PAC contributions is a real one even if there are few specifically stated quid pro quos. The participants understand what is going on. The process provides access and influence, and it affects decisions.

Here are three examples of how the system works:

A Common Cause study found that House members who voted on November 15, 1979 to kill hospital cost containment legislation had received almost four times as much in campaign contributions from the political committees of the American Medical Association as did supporters of the cost control bill.

1. The AMA, the nation's number one interest group campaign-giver, was a principal opponent of the hospital cost containment bill. The AMA's role in the successful defeat of the cost containment proposal was described as "absolutely critical" by Michael Bromberg, executive director of the Federation of American Hospitals. The House killed the proposal by voting 234-166 to substitute a national commission to study and monitor hospital costs for the cost control package. President Carter had estimated that his proposal would save Americans more than $40 billion during the next five years.

A Common Cause study found that 202 of the 234 House members who voted for the AMA-supported substitute received AMA campaign contributions totaling $6.1 million -- an average of more than $8,000 each. Forty-four of the 166 members who opposed the AMA-backed amendment received no AMA contributions. The remaining 122 representatives opposing the amendment had received substantially smaller AMA contributions than those who voted for the amendment – an average of $2,200.

2. In June 1979, a Common Cause study found that more than $1 million in political contributions by the political action committee of the National Association of Realtors (NAR) had paid off in a key legislative victory for the real estate industry. During the 1978 campaign, the NAR was the second largest interest group-giver in the nation.

The industry victory occurred on June 7, 1979, when the House of Representatives voted to block new enforcement powers for the Department of Housing and Urban Development (HUD) to be used against fraudulent land

314

developers. Proposed legislation would have allowed HUD to issue cease and desist orders where there was reasonable cause to believe that land developers had engaged in fraudulent activities in violation of the Interstate Land Sales Full Disclosure Act. By a vote of 245-145, the House adopted a NAR-backed amendment to eliminate the new enforcement provision from the bill.

The Common Cause study of campaign contributions made by the political action committee of the NAR to the 390 House members who voted on the amendment found that 83 percent of the members voting for the amendment had received campaign contributions from the NAR in the 1976 and 1978 campaigns. The average contribution was more than $3,600. In addition, 74 of the 145 representatives who voted against the NAR-backed amendment received no NAR contributions in these elections. The remaining 71 representatives who opposed the amendment received a smaller average contribution ($1,440) than did those who supported it.

3. A different kind of example was the special interest attack on the Federal Trade Commission (FTC). This agency, which serves consumers by policing monopolistic or deceptive economic competition, was picked apart by Congress at the instigation of a variety of special interests. During Senate consideration of the FTC authorization bill, the Senate reception room was crowded with lobbyists.

A Knight-Ridder Newspapers survey, based on Federal Election Commission records, found that $5.4 million was contributed to candidates for Congress by industries seeking to escape FTC regulation. The funeral industry and agricultural cooperatives that would benefit from the House-passed FTC bill contributed a total of $2.6 million to congressional races in the 1978 campaign. The used car, insurance and television advertising industries that would benefit from the Senate bill are recorded as contributing a total of $2.6 million to 1978 congressional campaigns.

To look more closely at one of these areas, the Knight-Ridder study found that the National Automobile Dealers Association, which opposes the FTC proposal to require a mandatory warranty or inspection before sale of a used car, had made substantial campaign contributions to Senate Commerce Committee members. Senator Jesse Helms (R-N.C.), who introduced the proposal to bar the FTC from requiring warranties, received $10,000 from

NADAPAC, the political action committee of the automobile dealers. The Knight-Ridder Newspapers also reported that "all five members of the Senate Commerce Committee elected in 1978 received money from the auto dealers. They are J.S. Exon (D-Neb.), $5,000; Howell Heflin (D-Ala.), $5,000; John Warner (R-Va.), $5,000; Larry Pressler (R-S.C.), $5,000; and Nancy Kassebaum (R-Kan.), $2,000."

III.

The explosive growth in the number and influence of PACs is the most significant development in the financing of congressional campaigns since 1974. Those PACs that are small financially will not remain small. PACs will grow in number, in size, in sophistication and in influence, unless changes are made in the campaign finance laws.

The basic reform needed for congressional elections is a public financing system that is matched by small contributions from individuals. Congress has not voted on the merits of this issue since 1974 when the Senate approved it and the House rejected it. In the meantime, what puts Congress as an institution in the auctioneer-bidder category is its refusal to do anything about limiting the power of PACs.

A bill introduced by Representative Obey (D-Wisc.) and Representative Railsback (R-Ill.), passed the House 217-198 in the fall of 1979. This bill would have reduced individual PAC contributions from a current maximum allowable of $10,000 per candidate, to $6,000 and, most importantly, would have placed an overall limit of $70,000 on the amount that a candidate could receive from all PACs.

For the first time, this bill would have limited the amount a House candidate can receive from PACs. Even though Congress was not willing to face the issue of public financing, the House of Representatives, looking the PACs squarely in the eye, did pass the Obey-Railsback legislation. The bill applied only to the House; a filibuster threat prevented the issue from being voted on in the Senate. In high and powerful places, obstructors from both parties did their best to prevent the bill from being debated and enacted.

In October 1979, Senator Baker (R-Tenn.), acting in his capacity as minority leader, said that he would be at the "forefront" of a filibuster to prevent PAC limitations for House races from being voted on in the Senate. Senator Baker practiced a double standard by accepting public money for his presidential campaign, but refused to allow the Senate to vote on PAC giving and spending in House races. In fact, Senator Baker received $370,868 in PAC contributions for his own 1978 Senate race, including funds donated after it was clear he would be safely reelected.

It is one thing to oppose legislation on the merits; that is the stuff of democratic debate. Senator Baker's filibuster threat, however, was pure and unadulterated obstruction. It was indefensible. By refusing to debate the PAC bill, the Senate — majority and minority members — acted as the agent of the PACs.

Limiting PAC giving would force the Congress to face the power of the special interest state. This legislation was fundamental to our ability to be fairly represented in an unrigged political marketplace.

PACs are a clear and present danger to achieving a political system free from corrupting influences. They are a direct threat to the legitimacy of congressional decision-making, and they threaten to totally drown out the voices of citizens. Without major changes in the campaign finance laws in the 97th Congress, PACs are likely to become an even greater problem in the future.

All of us have a stake in ending the pollution of the political process by special interest PACs. **PAC**

David Cohen, president of Common Cause, has been chief executive officer of the organization since April 1976. Cohen joined the Common Cause staff in July 1971 as director of field organization. He later served as vice president for operations and executive vice president before becoming president.

As a public interest lobbyist, Cohen has participated in numerous issue battles including civil rights, consumer affairs, urban affairs, anti-poverty and end the war legislation. He has published numerous articles on the need to revitalize Congress. His "Party Leaders in Congress" is a case study which has appeared in a college text.

Cohen served on the Secretary of the Treasury's Advisory Committee on Private Philanthropy and Public Needs; he was a non-lawyer member of the Ethics Committee of the District of Columbia Bar; and he was a member of the Synthesis Panel of the National Academy of Sciences' Committee on Nuclear and Alternative Energy Systems.

Before coming to Common Cause, Cohen was associate legislative director of the Council for Community Action from 1969 to 1971. While there, he concentrated on legislative and executive branch activities affecting the poor.

318

XIV. FUTURE TRENDS

The Future for PACs in Business

Edie Fraser
President, Fraser/Associates

Political action for business will continue to change the patterns of campaign financing and participation in American politics. Political action committees have become an institutional mechanism to provoke a new and heretofore missing stimulus for participation in the political process. The burgeoning of PACs and the surge of business involvement in the 1980 elections confirm this role.

The growth of business PACs is dramatic -- a quintupling in the last several years. Business PACs have raised more dollars than has labor. The surge in corporate PACs, coupled with the steady increase in the number of business-related trade association PACs, demonstrates that business is awakening to accept a new role in the political environment. Despite pressure to restrict business PACs, continued growth should be characteristic of the 1980s – despite the fact that the general economy is making it harder to raise dollars.

Businesses understand that significant results can be achieved by developing active constituencies to support candidates likely to share their interests. As a result, *PACs have become the most important vehicle of business political expression*. They are searching harder for candidates who match their ideological and partisan leanings. Many candidates, in turn, want PAC money.

PARTICIPATION ESSENTIAL

Participation is the key to PAC success. You can raise money, but finances alone do not buy success nor longevity. Clearly political action programs must recieve top management attention and corporate support to be effective. ARCO's program provides a striking example that voluntary, *personal* involvement by PAC members is an essential element of political action.

The use of an array of mechanisms to support business political participation is on the rise. Recognizing that political participation and effective persuasion in behalf of candidates are best demonstrated through the PAC mechanism, business is emphasizing the importance of political action committees. There are other vehicles, of course. These include institutional advertising; employee and shareholder political education programs; communications on issues to employees, stockholders, customers and other publics; and grassroots lobbying.

Reports confirm that U.S. business is increasingly politically active. A Conference Board study shows business is changing its approach: "defensive postures have been giving way to aggressive strategies." A *Harvard Business Review* article reveals that more and more business executives have come to realize that their well-being is politically tied to the direction the country takes. *The Wall Street Journal* reports that the ranks of government relations executives are swelling. And more and more chief executive officers are speaking out on the issues.

Yet business political action is still at its threshold; this is merely the beginning. Generally, corporate PACs have not utilized the in-kind contributions of employees and managers to foster their personal involvement in campaigns and elections. On the other hand, labor understands that personal involvement is one method that clearly brings results.

Trends likely to expand in the 1980s include:

BUSINESS PACS MORE SIGNIFICANT

Political action committees will become more significant, with approximately 1,200 corporate PACs on the FEC books as 1981 began. The number of corporate PACs should approach 1,600 by 1982 and 2,000 by 1984. Today there are approximately 600 for associations and 270 for trade unions. Association PACs will also grow in number.

Along with the increase of business PACs comes a push for "pro-business candidates." The 1980 elections demonstrated a recognition of "philosophy as significant to electibility." The National Chamber Alliance for Politics (NCAP) results find pro-business candidates were supported in 70 percent of 126 races targeted. NCAP selects only meaningful (very close) races which can result in victories for business philosophy. Congressional victors recognize the impact of business support and its growing sophistication.

TRAINING AND EDUCATION ALSO IMPORTANT

A new focus will be placed on *internal and operational procedures* to emphasize training and motivation of employees, managers and all business constituents -- stressing the need to generate genuine political participation and involvement. *First, inform and educate ;then, motivate to participate !* A great deal of added emphasis will be put on employees and stockholders. The initial objective will be to educate these groups about the nature of the political process, and to teach them why it is in their best interest to be active participants -- understanding how issues will impact employee and stockholder welfare.

As one corporate executive expressed it: "Business already earned the goodwill and support of its constituents. It has to earn it." Unions have provided more "in-kind" support -- valuable campaign workers and personal involvement. Business will need to increase its "in-kind" contributions in the coming years, recognizing that there is a definite humanizing effect to be gained from individual participation.

STATE FOCUS GROWS MORE SIGNIFICANT

Emergence of the *state legislature* as an ever-important political arena is inevitable. Recognizing our decentralized government, the traditional focus of business PACs on the Senate and House of Representatives is changing -- to the state legislatures. The PAC base is broadening to include more attention to state candidates and incumbents.

Although most corporate PACs nominally are established to support candidates for both federal and state offices, some 200 companies have separate state PACs. An excellent example of state political emphasis is provided by GOPAC. This Republican PAC (see chapter on States) is growing, using funds to aid Republican candidates for state legislatures. GOPAC officials have set a priority for their party to control as many legislatures as possible in 1981 and beyond. (Note GOPAC's 100 percent support of challengers and no incumbents). Other examples can be cited. One of the most interesting: ALCOA, with 13 state PACs.

All PACs at the federal level must register with the Federal Election Commission. PACs contributing to candidates for state office must register with the election commissions in each state in which donations might be made.

REPUBLICAN GAIN IN 1980

When Republicans captured control of the Senate and picked up 33 seats in the House in 1980, one reason was the role played by business PACs. They made a difference!

Democrats did not receive the hefty percentage of business PAC funds in 1980. Despite some continuity in giving to Democrats, particularly to incumbents, business PACs had stepped up their giving to Republican challengers and to Republicans in "open" races.

But business PACs also give to Democrats clearly in power positions. While the Democrat-supported labor PACs have been unable to generate much additional money, business PACs are optimistic about the future.

The 1980 trend is clear: Business PACs will continue to support Republican challengers against Democrats in "shaky" seats and some Democrats in "safe" seats deemed more responsive to business.

Joe Fanelli, BIPAC's president (see prior chapter), stated in 1980 there was a clear philosophical difference "between Republican challengers and Democratic incumbents." The National Conservative Political Action Committee overwhelmingly gave to Republicans. This challenge to Democrats: Either seek more PAC support from labor *and* business – or move to restrict PACs.

PUBLIC INTERESTS SPEAK OUT

Attempts to restrict PAC efforts will be accented by the public interest sector and labor unions. Organized labor and Common Cause today have reason to fear the growing political clout of business PACs. Despite the urgings of groups historically opposed to business influence in government, Congress will probably not curb PAC power, as was thought certain in 1980. Common Cause will lead the effort to limit contributions of PACs and to implement public financing of elections. *Though more business officials will understand the legitimacy and resources needed for business involvement in public affairs, so, too, will anti-business forces.*

Pleas for public financing may be heeded. In 1980, the Wisconsin legislature passed a bill encouraging candidates to accept public financing of campaigns. A realization exists that if the public becomes educated, public financing may be legislated.

A Harris survey of 1,200 Americans nationwide reports 61 percent of respondents believe that large sums spent on congressional campaigns constitute a "very serious" problem. The poll finds 58 percent oppose public financing of federal elections, compared with 42 percent in 1976. Note: 81 percent believe PACs have increased substantially; 71 percent say PACs are pouring in too much money. Therefore, a conclusion may be drawn that limits are necessary. It is against that background that labor unions, public interest groups and others will move to restrict business PACs in the 1980s.

325

Public interest groups are insistent that forcing business PACs to disclose details of their PAC operations in annual reports to shareholders will be a prominent public interest cry. Despite a public interest backlash to PACs, attempts to restrict PACs have failed, and will probably continue to do so in the near future. Despite reform group pressure for public funding, it certainly will not happen soon -- if at all.

MEDIA ATTENTION INCREASES

PACs are generating increased attention from national news media. The media will continue to focus on PAC power -- and will often be critical of business's political action involvement and suspicious of its aims. (Figures are often distorted. Corporate PACs have contributed only $20 million, or about 5.8 percent, to the more than 1,000 different federal candidates who spent over $350 million in 1980.) Still, the media are frequently critical, though the figures hardly "justify the gradual corporate purchase of the U.S. Congress." *The Wall Street Journal* has been in the minority in criticizing advocates of public financing of elections.

Stories about the power of oil and gas industry PACs as well as that of the utilities will be played heavily by the media. The *Christian Science Monitor*, which endorsed two congressmen, David Obey and Tom Railsback, in their legislative initiative to restrict PACs, has joined other media in contending that Americans need to know that the votes of members of Congress are not bought and paid for by PACs.

The media often fail to differentiate between corporate and other PACs. Consequently, the public is confused, and business PACs are viewed as all-powerful and somehow grouped in one monolithic structure. In reality, of course, they are as diverse as the objectives of the business organizations they represent.

CAUTION TO RIGHT

A word of caution is necessary. If business "blows its own horn" too forcefully in claiming credible results, and does not maintain a more balanced approach to political action and PACs, restriction of political action could become a reality. "New Right" PACs have announced that they are largely responsible for all 1980 PAC victories. Liberals respond, spotlighting the "New Right" corporate money.

Already, power attributed to PACs exceeds reality. Activities of independent PACs of the more right wing conservative groups have scared off many moderate business organizations.

FINANCIAL CEILINGS EXTENDED

The ceilings of $1,000 per individual contribution and $10,000 (primary and general) to a congressional candidate will probably be increased, rather than reduced. The 1980 political climate was conducive to calls for PAC restrictions. Yet in 1981, we believe, the Federal Election Commission and other political sophisticates will advocate raising the ceilings. Irony is evident, given the 1979-80 proposals to reform federal election laws, not only to curb but also to eliminate contributions from corporations.

Inflation is another reason why the $1,000 personal limit should be extended. Even the liberal-oriented *Washington Post* acknowledges that the statutory limit has not escaped inflationary pressures. The $1,000 limit enacted in 1974 is worth approximately $1,715 today. While some advocate maintaining the $1,000 ceiling on an indidvidual's gift to a PAC, allowing individuals to contribute up to $5,000 directly to a candidate, we predict the PAC limit will be raised.

The former Obey-Railsback legislation was designed to limit PAC spending to $70,000 per candidate for the House of Representatives from all PACs in a two-year period.

MANAGEMENT MORE INVOLVED

Senior corporate management is becoming more interested in the political process. Success of a corporate PAC in obtaining membership is often dependent on top management's efforts to communicate to employees its strong support for the PAC. When the chief executive and the senior management endorse a PAC, it becomes easier to raise money. And as corporate PACs find they are becoming increasingly lucrative sources of campaign funds, the PACs are receiving attention from federal, state and local candidates seeking support.

COERCION CHARGES

PAC participation must be voluntary. Business PACs must adhere to practices avoiding any membership solicitation of employees by their supervisors. Some employees have objected to perceived coercion, citing suggestions that part of their paychecks be used to contribute to PACs (despite denials by PAC administrators that pressure tactics are used). The International Association of Machinists case provides an example – a law suit to force the FEC to investigate whether ten corporations were coercing middle management. Increasingly, more PACs will establish safeguards to insure *voluntary* contribution to their PACs, i.e., Corning Glass, Boeing, Mead Corporation, General Electric and General Motors.

IRS AND TAX-EXEMPTIONS

The Internal Revenue Service (IRS) will continue to look askance at certain "clearly political" education initiatives. (Reference IRS regulations proposed in December '80 which limit action by tax-exempt groups.) IRS has activated its 1978 rule to ban most so-called voter education literature by which tax-exempt lobbying or charitable organizations inform members about the positions of specific politicians and candidates, warning such groups that they will lose their tax-exempt status if they issue partisan voter education material. One IRS preliminary ruling should be noted: Conservative PACs are told that contributions to "negative" campaigns are not eligible for tax credit.

FEDERAL ELECTION COMMISSION CHANGE

Former chairman Max Friedersdorf, working with the Reagan administration and with the Republican-led Senate, will assist in locating two new
Commission members to fill the 1981 vacancies -- members whose politics are
more conducive to a cohesive FEC.

The FEC will play an increasingly important role as PACs grow in
numbers and resources. And the roles of monitor and record-keeper will be
emphasized.

INDEPENDENTS ACTIVE

A surge of "independent" PACs will continue, despite concern they may
embarrass President Reagan and the Republicans. Such groups include the
Americans for Change, Americans for Reagan and the National Conservative
Political Action Committee (NCPAC).

Links between evangelical Christian groups and the "New Right"
emerged in 1980. These groups demonstrated vast fundraising potential, using
radio and television. The "Moral Majority" spent an estimated $5 million in
1980 and claimed to have recruited 72,000 ministers and four million lay
members.

The National Conservative PAC conducted extensive media campaigns
in 1980 -- designed specifically for the defeat of targeted Democratic
incumbents. The NCPAC crusade was ambitious and well-financed -- $1.2
million on five Senate races to defeat liberal incumbents. And it was
successful.

PROFESSIONAL GROUPS FIND PACS HELPFUL

There is no news in the fact that doctors, bankers, lawyers and other
professional groups have discovered the utility of PACs. The American
Medical Association's PAC raises millions. The American Bankers Association's political fundraising arm, BankPAC, raised approximately $1 million.

All major professional groups will recognize the importance of PAC action in the future as single-issue politics continue to dominate and as the hold of party loyalty and party unity continues to weaken.

INCUMBENTS vs. CHALLENGERS

The move to support Republican, business-oriented challengers is on. Before 1978, corporate PACs were often criticized for their typical all-out support for incumbents, regardless of ideology or orientation. The pattern was for corporate PACs to focus on heads of key committees and other such power factors. In 1978, a move to support challengers was evidenced, and it became a reality in 1980. Many examples can be cited: Frank Wolf (R-Va.) raised over $300,000 for his campaign, garnering support from both fundamentalist Christian groups and corporate PACs.

Challenger candidates supportive of business are far more apt to receive PAC funds in the 1980s. Combining the likelihood of victory with the need for funds and positions on the issues, corporate PACs have broadened their criteria for granting support to challengers. However, in close races, or in the case of identified party leaders, many will continue to give to both incumbents and challengers. Industry often plays it safe. Corporate contributions between incumbent Senator Robert Morgan and challenger John East in the 1980 North Carolina Senate race were equally divided.

CANDOR IS CRUCIAL

Openness was a characteristic of the 1980 elections and will be for the next decade. In the past, businesses and politicians alike were often secretive about campaign contributions.

Before the 1970s, the federal election laws were vague and not well-enforced. Hiding political contributions was sometimes characteristic. Executives borrowed to work on campaigns (while still on corporate payrolls) and were tucked away in campaign organizations. Slush funds were common, and cash was too often given without records or controls. Watergate helped bring about a recognition of the honest way to do business. Too many indictments of major corporations brought about reforms and procedures for legal methods to utilize business dollars in support of the political process.

Disclosure with open Federal Election Commission records is a characteristic of the present PAC system. The changes are clear. Lawyers often remind us, as do the media and interest groups, of the need for complete disclosure. What a PAC can do in fundraising and with contributions, and how these records are to be kept is now well-defined. What "in-kind" contributions can do, what independent contributions can do and how to heed the legal PAC parameters also are important lessons for PAC administrators. As the push toward openness is heightened, business PACs will respond.

TRADE ASSOCIATIONS CHALLENGE

The Federal Election Campaign Act will be challenged further, in an attempt to change its present prohibition against trade associations solicitating political contributions from PACs established by member organizations. The U.S. Supreme Court, in the past, refused to hear a challenge submitted by the National Chamber Alliance for Politics, but the Court *could* reconsider. Associations, in effect, should gain this solicitation right.

THE IMPORTANCE OF COMMUNICATIONS

One clear conclusion is that lawyers running a PAC without communications support can mean disaster. Building comprehensive communications is essential for a successful PAC. A systematic approach to communicating information about a PAC to employees and stockholders is not only warranted, it is essential.

Personal, face-to-face sessions are vital. Information about political issues and an introduction to what the PAC means to individual employees are part of attracting their interest and support. Excessive direct mail achieves little, but employee meetings "pay off." Suggestion: Try special events — dinners, parties, conferences and creative events — that help solicitations.

331

Graphic, easy-to-understand materials which "selfishly" describe to an employee how his/her PAC contribution is used are fundamental to success. Remember that all materials should be presented to evoke a response from the prospective member in terms of what can be done: a financial or in-kind contribution or a letter to a congressman. A regular employee newsletter serves both to distribute information and to educate. It must be vivid, clear, simple and demonstrate two-way communications.

Let employees know what is happening. Business needs to give PAC contributors periodic status reports – newsletters, bulletins or personal letters. Use of audiovisuals helps. Use of good video tapes, films, slides and graphs is suggested.

Listen to employees and solicit their ideas! Too often we forget to involve employees in the political process, but that is the only effective way. Involving all solicited employees in the allocation process often becomes cumbersome, but some mechanism to achieve active employee input is essential to success. Without it, PACs become what their critics charge – simple tools of management. Likewise, the allocation of PAC funds and other resources should be determined by a committee with the broadest possible participation.

Attracting employees (especially in this economy) to contribute voluntarily to a PAC requires an effective employee motivation and communications program. Such a program must be well-designed, comprehensive and visible in political "off years" as well as during campaign seasons.

MORE SOPHISTICATED BUDGETING, USE OF RESOURCES

Business PACs are becoming increasingly sophisticated in how they research candidates and analyze views. New intelligence networks rely on better computerized data. Seminars and meetings attended by PAC administrators across the country have led to the formation of a new intelligence network, assisting PAC members in evaluating candidates. PAC groups are trading information, evaluating prospects and devising new criteria to make their dollars *count*. Simply backing anticipated winners is no longer accepted by business, as proved by the 1980 elections. Business PACs will continue to

332

evaluate candidates in terms of potential for making a positive political impact on the economic interest of business. Exchange of information is assisting the support process.

Most business PACs still support a bipartisan approach, looking for candidates of either major party supportive of their own philosophy. For example, Grumman's PAC supports backers of more defense spending, while a pro-business PAC may have no interest in military preparedness; yet both generally are "pro-business."

PLANNING PAC EFFECTIVENESS

Establishing and meeting specific goals is significant to a business PAC. Measuring goals is also important to:

- Focus attention on specific economic and political issues confronting the business.

- Broaden substantially the number of employees and managers contributing.

- Increase the dollar value of funds raised.

- Target employees and stimulate an entire new sense of participation in election campaigns.

- Increase employees' level of political awareness, benefiting other corporate governmental and political programs.

- Broaden the scope and outreach of communications methods and techniques, measuring specific outreach.

- Measure results.

THE CHALLENGE AHEAD

PACs represent an unprecedented opportunity for business to *participate* in the governing process and to *influence* federal and state decisions which impact on each of us. There is strength in numbers. Because PACs are limited in how much they can raise, it takes thousands of individuals working through PACs to influence the political process. That is why PACs are a healthy democratic expression of political action.

Success of a PAC is dependent on many factors. Good communications, political education and participation are some essential ingredients. What other factors must exist?

- Clear goals and appropriate legal structures.

- A broad-based program, representing managers and employees at all levels.

- A plan and a budgeting process.

- An ongoing communications program, including simple and clear materials, personal approaches, extensive oral presentations and expression of two-way communications.

The sophistication of PACs is demonstrated by the importance that "criteria" have in the process. Criteria for selecting candidates will be emphasized, as will the following:

- A broad-based solicitation team,
- Expanded plant visits, and
- Payroll deduction plans.

What will result is the involvement of more people in the political process. If all goes well, PACs will be viewed by all constituencies as the best and most effective form of political expression by groups of individuals bound together by common interests.

334

PACs will continue their recent proliferation. What will result is a more legitimate interest and influence of business in politics. In 1980, PAC money made the difference in many races — especially those in which the winner received less than 55 percent of the popular vote. PACs will continue to make the difference. What seems certain in the early 1980s is that the political climate will reinforce the PAC concept. A more empathetic representation in Congress and a more politically aware work force already is evident from efforts to date.

For the 1980s, there is a need to develop step-by-step strategies designed to permit people to participate actively in a positive way. But remember: There never will be a substitute for voluntary participation.

BENEFITS FOR BUSINESS

In charting the experience of various corporations and associations, Fraser/Associates has found that the activities of the PAC *benefit business* in a variety of ways. The PAC:

- Encourages executives to become more aware of industry's position on political issues.

- Encourages executives to communicate with other management personnel across divisional or product lines.

- Provides corporations and trade associations with a legal and beneficial means of access to the political process.

- Allows corporation/association people to find a more personalized means of access to the political process.

- Represents the corporate/association sense of social responsibility, both externally and internally.

- Shows that corporations and associations are continually trying to find new ways of making our democratic system work for broad groups of people.

- Makes the corporation/association more visible.

- Helps elect candidates who know what kind of legislation business, which produces the capital and wealth of this country, needs to survive.

- Helps make specific business concerns known to politicians, underscoring the fact that private industry accounts for employment of about 80 million people whose security depends on business productivity.

PACS AID EMPLOYEES, TOO

The PAC also offers substantial benefits for employees. The PAC:

- Involves them individually in the political process.

- Gives strength and voice to their shared concerns.

- Allows the individual to participate actively in the electoral process by contributing across the board to candidates who would best preserve our economic system of free enterprise.

- Educates employees about politics and economics by providing the resources and information needed to make responsible voting decisions.

- Opens up additional ways in which the individual can participate in political campaigns.

- Enables employee family members to take an active part in or learn about the political process.

- Brings government closer to the individual, allowing that individual to see how government actions affect his or her daily life.

336

In the 1980 elections, PACs could claim a substantial contribution to the change in the Congress. Now, for the first time in 26 years, the Republicans have a majority in the Senate. In the House of Representatives, the GOP gained 33 seats while knocking down the powerful Democratic Committee chairman and the Majority Whip. Power in the states also shifted to the Republican column, though less than predicted. PACs *are* a "turning point" -- an historic influence on business to participate in politics. **PAC**

Edie Fraser, president of Fraser/Associates, has directed a wide variety of nationwide public affairs programs, all keyed to major policy issues. Clients have included corporations, trade associations, the Executive Branch and public interest organizations.

Prior to founding Fraser/Associates she directed consumer affairs for a major international public relations firm. She was director of communications in the Office of the Secretary for Health, Education and Welfare.

Fraser is a member of the Public Relations Society of America, is chairman of its public affairs section and is a PRSA counselor. She is on the advisory council of the Journalism School at the University of Tennessee and the Board of Directors of the Business School at the University of Maryland. Other memberships include the Public Affairs Council, the Chamber of Commerce of the U.S., National Association of Women Business Owners and the National Press Club.

She is a well-known writer and lecturer on public affairs issues and has written for such magazines as *Business and Society Review* and *Association Management*.

XV.   1980 ELECTIONS

Business PACs to Emerge as Major Issue in Wake of 1980 Elections

Wes Pedersen
Director, Communications, Public Affairs Council

The ink was hardly dry on the morning-after-election headlines before the attempts at credit-taking and blame-fixing began. "New Right" political action committees and moral superiority organizations announced they were responsible for victories large and small. "Liberals" pointed accusingly at business, indicating that a massive influx of "Sugar Daddy" corporate money had somehow persuaded millions of Americans -- many of whom the pollsters had said were undecided the day before the elections -- to vote against their own best interests.

As the weeks went by, the "what-went-wrong" and "what-went-Right" news stories subsided. But in the editorials and columns, four other words -- corporate political action committees -- began appearing more and more often.

Objective commentaries and analyses balanced the efforts of corporate PACs with those of labor. Typically, Herbert E. Alexander, Director of the Citizens' Research Foundation, wrote: "The business community generally was supportive of Reagan, but corporate PAC expenditures directed to employees and stockholders and their families did not approach those of labor."

Many commentaries, however, followed the Common Cause argument that corporate political action committees distort the electoral system with – as *The New York Times* put it in reporting the Common Cause position – "their huge, issues-oriented expenditures on behalf of selected candidates."

The stage was set for a new round of attacks on business PACs. The campaign can be expected to intensify as the key 1982 congressional and state elections draw closer and as 1984 appoaches (in the political, not Orwellian sense).

The Washington Post, for one, wants Congress to "curb the growing clout of political action committees" through endorsement of the Obey-Railsback amendment by both Houses. The *Post* is unhappy because "more and more candidates have sought and received contributions from political action committees ... especially from corporate PACs." In 1974, according to the *Post*, there were 89 corporate PACs; by 1980, there were "1,153 registered with the Federal Election Commission" (actually, the total registered stood at 1,106, some 300 of which never raised or contributed a single cent). That kind of growth, the newspaper says, has enabled PACs of all kinds to play "an ever bigger role in House elections" and in Senate races as well. The paper sees the possibility that "the House will be PAC'd."

As one solution to "the PAC problem," the *Post* is pushing for action by Congress to encourage individual contributions by reversing the present law which "limits the individual gift to $1,000 and ... allows PAC contributions to the same candidate in the same race to be $5,000."

Individual contributions, the newspaper maintains, should be preferred over "institutional or group contributions" because:

> "The candidate's perspective is important in the matter of contributions. A gift from an individual citizen is a contribution from a kind of one-person multiple source: consumer, employer or employee, family member, man or woman, a certain age, experience and education. Most citizens who do contribute have more than a single interest or objective. Too often, the same cannot be said of the narrow-based PACs. Typically, the PAC to Preserve the Upper Great Lakes

Widget Industry cares only how the legislator votes in the subcommittee on widgets. Little, if any, attention is given to the legislator's votes on widows, orphans, veterans, MXs or B-1s.   Individuals generally have wider interests than PACs."

The *Post* is quoted at length here because its viewpoints are shared by enough editors, commentators, legislators and interest groups to make it a fairly representative spokesman for those who appear to have anti-PAC sentiments.

And this point must be emphasized: the role of the political action committee – particularly the corporate PAC – will come under increasingly heavy fire from its opponents as the months pass.

Many Democratic leaders will play key roles in the anti-PAC drive. True, enough Democrats attracted money from corporate and trade PACs so that nearly half their campaign revenues were derived from the committees. But PACs have always tended to favor incumbents regardless of party, and that favor will now turn from Democratic officeholders to Republicans, given the magnitude of the GOP's victories in the 1980 elections. Keeping money away from Republican incumbents will now become a major goal of many Democratic officials.

What about labor PACs? They are less susceptible to attack because, in the words of COPE spokesman Ben Albert, "We have just a finite number of unions and we've reached our level."

In any event, there is little question that Walter Mondale is right when, in reponding to queries about the role of PACs, he declares that "not too long from now," the question of political action committee contributions "will become a great issue." As Mondale sees it, the real issue is one of "big money casting a dark cloud over the integrity of the American political system ... and the American people will demand a stop to it."

Against that background, it is essential that corporate public affairs officers lose no time in presenting to the public the facts about business PACs. The PAC story needs to be told in true perspective.

343

The idea that a PAC – corporate or labor – can "buy" a U.S. Senator or Representative, a governor or state legislator, is implicit in the attacks by the critics of political action committees. It is precisely the sort of thing a rather large segment of the public would probably like to believe, but it is simply not true, and individuals such as Walter Mondale do their political colleagues no favor by implying that they are up for grabs.

Those critical of political action committees generally talk of corporate money with no reference to the voluntary and personal nature of the PACs. Some writers point out that 50,000 corporations are eligible to form PACs – as if nearly 49,000 of them are about to spring into being overnight.

Business needs to refute innuendos, misleading statements and misinformation about political action committees. It needs to ask the critics of the PACs a few questions. For example:

Has it occurred to them that corporate PACs are, in fact, legal? Congress wrote the law, the Federal Election Commission interpreted the law, and the Supreme Court has upheld the law. Companies are obeying the law. Why should they now be treated as villains?

Candidates for federal office spent approximately $350 million in 1980. Corporate PACs contributed about $20 million to more than 1,000 different candidates at the federal level. Corporate PACs, in other words, contributed approximately 5.8 percent of the total spent at the federal level. How can this percentage possibly be considered "excessive"? How can it for one moment be portrayed as signifying the "corporate purchase" of the U.S. Senate?

And if the corporate political action committees are really as powerful, as threatening as some would paint them, why did so many of the incumbents they backed lose their races for re-election?

The Public Affairs Council believes in the concept, the purposes and the principles of the corporate PACs. It does not, however, believe that they possess anything remotely like the power attributed to them by their detractors. The Council regards them as highly positive institutions whose work is needed and should be increased, not "curbed."

The media of the nation have demonstrated no appreciable success in persuading large numbers of the American populace to take active roles in the political system. Because PAC action *does* result in increased public participation, the committees should be praised -- not rebuked.

To sum up, the question of political action committees will become a major issue as the anti-PAC campaign intensifies. It is an issue on which business could lose if it fails to tell the facts as they really are. The story of corporate PACs and their contributions to the American political system is a highly positive, impressive one. There is no room in it for the myth that corporate money is "clouding" the political skies. **PAC**

Wes Pedersen is director of communications of the Public Affairs Council, editor of the *Public Affairs Review*, columnist for the *Public Relations Journal*, and member of the editorial boards of the *Public Relations Quarterly* and the *Foreign Service Journal*. A former city editor, foreign affairs columnist and federal official, he is the founding chairman of the National Institute for Government Public Information Research at The American University and is the former president of the National Association of Government Communicators. He is the editor of some two dozen books and the author of others, including the international best-seller, *Legacy of a President*. He is profiled in *Who's Who in the World*, *Who's Who in America* and other reference works.

Business Political Action Committees:
A Significant Factor in 1980 Election Results

H. Richard Mayberry , Esq .
Law Offices of H .Richard Mayberry ,Jr .

INTRODUCTION

Nineteen -eighty is a watershed year in American politics and may turn out to be one of the most significant elections of the century . A conservative mood prevailed and the American electorate put forth a mandate to the Reagan administration to bring a new approach to governing the nation. Within this political milieu , business political action committees, or PACs, prospered in significant growth and influence, and continue to be an important component in the financing of modern -day federal elections. This article will examine the role of business PACs in the dramatic 1980 elections.

With the election of President Reagan and with substantial Republican gains in Congress, there appears to be a shift in power away from long-standing supremacy of the Democratic Party . Only time will tell the true extent of this apparent realignment. The question is whether the 1980 election is more akin to 1932 in which Democrats took the White House and Congress and would remain in power for approximately 20 years, or, to 1952 when the Republicans captured majority status, and would soon thereafter lose it on the next election two years later. Most political commentators are saying at least two subsequent elections will be needed in order to judge the true significance of the resurgency of Republican political strength in 1980.

With 53 seats (53R, 47D), the Republicans are the majority party of the U.S. Senate in the 97th Congress. They are sure to find increased power in the House of Representatives (192R, 243D) with a net gain of 33 seats. In light of the clear and unequivocal message from the American people to the Democratic majority that old approaches to present problems are no longer acceptable and that incumbents cannot assume automatic re-election, Republican influence in the House of Representatives is sure to be enhanced despite a lack of a voting majority.

It is clear that the American voters agree with Mr. Brock and the Republican National Committee that it is indeed "a time for change" in American government. This national resolve provides the backdrop of political sentiments in which business PACs functioned in 1980.

VOICE FOR BUSINESS

Political action committees, or "separate segregated funds" as they are defined in applicable election law, provide an important political voice for business. They are a lawful, congressionally sanctioned vehicle for political association and expression by corporations and their trade associations.

Although a corporation cannot directly contribute funds to federal candidates, companies may sponsor political action committees. All costs associated with the formation, administration and solicitation of voluntary contributions for a PAC may be directly paid from the corporate treasury and are not reportable to the Federal Election Commission (FEC). These so-called "soft dollars" provide a tremendous advantage for political participation by business. Other political committees and parties must pay all overhead costs from the monies they can raise from individuals and other groups. (Diagram 1 illustrates the financing system of a political action committee.)

The corporate PAC, in turn, is able to collect voluntary contributions, often through personal appeals and direct mail, from employees and stockholders. Since administration costs are assumed by the corporation, virtually every dollar raised can be directed to support federal candidates. These contributions are often referred to as "hard dollars" for the process of political fundraising has the attendant difficulties of charitable fundraising and is closely regulated by law.

347

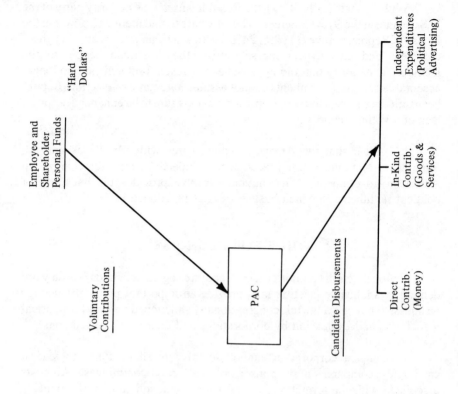

Corporate Treasury

"Soft
Dollars"

Used to Pay Costs of
Organization, Administration
and Solicitation.

Voluntary
Contributions

Employee and
Shareholder
Personal Funds

"Hard
Dollars"

PAC

Candidate Disbursements

Direct
Contrib.
(Money)

In-Kind
Contrib.
(Goods &
Services)

Independent
Expenditures
(Political
Advertising)

Diagram 1.

348

A political action committee has tremendous potential for bringing the voice of business to the electoral process. Through the "pooling of many small individual contributions," persons with an interest in government policies vis-a-vis the business community have their individual voices amplified through collective and unified political action.

Accordingly, a qualified multi-candidate PAC may contribute up to $5,000 per candidate for each election (primary and general are treated as separate elections) and is not limited to the aggregate contributions which can be made in any one year. (See Diagram 2.)

By way of comparison and illustrated in Diagram 2, an individual may not contribute more than $1,000 per candidate per election, and may not expend more than $25,000 in political contributions (federal) in a calendar year.

PAC GROWTH

The last decade witnessed a surge in the number of political action committees, and many commentators now openly refer to a "PAC movement." The advent of this movement can be at least partially attributed to clarification of the absolute right of corporations to form PACs, and an increased realization by many businesses of the need to communicate their policy positions in the political arena.

An evaluation of this growth should be made in both absolute and relative terms. The number of PACs in comparison with the number of corporations in America is fairly small. With approximately 2 million corporations of varying size, 1,204 had formed and registered PACs in 1980. More companies, especially small businesses, can be expected to register PACs with the FEC in 1981.

However, PACs are a "growth industry" for the business community, as evidenced in Diagram 3.

Twelve hundred and four PACs represent a significant increase in the numbers from the early seventies. In 1974, 89 corporations sponsored PACs. With a moderate increase in 1975 to 139, a trend reflecting significant growth

Contribution Limitations

Entity	Per Candidate Each Election	Aggregate Each Year (Calendar)
Individual	$ 1,000	$ 25,000
Qualified Multicandidate Political Action Committee (registered for 6 months, received contributions from more than 50 contributors, made contributions to at least 5 federal candidates)	$ 5,000	Unlimited

Diagram 2.

Number of PACs

(Source: FEC Press Release, 1/16/81)

Type of PAC	1974	1976	1978	1980
Corporate	89	433	784	1204
Membership Organizations (Trade, Professional, Health)	318	489	451	574
Labor	201	224	217	297
Independent	NA	NA	165	378
Total, including other type PACs, as cooperatives	608	1146	1653	2551

Diagram 3.

351

Listing of Largest Ten PACs

Name	Candidate Contributions (as of 9/25/80)
1) American Medical PAC (American Medical Association)	$ 596,435
2) Automobile and Truck Dealers Election Action Committee (National Automobile Dealers Association)	512,526
3) Realtors PAC (National Association of Realtors)	465,647
4) UAW–V–CAP (UAW Voluntary Community Action Program) (United Auto Workers)	449,816
5) AFL–CIO COPE Political Contributions Committee (AFL–CIO)	381,922
6) Carpenters' Legislative Improvement Committee (Carpenters and Joiners of America)	333,408
7) Committee for Thorough Agricultural Political Education of Associated Milk Producers, Inc. (Associated Milk Producers, Inc.)	331,489
8) Machinists Non-Partisan Political League (Machinists and Aerospace Workers)	325,785
9) Transportation Political Education League (United Transportation Union)	302,435
10) National Association of Life Underwriters PAC (National Association of Life Underwriters)	295,637

Diagram 4

352

followed throughout the 1970s. From 433 corporate PACs in 1976, there were 784 business PACs in 1978, and as previously mentioned, slightly over 1,200 corporate PACs in this last election year.

While corporate PACs may have formed in greater numbers than labor PACs, further comparison is difficult and fraught with difficulties in evaluating relative political strengths. PACs are only one element in such an evaluation, and do not account for unreportable organized volunteer efforts nor effective partisan communications and endorsements. With this preface, it is interesting to undertake a partial comparison.

Labor organizations' first PACs were formed prior to the decade of corporate PAC development in the 1970s. Most unions have a connected PAC. Familiarity with use of the PAC vehicle probably has an impact on the effectiveness of the individual labor PAC, which currently number about 300.

Of the ten largest PACs in 1980 which are listed in Diagram 4, five were labor committees. They included, among others, the AFL-CIO, Machinists, and United Transportation Unions. The remaining five largest PACs belong to trade and professional associations which, by and large, carry a pro-business viewpoint. Notably, not one corporate PAC qualified in size for the list of ten largest PACs shown in Diagram 5.

All PACs contributed significant sums of money to federal candidates in 1980. Total PAC-related contributions to federal candidates totaled $42.2 million for congressional elections, including $28 million to House candidates and $12.5 million to Senate candidates. (See Diagram 6. *Caveat*: The FEC Press Office urges caution in use of the data in this table. The information is incomplete. For purposes of this article, data use is limited to trend analysis.)

These PAC disbursements accounted for approximately 18 percent of all House and Senate candidate funds raised by candidates. Again, as was true in previous elections, direct contributions from individuals and national party congressional campaign committees were the primary source of financing for federal office-seekers.

Corporate PACs contributed approximately $13.6 million to candidates which was divided with $8.1 million going to House candidates and $4.4 million to Senate candidates. The propensity toward House candidates

353

Typology of Largest Ten PACs

Type	In Top Ten
Corporate	0
Membership	5
Labor	5
Independent	0
	10

Diagram 5.

DETAILS OF CONTRIBUTIONS TO CANDIDATES
(Data relating solely to 1980 House and Senate races shown in parenthesis)

	Contributions To Candidates		By Type of Candidate			By Candidate Status			By Party Affiliation		
	Comm	Amount	Presidential	Senate	House	Incumbent	Challenger	Open Seat	Democrat	Republican	Other
Corporation	905	$13,611,042 (11,301,599)	$1,041,318	$4,416,760 (3,660,095)	$8,152,964 (7,641,504)	$8,903,250 (7,513,125)	$3,540,365 (2,624,047)	$1,167,427 (1,164,427)	$5,627,111 (4,855,005)	$7,966,182 (6,440,994)	$17,749 (5,600)
Labor Organization	201	$11,109,685 (10,265,498)	$231,268	$3,352,561 (3,043,557)	$7,525,856 (7,232,941)	$8,137,017 (7,508,976)	$1,739,347 (1,536,701)	$1,233,321 (1,230,821)	$10,394,293 (9,622,981)	$710,792 (649,917)	$4,600 (3,600)
No-Connected Org.	153	$2,854,490 (2,651,153)	$63,789	$1,047,313 (997,315)	$1,743,388 (1,653,838)	$948,773 (860,840)	$1,371,038 (1,257,750)	$534,679 (532,563)	$950,464 (872,844)	$1,876,214 (1,753,097)	$27,812 (25,212)
Trade/Member/Health	403	$13,135,267 (12,064,520)	$248,546	$3,320,643 (2,852,168)	$9,566,078 (9,212,352)	$9,129,630 (8,316,870)	$2,508,851 (2,257,714)	$1,496,786 (1,489,936)	$5,999,238 (5,526,643)	$7,110,613 (6,531,127)	$25,416 (6,750)
Cooperative	28	$1,226,344 (1,097,607)	$41,950	$311,137 (261,200)	$873,257 (836,407)	$1,045,406 (941,269)	$46,490 (23,890)	$134,448 (132,448)	$820,461 (756,424)	$405,883 (341,183)	$0 (0)
Comp. N/O Stock	36	$267,515 (211,516)	$37,149	$65,560 (54,160)	$164,806 (157,356)	$212,798 (185,881)	$46,317 (17,235)	$8,400 (8,400)	$184,318 (154,401)	$81,997 (57,115)	$1,200 (0)
Total	1,726	$42,204,343 ($37,602,893)	$1,664,020	$12,513,974 ($10,868,495)	$28,026,349 ($26,734,398)	$28,376,874 ($25,326,961)	$9,252,408 ($7,717,337)	$4,575,061 ($4,558,595)	$23,975,885 ($21,788,298)	$18,151,681 ($15,773,433)	$76,777 ($41,162)

1. Total receipt and disbursement figures include monies transferred between affiliated committees. For that reason, they are somewhat inflated.
2. Adjusted receipt and disbursement figures do not include monies transferred between affiliated committees, and therefore are more representative of actual receipts and disbursements.
3. The number of committees included in this report DOES NOT represent the number active as of a particular date.

Diagram 6.

Source: FEC Press Release, 1/13/81

reflects a belief that dollar for dollar, PAC money is more important in the smaller budgeted, more manageable House campaigns.

IMPACT OF BUSINESS PACS

Many complex socio-economic and political dynamics affected the 1980 election. The most significant factor in 1980, as in every election, was the underlying political climate in the year preceding the election. In 1980, the country found itself plagued by double-digit inflation and rising unemployment. The Iranian crisis consumed a considerable amount of former President Carter's time, captivated the national press and instilled deep emotions in the American people. The national mood was "anti-misery index, anti-Carter, anti-mistake," as recently described in an exceptionally informative symposium on the issue of governance held at The George Washington University. This restive electorate would bring their frustrations to the election polls when they cast their votes. (Almost 54 percent of eligible American voters cast their ballots in the 1980 elections. The turbulent times did not mean a greater voter turnout, but did affect those that voted.)

Being elected in any time period, and even more so in a turbulent era, is a function of many factors, some candidate-controllable and others not. Specific dynamics in the 1980 elections which must be factored into the impact analysis of business PACs included, among other things, the following.

First, all candidates would have to cope with anti-Carter sentiments, and the Reagan "coattails effect." Second, there were a number of liberal members of Congress from western states whose policy positions and record votes were "out of step" with their constituents'. They consequently would be more vulnerable to defeat, and included Senators McGovern, Bayh, Church and other well-known senators and congressmen. Third, government corruption investigations and subsequent convictions would be a bar to the re-election of many incumbents with considerable seniority from the eastern region of the country, including the likes of powerful Frank Thompson of New Jersey.

In addition to these factors, the age-old question of whether money wins elections must be addressed in relation to the impact of PAC contributions. Generally, substantial constituent appeal and support, *and* adequate campaign

356

resources are required to win elections; and the two are inexoribly inter-dependent. A candidate must have voter support to win a majority vote, but capturing a majority of the votes cast may be dependent upon having enough money to reach the voter through political broadcast, which is very expensive. It is probably safe to say that without money it is extremely difficult to be elected, but that money alone will not necessarily guarantee victory. The defeat of many of the previously mentioned liberal senators from western states evidences this conclusion, for they all had sufficient campaign resources. The lesson learned is money alone will not buy a seat in Congress, regardless if the source is a PAC or inheritance.

Therefore, at the outset, I cannot subscribe to the notion that "but for" political action committees, the 1980 election results would have been different. I *do* believe that PACs, especially business PACs, were an "important and significant contributing factor" in the election results.

1. Increased PAC activity meant more campaign resources to more candidates. The enactment of the Federal Election Campaign Act of 1971, as amended, placed contribution ceilings on political gifts by individuals and organizations. The contribution limitations greatly restricted access to large individual contributions, and forced candidates to new and more expensive fundraising devices, such as direct mail.

Correspondingly, inflation was driving up the cost of campaigning, creating a push-pull effect on campaign financing: More money was needed for a competitive campaign while the legal restrictions made the money harder to raise.

The Campaign Act containing these contribution limitations also had enabling provisions clarifying the right of certain economic interests to sponsor a political committee. These political action committees grew in number and strength and provided a new source for candidates to secure needed campaign resources. In 1980, all PACs contributed over $42.2 million dollars to all federal candidates and helped to alleviate to some extent the chronic problems of the under-financed campaign.

2. Shift in contribution patterns meant more campaign resources to different types of candidates. Not only was there more PAC money available in the 1980 elections, PAC resources were going to different types of

357

candidates -- many of whom would, against great odds, be elected to public office. There now appears to be evidence that business PACs were shying away from past contributions patterns comprised of giving more to a Democratic over a Republican candidate; disregarding challengers and open seats in deference to incumbents; and allocating few contributions in the early period of a campaign.

(a) The corporate preference for Republican candidates became more pronounced than in previous elections. A post-election study by *Congressional Quarterly* of the finance reports of ten large PACs appears to document this. (Larry Light, "Democrats May Lose Edge in Contributions from PACs," *Congressional Quarterly Weekly Report,* 11/22/80, pp. 3405-9):

> "Of contributions made in the 1979-80 election cycle, FEC data show that through August 31 Democrats had gotten $5.2 million and Republicans $6.6 million from all corporate PACs. And after Labor Day ,when most contributions were made, business PACs began pouring even more of their money into Republican coffers, CQ's study of FEC records shows."

January FEC figures confirm this trend, and the yet incomplete FEC data show $5.6 million to Democrats and nearly $8 million going to Republicans.

Examples of increased PAC funding of Republican challengers who were successful include, among others, Eugene Johnston's defeat of Rep. Richardson Preyer, North Carolina - 6; Sid Morrison's defeat of Mike McCormack in Washington - 4; and Larry Hopkins' re-election in Kentucky - 6, in which he defeated Mr. Easterly a second time -- all in which business PAC contributions were important.

Since a Republican President was elected and Republican candidates prevailed in so many congressional races, business PACs surely were an important contributing factor in the 1980 Republican election gains.

(b) According to numerous interviews with PAC executives and members of the national press responsible for observing the PAC movement, challengers and candidates in open seats started receiving more contributions from business PACs in 1980. FEC data show corporate PACs contributed over $3.5 million to challengers, and $1.2 million in open seats.

An example of PAC preference for a Republican challenger is the three-way New York Senate race. Alfonse D'Amato received considerable PAC funds and in a relatively close election beat Rep.Elizabeth Holtzman by about 200,000 votes. Incumbent Jacob Javits placed third (and had not survived the Republican primary). PAC contributions helped purchase TV time, which is crucial to New York elections, and very expensive.

Movement away from incumbency giving remains at best an incipient trend. Incumbents still received the "lion's share" of corporate PAC money, approximately $8.9 million.

However, movement towards non-incumbency giving is significant. Even if relatively small in this last election, it may have been a contributing factor in 1980 election results in which many incumbents would not be returned to Congress.

(c) Another discernible trend was the making of PAC contributions in earlier time periods in campaigns. Early money is extremely important to candidates. For example, Richard Huff ran a close election against Mo Udall (Arizona - 2) in what ended up a 58-42 percent Udall victory. With early PAC money, Huff used extensive TV campaigning in 1979 in an attempt to create greater name recognition in the district, and gave pause to the veteran Udall.

COMING OF AGE:
THE MATURATION OF BUSINESS PACS
AND OTHER DEVELOPMENTS

This heightening of campaign giving to Republicans and increase in support for non-incumbents with early money evidences an underlying phenomena: the "maturation" of the business PAC movement. Instead of contributing to incumbents to insure legislative access which is often of questionable worth, decisions are now more than before being predicated strongly upon the philosophical leaning of the candidate on business issues and electability. In the past, many PACs were solely "incumbency PACs," which

359

based their decision to support a candidate primarily on whether that person was an incumbent with important committee assignments and party seniority.

This development is, of course, not without its exceptions. Consider Democratic Rep. Al Ullman (Oregon - 2), "whose authority over tax matters as chairman of the House Ways and Means Committee commanded the defense of the business community" -- despite his position on many business issues. For example, Ullman was the chief draftsman and architect of "Windfall Profits Tax" legislation. Furthermore, one business federation evaluated his cumulative voting performance as being correct in accordance with the organization's stance of selected issues only 43 percent of the time.

Add to this early indication showing Ullman vulnerable to defeat. Mr. Ullman squeaked by his primary with only 55.6 percent of the vote. Still, Mr. Ullman received nearly $400,000 in business money from PACs and executives. On the other hand, conservative challenger and now Congressman Denny Smith received less than $30,000 prior to August and $150,000 for the entire campaign. Even so, sources close to the Smith campaign say this late PAC money was absolutely essential to purchase media time in this close election. Smith won by approximately 3,800 votes.

The move of ideological PACs, such as the National Conservative Political Action Committee, or NCPAC, to in-kind contributions and independent expenditures is worthy of note. Dedicated to promoting conservative candidates and causes (many of which are consonant with a business viewpoint on economic issues), NCPAC made extensive use of public opinion surveys to target their resources towards vulnerable incumbents. Identifying those candidates, NCPAC was able to share campaign management expertise as in-kind contributions, and use independent expenditures (in different races) to purchase political advertisements highlighting the voting records of candidates they targeted for defeat. Ideological PACs were not alone in use of modern campaign technology, but they surely were on the forefront and cutting edge of this new development.

FUTURE PAC DEVELOPMENT

PACs will continue to be an important force in American politics. Legislation curtailing the ability of business PACs to participate fully will not be passed in the 97th Congress. In 1981, PACs will continue to "fine-tune" their methodology used in candidate selection and bring this art toward a more scientific analysis.

Extensive analysis of which candidates will receive PAC money is a logical concomitant in the maturation of PACs. A cadre of professional PAC executives are spending more time examining the historical positions of candidates on business issues before making any decision.

For example, one of the largest health association PACs is spending considerable resources analyzing organizational ratings of candidates, and evaluating the meaning of specific votes on certain issues toward a determination using both a quantitative and qualitative analysis. The new holistic approach to candidate selection is a step forward in accepting the business concept of "investment capital" in supporting challengers to incumbents and entering "open seats."

The management skills applied to fundraising and operations of PACs have profoundly developed from a part-time responsibility of a government affairs officer to staffing, ample budgets, and the modern use of computer technology. Payroll deduction, a less painful fundraising device, will continue to grow as a predominant tool in raising PAC monies.

Off-election year PAC activity is turning into a full-time pursuit in not only evaluating candidates -- but identifying candidates, encouraging them to run and providing them resources. The ongoing evaluation, combined with the restive mood of the electorate, will increase the accountability of Congress to their constituents and enhance the ability of lobbyists to communicate their message to Congress.

In summation, business PACs were a significant force in the 1980 election, and the prognosis for the future is bright. **PAC**

APPENDIX

STATEMENT OF ORGANIZATION

(see reverse side for instructions)

1. (a) Name of Committee (in Full) ☐ Check if name or address is changed.	2. Date
(b) Address (Number and Street)	3. FEC Identification Number
(c) City, State and ZIP Code	4. Is this an amended Statement? ☐ YES ☐ NO

5. TYPE OF COMMITTEE (check one):

☐ (a) This committee is a principal campaign committee. (Complete the candidate information below.)

☐ (b) This committee is an authorized committee, and is NOT a principal campaign committee. (Complete the candidate information below.)

Name of Candidate	Candidate Party Affiliation	Office Sought	State/District

☐ (c) This committee supports/opposes only one candidate _____ and is NOT an authorized committee.
(name of candidate)

☐ (d) This committee is a _____ committee of the _____ Party.
(National, State or subordinate)   (Democratic, Republican, etc.)

☐ (e) This committee is a separate segregated fund.

☐ (f) This committee supports/opposes more than one Federal candidate and is NOT a separate segregated fund nor a party committee.

6. Name of Any Connected Organization or Affiliated Committee	Mailing Address and ZIP Code	Relationship

If the registering political committee has identified a "connected organization" above, please indicate type of organization:

☐ Corporation   ☐ Corporation w/o Capital Stock   ☐ Labor Organization   ☐ Membership Organization   ☐ Trade Association   ☐ Cooperative

7. **Custodian of Records:** Identify by name, address (phone number — optional) and position, the person in possession of committee books and records.

Full Name	Mailing Address and ZIP Code	Title or Position

8. **Treasurer:** List the name and address (phone number — optional) of the treasurer of the committee; and the name and address of any designated agent (e.g., assistant treasurer).

Full Name	Mailing Address and ZIP Code	Title or Position

9. **Banks or Other Depositories:** List all banks or other depositories in which the committee deposits funds, holds accounts, rents safety deposit boxes or maintains funds.

Name of Bank, Depository, etc.	Mailing Address and ZIP Code

I certify that I have examined this Statement and to the best of my knowledge and belief it is true, correct and complete.

Type or Print Name of Treasurer	SIGNATURE OF TREASURER	Date

NOTE: Submission of false, erroneous, or incomplete information may subject the person signing this Statement to the penalties of 2 U.S.C. §437g.

For further information contact: Federal Election Commission, Toll Free 800-424-9530, Local 202-523-4068

FEC FORM 1 (3/80)

APPENDIX B

XYZ, INC.
POLITICAL ACTION COMMITTEE

BYLAWS

ARTICLE I

Name

The name of this association shall be XYZ, Inc.
Political Action Committee (hereinafter "XYZ PAC").

ARTICLE II

Principal Office and Address

The principal office of XYZ PAC shall be located at,
and its address shall be _____.

ARTICLE III

Organization

XYZ PAC shall be a voluntary, non-profit, unincorporated
political association composed of its members, who shall be
individuals. XYZ PAC shall be independent of any political party,
candidate, or organization except that XYZ, Inc. shall defray all
costs and expenses incurred in the establishment and administration
of, and in the solicitation of contributions to XYZ PAC.

ARTICLE IV

Purposes and Powers

The purposes of XYZ PAC shall be to encourage the
growth of the XYZ industry, support the objectives of XYZ Inc.,
to promote the election of responsible, qualified candidates to

public office, regardless of party affiliation, and, in particular,
to support candidates for public office who understand and appreciate the goals and objectives of XYZ, Inc. generally and the XYZ
industry specifically.

To achieve these purposes, XYZ PAC may solicit voluntary
contributions from members of XYZ, Inc. and from its executive
or management personnel and their families, may accept contributions from those persons and others, and may in turn make
contributions and expenditures to influence the nomination for
election, and the election, of candidates for federal, state or
local elective public office who are believed to be in general
agreement with any purpose of XYZ PAC. XYZ PAC may also make contributions to national, state, and local committees of national
political parties. XYZ PAC is further empowered, within limits
approved by law, to do such other and further things not inconsistent
with the foregoing as may be necessary or desirable for the
attainment of the purposes above stated.

ARTICLE V

Membership

Section 1. Members of the Contribution and Advisory
Committees and officers of XYZ PAC shall automatically become
members of XYZ PAC upon his or her election or appointment as
such and he or she shall continue as a member of XYZ PAC so long
as he or she occupies such position or office.

Section 2. Any member of XYZ PAC may be removed for any cause by a majority vote of the members of XYZ PAC and such removal shall be effective upon receipt of written notice by the Secretary of XYZ PAC.

Section 3. Any member may resign from membership in the XYZ PAC at any time and such resignation shall be effective upon receipt of written notice by the Secretary of XYZ PAC. Membership in XYZ PAC shall cease automatically upon cessation of employment with XYZ, Inc.

ARTICLE VI

Contributions and Expenditures/Separate Segregated Fund

Section 1. All contributions to XYZ PAC shall be voluntary, and no contributions to XYZ PAC shall be solicited or secured by physical force, job discrimination, or financial reprisal, or the threat thereof, or as a condition of membership in or employment by XYZ, Inc. In addition, each individual who is solicited for a contribution to XYZ PAC shall be informed of the political purposes of the fund and of his or her right to refuse to contribute without any reprisal.

Section 2. No member of XYZ PAC, or contributor thereto. shall have a right to share personally in any of the funds or assets of XYZ PAC upon its dissolution, or at any other time.

Section 3. The expenditure and disbursement of the XYZ PAC funds shall be within the sole discretion of XYZ PAC's Contribution Committee, subject to Article VIII hereof.

Section 4. All contributions to XYZ PAC shall be maintained by XYZ PAC as a separate, segregated fund, and all expenditures and disbursements by XYZ PAC in support of any candidate or political committee shall be made from such fund and from no other source.

ARTICLE VII

Officers

Section 1. The officers of XYZ PAC shall include: a Chairman, Treasurer, Assistant Treasurer and Secretary, all of whom shall be appointed by the Board of Directors of XYZ, Inc. Except as set forth in Article V of these Bylaws, each officer of XYZ PAC shall continue to serve in his office until his successor is appointed.

Section 2. The Chairman shall be the principal executive officer of XYZ PAC and shall supervise and control all of the business and affairs of XYZ PAC, preside at all meetings of XYZ PAC and execute such powers of attorney appointing other corporations, partnerships, or individuals the agent of XYZ PAC, as he deems necessary for the efficient operation of XYZ PAC.

Section 3. The Treasurer shall be the chief financial officer of XYZ PAC. The Treasurer, subject to the provisions of these Bylaws shall have the general responsibility for all funds collected and all disbursements made by XYZ PAC. The Treasurer shall keep correct and complete records of account, showing accurately at all times the financial condition of XYZ PAC. He shall be the legal custodian of all monies, notes, and other valuables that may from time to time come into the possession of XYZ PAC. Within 5 days of receipt, he shall deposit all funds of XYZ PAC in some reliable bank or other depository, and shall keep this bank account in the name of the XYZ PAC. He shall furnish at meetings of the Contribution Committee, or whenever requested, a statement of the financial condition of XYZ PAC, and shall perform such other duties as these Bylaws, or the Chairman may prescribe. He shall prepare, sign, file, and maintain copies of all reports which are required by law to be made or maintained by XYZ PAC.

Section 4. During the absence or incapacity of the Chairman, the Treasurer shall automatically assume the duties and exercise the powers of the Chairman.

Section 5. During the absence or incapacity of the Treasurer, the Assistant Treasurer shall automatically assume the duties and functions, and exercise the powers of the Treasurer. The Assistant Treasurer shall also perform such other duties as may be assigned to him by these Bylaws or by the Chairman of XYZ PAC.

Section 6. The Secretary shall prepare and keep proper records pertaining to his office. He shall give notice of the meetings of the Contribution Committee.

Section 7. The office of Chairman and Treasurer may not be held by the same person. No contribution shall be accepted, and no expenditure shall be made, by or on behalf of XYZ PAC when the office of the Treasurer is vacant.

ARTICLE VIII

Contribution Committee

Section 1. The financial affairs of XYZ PAC, including the solicitation of contributions to and the disbursement of monies from XYZ PAC shall be supervised and directed by the Contribution Committee. The Treasurer of XYZ PAC shall serve as Chairman of the Contribution Committee; other members shall include the Chairman of XYZ PAC, the Secretary of XYZ PAC, and such other XYZ PAC members, if any, as may be designated by XYZ Inc. A quorum of the Contribution Committee for the transaction of business shall consist of a majority of its members, at least one of whom must be the Treasurer or Chairman.

Section 2. The Contribution Committee may delegate to the Treasurer, subject to the general direction of the Committee, the responsibility for managing the financial affairs of XYZ PAC, including the determination of the candidates and/or political committees that XYZ PAC shall support.

ARTICLE IX

Advisory Committee

Section 1. An Advisory Committee consisting of two or more persons shall be designated by the Board of Directors of XYZ, Inc. The Advisory Committee shall submit their recommendations for contributions and expenditures to the Contribution Committee.

Section 2. The Advisory Committee shall have no power or authority to make any contributions, but shall act solely to provide recommendations to the Contribution Committee.

Section 3. Members of the Advisory Committee shall become XYZ PAC members by virtue of their position as members of the Advisory Committee.

ARTICLE X

Audit

The Chairman may annually appoint an independent public accounting firm to audit the books of XYZ PAC for each year.

ARTICLE XI

Meetings

Section 1. A meeting of the Contribution Committee may be called by the Chairman of XYZ PAC, by the Chairman of the Contribution Committee or by a majority of its members whenever either Chairman or such members deem it necessary.

Section 2. Any action that may be taken at a meeting of the Contribution Committee may be taken without a meeting if a consent in writing, setting forth the action so to be taken, shall be signed before the action is taken by no less than a majority of the members of the Contribution Committee.

Section 3. Meetings of the members of XYZ PAC may be called by a majority of the members of XYZ PAC or the Chairman thereof, as they deem necessary.

Section 4. Meetings shall be held at the principal office of XYZ PAC, unless otherwise determined.

ARTICLE XII

Adoption and Amendments

Section 1. These Bylaws shall be adopted effective Month day, year.

Section 2. These Bylaws may be amended from time to time by action of the Board of Directors of XYZ, Inc.

ARTICLE XIII

Dissolution

Although the duration of XYZ PAC is to be perpetual, XYZ PAC may be dissolved at any time by action of the Board of Directors of XYZ, Inc. In the event of such dissolution, all surplus funds of XYZ PAC shall be promptly distributed to candidates or committees or expended in a manner consistent with Article VIII, and for the purposes set forth in Article IV hereof.

RESOLUTION TO ESTABLISH A
POLITICAL ACTION COMMITTEE

WHEREAS, it has been determined that it would be in the best interests of this Corporation to establish a political action committee, and

WHEREAS, there has been presented to this meeting the proposed Bylaws of the XYZ, Inc. Political Action Committee ("XYZ PAC").

NOW, THEREFORE, BE IT RESOLVED that the Bylaws of the XYZ, Inc. Political Action Committee as presented to this meeting are hereby authorized and approved.

RESOLVED FURTHER, that _____, _____ of this Corporation is hereby elected Chairman of the XYZ PAC with the powers and duties set forth in the Bylaws.

RESOLVED FURTHER, that _____, _____ of this Corporation is hereby elected Treasurer of XYC PAC with the powers and duties set forth in the Bylaws.

RESOLVED FURTHER, that _____, _____ of this Corporation is hereby elected Assistant Treasurer of the XYZ PAC with the powers and duties set forth in the Bylaws.

RESOLVED FURTHER, that _____, _____ of this Corporation is hereby elected Secretary of XYZ PAC with the powers and duties set forth in the Bylaws.

RESOLVED FURTHER, that _____, _____ and _____ are hereby elected to the Contribution Committee of XYZ PAC with the powers and duties set forth in the Bylaws.

RESOLVED FURTHER, that the aforementioned Officers and Contribution Committee shall serve in their stated capacities until their successors are elected by action of this Board of Directors.

Form **1120-POL**
Department of the Treasury
Internal Revenue Service

U.S. Income Tax Return
for Certain Political Organizations
To be filed by those organizations having taxable income (line 19).
(Under Section 527 of the Internal Revenue Code)

1980

For calendar year 1980 or other tax year beginning _____ , 1980 and ending _____ , 19 ___ .

Note: If you are a section 501(c) organization (see instruction A.3) or a separate segregated fund described in section 527(f)(3), check here ▶ ☐.

Name of organization	Employer identification number (see instruction O)
Number and street	Date organization formed
City or town, State and ZIP code	Were the required Forms 1087, 1096, and 1099 filed? . . . . ☐ Yes ☐ No

(Please print or type)

Enter name of candidate ▶
The books are in care of ▶ ....   Telephone No. ▶ ....
Located at ▶

Important—Fill in all applicable lines and schedules.

Gross Income

1 Dividends (attach schedule)	1	
2 Interest on obligations of the United States and U.S. instrumentalities	2	
3 Other interest	3	
4 Gross rents	4	
5 Gross royalties	5	
6 (a) Capital gain net income from Schedule D, line 9	6(a)	
(b) Net gain or (loss) from Form 4797, line 11(a), Part II (attach Form 4797)	6(b)	
7 Other income (see "Note" in instruction D—attach schedule)	7	
8 Total income (add lines 1 through 7)	8	

Deductions

9 (a) Salaries and wages ....,		
(b) Less WIN credit from Form 4874, line 12 .... Balance ▶	9(c)	
10 Repairs	10	
11 Rents	11	
12 Taxes	12	
13 Interest	13	
14 Depreciation from Form 4562 (attach Form 4562) ...., less depreciation claimed elsewhere on the return .... Balance ▶	14	
15 Other deductions (attach schedule)	15	
16 Total deductions (add lines 9 through 15)	16	
17 Taxable income before specific deduction of $100 (line 8 less line 16). (Section 501(c) organizations show: (a) amount of net investment income (see instruction A3(b)(ii)) ▶.............................., (b) aggregate amount expended for an exempt function (attach schedule) ▶.............................. and enter on line 17, the lesser of (a) or (b)):	17	
18 Less specific deduction of $100 (not allowed for newsletter funds defined under section 527(g)) . .	18	
19 Taxable income (subtract line 18 from line 17)	19	

Tax

20 Total tax (from Schedule A, line 6)	20	
21 Credits: (a) Tax deposited with Form 7004		
(b) Tax deposited with Form 7005 (attach copy)		
(c) Credit from regulated investment companies (attach Form 2439) . .	21	
22 Tax due (subtract line 21 from line 20). See instruction I for depositary method of payment . . .	22	
23 Overpayment (subtract line 20 from line 21)	23	

Foreign Financial Accounts and Foreign Trusts

1 At any time during the tax year, did you have an interest in or a signature or other authority over a bank account, securities account, or other financial account in a foreign country (see instruction T)? . . . . ☐ Yes ☐ No

2 Were you the grantor of, or transferor to, a foreign trust which existed during the current tax year, whether or not you have any beneficial interest in it? . . . . ☐ Yes ☐ No
If "Yes," you may have to file Forms 3520, 3520–A or 926.

Please Sign Here

Under penalties of perjury, I declare that I have examined this return, including accompanying schedules and statements, and to the best of my knowledge and belief, it is true, correct, and complete. Declaration of preparer (other than taxpayer) is based on all information of which preparer has any knowledge.

Signature of officer	Date	Title

Paid Preparer's Use Only

Preparer's signature and date ▶	Check if self-employed ▶ ☐	Preparer's social security no.
Firm's name (or yours, if self-employed) and address ▶	E.I. No. ▶ ZIP code ▶	

Schedule L.—Balance Sheets

Assets	Beginning of Tax Year		End of Tax Year	
	(A)	(B)	(C)	(D)
1 Cash: (a) Savings and interest-bearing accounts . . .				
(b) Other				
2 Accounts receivable net				
3 Notes receivable net (attach schedule)				
4 Inventories				
5 Government obligations: (a) U.S. and instrumentalities . .				
(b) State, subdivisions thereof, etc.				
6 Investments in nongovernmental bonds, etc. (attach schedule) .				
7 Investments in corporate stocks (attach schedule)				
8 Loans:				
(a) Mortgage loans (number of loans ▶ _____) . .				
(b) Other loans (attach schedule)				
9 Other investments (attach schedule)				
10 Depreciable (depletable) assets (attach schedule):				
(a) Held for investment purposes				
(b) Less accumulated depreciation				
(c) Held for campaign purposes				
(d) Less accumulated depreciation				
11 Land: (a) Held for investment purposes				
(b) Held for campaign purposes				
12 Other assets (attach schedule)				
13 Total assets				
Liabilities				
14 Accounts payable				
15 Contributions, gifts, grants, etc. payable				
16 Mortgages and notes payable (attach schedule)				
17 Other liabilities (attach schedule)				
18 Total liabilities				
Net Worth (Fund Balances)				
19 Principal Fund _____				
20 Income Fund _____				
21 Total Net Worth (Fund Balances)				
22 Total liabilities and Net Worth (line 18 plus line 21) . . .				

Schedule M.—Analysis of Changes in Net Worth

1 Total net worth at beginning of year—from Schedule L, line 21, column (B)	1	
2 Enter amount from line 17, page 1	2	
3 Nontaxable income from contributions	3	
4 Nontaxable income from other sources	4	
5 Other increases not included above (itemize) ▶ _____	5	
6 Total (add lines 1 through 5)	6	
7 Campaign expenses	7	
8 Expenses attributable to other nontaxable income	8	
9 Other decreases not included above (itemize) ▶ _____	9	
10 Total of lines 7 through 9	10	
11 Total net worth at end of year (subtract line 10 from line 6)—This equals Schedule L, line 21, column (D) .	11	

(FRB) servicing the geographic area where the organization is located. Records of deposits will be sent to IRS for crediting to the organization's account. See the instructions on the back of Form 503 for more information and exceptions.

In Schedule K, list all deposits on FTD Form 503 that relate to the tax year for which this return is filed and which were made before or at the same time this form was filed.

You may apply for these FTD Forms 503 from the Internal Revenue Service Center where the organization files its return. If you do not have these forms when a deposit is due, mail your payment to the Internal Revenue Service Center where the organization files its return. When applying for FTD Form 503 (and also when making a deposit without FTD Form 503), include the organization's name, identification number, address, and the tax year to which the deposits relate.

J. Change in Accounting Period.—Before you can change an accounting period, you must get the Commissioner's approval (section 1.442-1 of the regulations) by filing Form 1128, Application for Change in Accounting Period. Also see **Publication 538,** Accounting Periods and Methods.

K. Accounting Methods.—Taxable income must be computed using the method of accounting regularly used in keeping' the organization's books and records. In all cases, the method adopted must clearly reflect taxable income. (See section 446.)

Unless the law specifically permits otherwise, the organization may change the method of accounting used to report taxable income in earlier years (for income as a whole or for any material item) only by first getting consent on Form 3115, Application for Change in Accounting Method. Also see **Publication 538,** Accounting Periods and Methods.

L. Rounding Off.—You may show money items as whole-dollar amounts by dropping amounts under 50 cents and increasing amounts from 50 to 99 cents to the next higher dollar.

M. Attachments.—If you need more space on forms or schedules, attach separate sheets to the back of Form 1120-POL. Attach schedules in alphabetical order and forms in numerical order. Be sure to put the taxpayer's name and employer identification number (EIN) on each sheet.

N. Signature.—The return must be signed and dated by the president, vice president, treasurer, assistant treasurer, chief accounting officer, or any other officer (such as tax officer) authorized to sign. A receiver, trustee, or assignee must sign and date any return required to be filed on behalf of an organization.

If your organization officer filled in Form 1120-POL, the Paid Preparer's space under "Signature of officer" should remain

blank. If someone prepares Form 1120-POL and does not charge the organization, that person should not sign the return. Certain others who prepare Form 1120-POL should not sign. For example, a regular, full-time employee of the organization such as clerk, secretary, etc. does not have to sign. (This list is not all inclusive.)

Generally, anyone who is paid to prepare Form 1120-POL must sign the return and fill in the other blanks in the Paid Preparer's Use Only area of the return.

If the preparer is self-employed (that is, is not employed by any person or business entity to prepare the return), he or she should check the "self-employed" box.

If you have questions about whether a preparer is required to sign Form 1120-POL, please contact an IRS office.

The preparer required to sign the return MUST complete the required preparer information and:

● Sign it, by hand, in the space provided for the preparer's signature. (Signature stamps or labels are not acceptable.)

● Give a copy of Form 1120-POL to the taxpayer in addition to the copy filed with IRS.

Tax return preparers should be familiar with their responsibilities. **Publication 1045,** Information and Order Blanks for Preparers of Federal Income Tax Returns, lists some of the preparers' other responsibilities and penalties for which they may be liable. The publication also contains the regulation citations which govern their work.

O. Employer Identification Number.—All political organizations (including separate segregated funds described in section 527(f)(3) and newsletter funds) must use an employer identification number (EIN).

An organization that does not have an EIN should apply for one on Form SS-4, Application for Employer Identification Number. You can get this form at any IRS or Social Security Administration office. Send Form SS-4 to the same Internal Revenue Service Center to which you send Form 1120-POL. If you have not received the EIN by the filing time for Form 1120-POL write "Applied for" in the space for the EIN.

P. Penalties.—

Avoid penalties and interest by correctly filing and paying the tax when due. The organization may have to pay the following penalties unless it can show that failure to file or to pay was due to reasonable cause and not willful neglect. (These penalties are in addition to the interest charge on unpaid tax at a rate under section 6621.)

● A political organization that fails to file its tax return when due (including any extensions of time for filing) may be subject to a penalty of 5% a month, up to a maximum of 25%, for each month the return is not filed. (The penalty is imposed

on the net amount due.)

● A political organization that fails to pay the tax when due may be subject to a penalty of ½% a month or fraction of a month, up to a maximum of 25%, for each month the tax is not paid. (The penalty is imposed on the net amount due.)

Q. Possessions Tax Credit.—See Form 5712 for rules on how to elect to claim the possessions tax credit (section 936). Compute the credit on Form 5735, and include the amount of the credit in the total for Schedule A (Form 1120-POL), line 5. Write in the margin, next to the entry on line 5, the amount of the credit and identify it as a section 936 credit.

R. Estimated Tax, Minimum Tax, Investment Credit and Jobs Credit.—Estimated tax, minimum tax, investment credit, and jobs credit do not apply to political organizations defined in section 527.

S. Financial Statements.—Section 501 (c) organizations do not have to complete Schedules L and M.

T. Foreign Financial Accounts and Foreign Trusts.—

Question 1: Check the Yes box if either 1 or 2 below applies to you.

1. At any time during the year you had an interest in or signature or other authority over a bank account, securities account, or other financial account in a foreign country. *Exception:* Check No if any of the following apply to you:

● The combined value of the accounts was $1,000 or less during the whole year.

● The accounts were with a U.S. military banking facility operated by a U.S. financial institution.

2. You own more than 50% of the stock in any corporation that owns one or more foreign bank accounts.

Get Form 90-22.1 to see if you are considered to have an interest in or signature or other authority over a bank account, securities account, or other financial account in a foreign country.

If you checked Yes for Question 1, file Form 90-22.1 by June 30, 1981, with the Department of the Treasury at the address shown on the form. Form 90-22.1 is not a tax return, so do not file it with the IRS. But be sure to file your Form 1120-POL with the IRS.

You can get Form 90-22.1 from many IRS offices.

Question 2: Check the Yes box if you were a grantor of, or a transferor to, a foreign trust that existed during the tax year.

Instructions for Schedule D

Purpose

Schedule D should be used by organizations to report sales or exchanges of capital assets. Sales or exchanges of property

(Continued on page 6)

REPORT OF RECEIPTS AND DISBURSEMENTS
For a Political Committee Other Than an Authorized Committee

(Summary Page)

1. Name of Committee (in Full)	4. TYPE OF REPORT (check appropriate boxes)

4. TYPE OF REPORT (check appropriate boxes)

(a) ☐ April 15 Quarterly Report

☐ July 15 Quarterly Report

☐ October 15 Quarterly Report

☐ January 31 Year End Report

☐ July 31 Mid Year Report (Non-election Year Only)

☐ Monthly Report for _____

☐ Twelfth day report preceding _____
(Type of Election)

election on _____ in the State of _____

☐ Thirtieth day report following the General Election

on _____ in the State of _____

☐ Termination Report

Address (Number and Street)

City, State and ZIP Code

☐ Check if address is different than previously reported.

2. FEC Identification Number

3. ☐ This committee qualified as a multicandidate committee during this Reporting Period on _____ (date)

(b) Is this Report an Amendment?
☐ YES   ☐ NO

SUMMARY

	Column A This Period	Column B Calendar Year-to-Date
5. Covering Period _____ Through _____		
6. (a) Cash on Hand January 1, 19___		$
(b) Cash on Hand at Beginning of Reporting Period	$	
(c) Total Receipts (from Line 18)	$	$
(d) Subtotal (add lines 6(b) and 6(c) for Column A and lines 6(a) and 6(c) for Column B)	$	$
7. Total Disbursements (from Line 28)	$	$
8. Cash on Hand at Close of Reporting Period (subtract line 7 from 6(d)) . . .	$	$
9. Debts and Obligations Owed TO the Committee (Itemize all on Schedule C or Schedule D)	$	
10. Debts and Obligations Owed BY the Committee (Itemize all on Schedule C or Schedule D)	$	

I certify that I have examined this Report and to the best of my knowledge and belief it is true, correct and complete.

For further information, contact:

Federal Election Commission
Toll Free 800-424-9530
Local 202-523-4068

Type or Print Name of Treasurer

SIGNATURE OF TREASURER   Date

NOTE: Submission of false, erroneous, or incomplete information may subject the person signing this Report to the penalties of 2 U.S.C. §437g.

All previous versions of FEC FORM 3 and FEC FORM 3a are obsolete and should no longer be used.

FEC FORM 3X (3/80)

DETAILED SUMMARY PAGE
of Receipts and Disbursements
(Page 2, FEC FORM 3X)

Name of Committee (in Full)	Report Covering the Period:	
	From: To:	
	COLUMN A Total This Period	**COLUMN B** Calendar Year-to-Date
I. RECEIPTS		
11. CONTRIBUTIONS (other than loans) FROM:		
(a) Individuals/Persons Other Than Political Committees		
(Memo Entry Unitemized $_____)		
(b) Political Party Committees.		
(c) Other Political Committees		
(d) TOTAL CONTRIBUTIONS (other than loans) (add 11a, 11b and 11c)		
12. TRANSFERS FROM AFFILIATED/OTHER PARTY COMMITTEES		
13. ALL LOANS RECEIVED		
14. LOAN REPAYMENTS RECEIVED		
15. OFFSETS TO OPERATING EXPENDITURES (Refunds, Rebates, etc.)		
16. REFUNDS OF CONTRIBUTIONS MADE TO FEDERAL CANDIDATES AND OTHER POLITICAL COMMITTEES		
17. OTHER RECEIPTS (Dividends, Interest, etc.)		
18. TOTAL RECEIPTS (Add 11d, 12, 13, 14, 15, 16 and 17).		
II. DISBURSEMENTS		
19. OPERATING EXPENDITURES		
20. TRANSFERS TO AFFILIATED/OTHER PARTY COMMITTEES.		
21. CONTRIBUTIONS TO FEDERAL CANDIDATES AND OTHER POLITICAL COMMITTEES.		
22. INDEPENDENT EXPENDITURES (Use Schedule E)		
23. COORDINATED EXPENDITURES MADE BY PARTY COMMITTEES (2 U.S.C. §441a(d)) (Use Schedule F)		
24. LOAN REPAYMENTS MADE		
25. LOANS MADE		
26. REFUNDS OF CONTRIBUTIONS TO:		
(a) Individuals/Persons Other Than Political Committees		
(b) Political Party Committees.		
(c) Other Political Committees		
(d) TOTAL CONTRIBUTION REFUNDS (add 26a, 26b and 26c)		
27. OTHER DISBURSEMENTS.		
28. TOTAL DISBURSEMENTS (Add Lines 19, 20, 21, 22, 23, 24, 25, 26d and 27). . .		
III. NET CONTRIBUTIONS AND NET OPERATING EXPENDITURES		
29. TOTAL CONTRIBUTIONS (other than loans) from Line 11d		
30. TOTAL CONTRIBUTION REFUNDS from Line 26d		
31. NET CONTRIBUTIONS (other than loans) (subtract Line 30 from Line 29)		
32. TOTAL OPERATING EXPENDITURES from Line 19		
33. OFFSETS TO OPERATING EXPENDITURES from Line 15.		
34. NET OPERATING EXPENDITURES (subtract Line 33 from Line 32)		

SCHEDULE A

Page _____ of _____ for
LINE NUMBER _____
(Use separate schedule(s) for each category of the Detailed Summary Page)

ITEMIZED RECEIPTS

Any information copied from such Reports or Statements may not be sold or used by any person for the purpose of soliciting contributions or for commercial purposes, other than using the name and address of any political committee to solicit contributions from such committee.

Name of Committee (in Full)

A. Full Name, Mailing Address and ZIP Code	Name of Employer	Date (month, day, year)	Amount of Each Receipt this Period
	Occupation		
Receipt For: ☐ Primary ☐ General ☐ Other (specify):	Aggregate Year-to-Date—$		

B. Full Name, Mailing Address and ZIP Code	Name of Employer	Date (month, day, year)	Amount of Each Receipt This Period
	Occupation		
Receipt For: ☐ Primary ☐ General ☐ Other (specify):	Aggregate Year-to-Date—$		

C. Full Name, Mailing Address and ZIP Code	Name of Employer	Date (month, day, year)	Amount of Each Receipt This Period
	Occupation		
Receipt For: ☐ Primary ☐ General ☐ Other (specify):	Aggregate Year-to-Date—$		

D. Full Name, Mailing Address and ZIP Code	Name of Employer	Date (month, day, year)	Amount of Each Receipt This Period
	Occupation		
Receipt For: ☐ Primary ☐ General ☐ Other (specify):	Aggregate Year-to-Date—$		

E. Full Name, Mailing Address and ZIP Code	Name of Employer	Date (month, day, year)	Amount of Each Receipt This Period
	Occupation		
Receipt For: ☐ Primary ☐ General ☐ Other (specify):	Aggregate Year-to-Date—$		

F. Full Name, Mailing Address and ZIP Code	Name of Employer	Date (month, day, year)	Amount of Each Receipt This Period
	Occupation		
Receipt For: ☐ Primary ☐ General ☐ Other (specify):	Aggregate Year-to-Date—$		

G. Full Name, Mailing Address and ZIP Code	Name of Employer	Date (month, day, year)	Amount of Each Receipt This Period
	Occupation		
Receipt For: ☐ Primary ☐ General ☐ Other (specify):	Aggregate Year-to-Date—$		

SUBTOTAL of Receipts This Page (optional) . . . .

TOTAL This Period (last page this line number only) . . . .

Page _____ of _____ for
LINE NUMBER _____
(Use separate schedule(s) for each
category of the Detailed
Summary Page)

SCHEDULE A

ITEMIZED RECEIPTS

Any information copied from such Reports or Statements may not be sold or used by any person for the purpose of soliciting contributions or for commercial purposes, other than using the name and address of any political committee to solicit contributions from such committee.

Name of Committee (in Full)

A. Full Name, Mailing Address and ZIP Code	Name of Employer	Date (month, day, year)	Amount of Each Receipt this Period
	Occupation		
Receipt For: ☐ Primary ☐ General ☐ Other (specify):	Aggregate Year-to-Date—$		
B. Full Name, Mailing Address and ZIP Code	Name of Employer	Date (month, day, year)	Amount of Each Receipt This Period
	Occupation		
Receipt For: ☐ Primary ☐ General ☐ Other (specify):	Aggregate Year-to-Date—$		
C. Full Name, Mailing Address and ZIP Code	Name of Employer	Date (month, day, year)	Amount of Each Receipt This Period
	Occupation		
Receipt For: ☐ Primary ☐ General ☐ Other (specify):	Aggregate Year-to-Date—$		
D. Full Name, Mailing Address and ZIP Code	Name of Employer	Date (month, day, year)	Amount of Each Receipt This Period
	Occupation		
Receipt For: ☐ Primary ☐ General ☐ Other (specify):	Aggregate Year-to-Date—$		
E. Full Name, Mailing Address and ZIP Code	Name of Employer	Date (month, day, year)	Amount of Each Receipt This Period
	Occupation		
Receipt For: ☐ Primary ☐ General ☐ Other (specify):	Aggregate Year-to-Date—$		
F. Full Name, Mailing Address and ZIP Code	Name of Employer	Date (month, day, year)	Amount of Each Receipt This Period
	Occupation		
Receipt For: ☐ Primary ☐ General ☐ Other (specify):	Aggregate Year-to-Date—$		
G. Full Name, Mailing Address and ZIP Code	Name of Employer	Date (month, day, year)	Amount of Each Receipt This Period
	Occupation		
Receipt For: ☐ Primary ☐ General ☐ Other (specify):	Aggregate Year-to-Date—$		

SUBTOTAL of Receipts This Page (optional) . . . .

TOTAL This Period (last page this line number only) . . . .

SCHEDULE A   **ITEMIZED RECEIPTS**

Page _____ of _____ for
LINE NUMBER _____
(Use separate schedule(s) for each
category of the Detailed
Summary Page)

Any information copied from such Reports or Statements may not be sold or used by any person for the purpose of soliciting contributions or for commercial purposes, other than using the name and address of any political committee to solicit contributions from such committee.

Name of Committee (in Full)

A. Full Name, Mailing Address and ZIP Code	Name of Employer	Date (month, day, year)	Amount of Each Receipt this Period
	Occupation		
Receipt For: ☐ Primary ☐ General ☐ Other (specify):	Aggregate Year-to-Date—$		
B. Full Name, Mailing Address and ZIP Code	Name of Employer	Date (month, day, year)	Amount of Each Receipt This Period
	Occupation		
Receipt For: ☐ Primary ☐ General ☐ Other (specify):	Aggregate Year-to-Date—$		
C. Full Name, Mailing Address and ZIP Code	Name of Employer	Date (month, day, year)	Amount of Each Receipt This Period
	Occupation		
Receipt For: ☐ Primary ☐ General ☐ Other (specify):	Aggregate Year-to-Date—$		
D. Full Name, Mailing Address and ZIP Code	Name of Employer	Date (month, day, year)	Amount of Each Receipt This Period
	Occupation		
Receipt For: ☐ Primary ☐ General ☐ Other (specify):	Aggregate Year-to-Date—$		
E. Full Name, Mailing Address and ZIP Code	Name of Employer	Date (month, day, year)	Amount of Each Receipt This Period
	Occupation		
Receipt For: ☐ Primary ☐ General ☐ Other (specify):	Aggregate Year-to-Date—$		
F. Full Name, Mailing Address and ZIP Code	Name of Employer	Date (month, day, year)	Amount of Each Receipt This Period
	Occupation		
Receipt For: ☐ Primary ☐ General ☐ Other (specify):	Aggregate Year-to-Date—$		
G. Full Name, Mailing Address and ZIP Code	Name of Employer	Date (month, day, year)	Amount of Each Receipt This Period
	Occupation		
Receipt For: ☐ Primary ☐ General ☐ Other (specify):	Aggregate Year-to-Date—$		

SUBTOTAL of Receipts This Page (optional) . . . .

TOTAL This Period (last page this line number only) . . . .

SCHEDULE A

ITEMIZED RECEIPTS

Page _____ of _____ for
LINE NUMBER _____
(Use separate schedule(s) for each
category of the Detailed
Summary Page)

Any information copied from such Reports or Statements may not be sold or used by any person for the purpose of soliciting contributions or for commercial purposes, other than using the name and address of any political committee to solicit contributions from such committee.

Name of Committee (in Full)

A. Full Name, Mailing Address and ZIP Code	Name of Employer	Date (month, day, year)	Amount of Each Receipt this Period
	Occupation		
Receipt For: ☐ Primary ☐ General ☐ Other (specify):	Aggregate Year-to-Date—$		

B. Full Name, Mailing Address and ZIP Code	Name of Employer	Date (month, day, year)	Amount of Each Receipt This Period
	Occupation		
Receipt For: ☐ Primary ☐ General ☐ Other (specify):	Aggregate Year-to-Date—$		

C. Full Name, Mailing Address and ZIP Code	Name of Employer	Date (month, day, year)	Amount of Each Receipt This Period
	Occupation		
Receipt For: ☐ Primary ☐ General ☐ Other (specify):	Aggregate Year-to-Date—$		

D. Full Name, Mailing Address and ZIP Code	Name of Employer	Date (month, day, year)	Amount of Each Receipt This Period
	Occupation		
Receipt For: ☐ Primary ☐ General ☐ Other (specify):	Aggregate Year-to-Date—$		

E. Full Name, Mailing Address and ZIP Code	Name of Employer	Date (month, day, year)	Amount of Each Receipt This Period
	Occupation		
Receipt For: ☐ Primary ☐ General ☐ Other (specify):	Aggregate Year-to-Date—$		

F. Full Name, Mailing Address and ZIP Code	Name of Employer	Date (month, day, year)	Amount of Each Receipt This Period
	Occupation		
Receipt For: ☐ Primary ☐ General ☐ Other (specify):	Aggregate Year-to-Date—$		

G. Full Name, Mailing Address and ZIP Code	Name of Employer	Date (month, day, year)	Amount of Each Receipt This Period
	Occupation		
Receipt For: ☐ Primary ☐ General ☐ Other (specify):	Aggregate Year-to-Date—$		

SUBTOTAL of Receipts This Page (optional) . . . .

TOTAL This Period (last page this line number only) . . . .

Page ____ of ____ for
LINE NUMBER ____
(Use separate schedule(s) for each
category of the Detailed
Summary Page)

SCHEDULE B   **ITEMIZED DISBURSEMENTS**

Any information copied from such Reports and Statements may not be sold or used by any person for the purpose of soliciting contributions or for commercial purposes, other than using the name and address of any political committee to solicit contributions from such committee.

Name of Committee (in Full)

A. Full Name, Mailing Address and ZIP Code	Purpose of Disbursement	Date (month, day, year)	Amount of Each Disbursement This Period
	Disbursement for: ☐ Primary ☐ General ☐ Other (specify):		
B. Full Name, Mailing Address and ZIP Code	Purpose of Disbursement	Date (month, day, year)	Amount of Each Disbursement This Period
	Disbursement for: ☐ Primary ☐ General ☐ Other (specify):		
C. Full Name, Mailing Address and ZIP Code	Purpose of Disbursement	Date (month, day, year)	Amount of Each Disbursement This Period
	Disbursement for: ☐ Primary ☐ General ☐ Other (specify):		
D. Full Name, Mailing Address and ZIP Code	Purpose of Disbursement	Date (month, day, year)	Amount of Each Disbursement This Period
	Disbursement for: ☐ Primary ☐ General ☐ Other (specify):		
E. Full Name, Mailing Address and ZIP Code	Purpose of Disbursement	Date (month, day, year)	Amount of Each Disbursement This Period
	Disbursement for: ☐ Primary ☐ General ☐ Other (specify):		
F. Full Name, Mailing Address and ZIP Code	Purpose of Disbursement	Date (month, day, year)	Amount of Each Disbursement This Period
	Disbursement for: ☐ Primary ☐ General ☐ Other (specify):		
G. Full Name, Mailing Address and ZIP Code	Purpose of Disbursement	Date (month, day, year)	Amount of Each Disbursement This Period
	Disbursement for: ☐ Primary ☐ General ☐ Other (specify):		
H. Full Name, Mailing Address and ZIP Code	Purpose of Disbursement	Date (month, day, year)	Amount of Each Disbursement This Period
	Disbursement for: ☐ Primary ☐ General ☐ Other (specify):		
I. Full Name, Mailing Address and ZIP Code	Purpose of Disbursement	Date (month, day, year)	Amount of Each Disbursement This Period
	Disbursement for: ☐ Primary ☐ General ☐ Other (specify):		

SUBTOTAL of Disbursements This Page (optional) . . . .

TOTAL This Period (last page this line number only) . . . .

Page _____ of _____ for
LINE NUMBER _____
(Use separate schedule(s) for each
category of the Detailed
Summary Page)

SCHEDULE B   **ITEMIZED DISBURSEMENTS**

Any information copied from such Reports and Statements may not be sold or used by any person for the purpose of soliciting contributions or for commercial purposes, other than using the name and address of any political committee to solicit contributions from such committee.

Name of Committee (in Full)

A. Full Name, Mailing Address and ZIP Code	Purpose of Disbursement	Date (month, day, year)	Amount of Each Disbursement This Period
	Disbursement for: ☐ Primary ☐ General ☐ Other (specify):		
B. Full Name, Mailing Address and ZIP Code	Purpose of Disbursement	Date (month, day, year)	Amount of Each Disbursement This Period
	Disbursement for: ☐ Primary ☐ General ☐ Other (specify):		
C. Full Name, Mailing Address and ZIP Code	Purpose of Disbursement	Date (month, day, year)	Amount of Each Disbursement This Period
	Disbursement for: ☐ Primary ☐ General ☐ Other (specify):		
D. Full Name, Mailing Address and ZIP Code	Purpose of Disbursement	Date (month, day, year)	Amount of Each Disbursement This Period
	Disbursement for: ☐ Primary ☐ General ☐ Other (specify):		
E. Full Name, Mailing Address and ZIP Code	Purpose of Disbursement	Date (month, day, year)	Amount of Each Disbursement This Period
	Disbursement for: ☐ Primary ☐ General ☐ Other (specify):		
F. Full Name, Mailing Address and ZIP Code	Purpose of Disbursement	Date (month, day, year)	Amount of Each Disbursement This Period
	Disbursement for: ☐ Primary ☐ General ☐ Other (specify):		
G. Full Name, Mailing Address and ZIP Code	Purpose of Disbursement	Date (month, day, year)	Amount of Each Disbursement This Period
	Disbursement for: ☐ Primary ☐ General ☐ Other (specify):		
H. Full Name, Mailing Address and ZIP Code	Purpose of Disbursement	Date (month, day, year)	Amount of Each Disbursement This Period
	Disbursement for: ☐ Primary ☐ General ☐ Other (specify):		
I. Full Name, Mailing Address and ZIP Code	Purpose of Disbursement	Date (month, day, year)	Amount of Each Disbursement This Period
	Disbursement for: ☐ Primary ☐ General ☐ Other (specify):		

SUBTOTAL of Disbursements This Page (optional) . . . .

TOTAL This Period (last page this line number only) . . . .

SCHEDULE B   ITEMIZED DISBURSEMENTS

Page _____ of _____ for
LINE NUMBER _____
(Use separate schedule(s) for each
category of the Detailed
Summary Page)

Any information copied from such Reports and Statements may not be sold or used by any person for the purpose of soliciting contributions or for commercial purposes, other than using the name and address of any political committee to solicit contributions from such committee.

Name of Committee (in Full)

A. Full Name, Mailing Address and ZIP Code	Purpose of Disbursement	Date (month, day, year)	Amount of Each Disbursement This Period
	Disbursement for: ☐ Primary ☐ General ☐ Other (specify):		
B. Full Name, Mailing Address and ZIP Code	Purpose of Disbursement	Date (month, day, year)	Amount of Each Disbursement This Period
	Disbursement for: ☐ Primary ☐ General ☐ Other (specify):		
C. Full Name, Mailing Address and ZIP Code	Purpose of Disbursement	Date (month, day, year)	Amount of Each Disbursement This Period
	Disbursement for: ☐ Primary ☐ General ☐ Other (specify):		
D. Full Name, Mailing Address and ZIP Code	Purpose of Disbursement	Date (month, day, year)	Amount of Each Disbursement This Period
	Disbursement for: ☐ Primary ☐ General ☐ Other (specify):		
E. Full Name, Mailing Address and ZIP Code	Purpose of Disbursement	Date (month, day, year)	Amount of Each Disbursement This Period
	Disbursement for: ☐ Primary ☐ General ☐ Other (specify):		
F. Full Name, Mailing Address and ZIP Code	Purpose of Disbursement	Date (month, day, year)	Amount of Each Disbursement This Period
	Disbursement for: ☐ Primary ☐ General ☐ Other (specify):		
G. Full Name, Mailing Address and ZIP Code	Purpose of Disbursement	Date (month, day, year)	Amount of Each Disbursement This Period
	Disbursement for: ☐ Primary ☐ General ☐ Other (specify):		
H. Full Name, Mailing Address and ZIP Code	Purpose of Disbursement	Date (month, day, year)	Amount of Each Disbursement This Period
	Disbursement for: ☐ Primary ☐ General ☐ Other (specify):		
I. Full Name, Mailing Address and ZIP Code	Purpose of Disbursement	Date (month, day, year)	Amount of Each Disbursement This Period
	Disbursement for: ☐ Primary ☐ General ☐ Other (specify):		

SUBTOTAL of Disbursements This Page (optional) . . . .

TOTAL This Period (last page this line number only) . . . .

ITEMIZED DISBURSEMENTS

Page _____ of _____ for
LINE NUMBER _____
(Use separate schedule(s) for each
category of the Detailed
Summary Page)

Name of Committee (in Full)

A. Full Name, Mailing Address and ZIP Code	Purpose of Disbursement	Date (month, day, year)	Amount of Each Disbursement This Period
	Disbursement for: ☐ Primary ☐ General ☐ Other (specify):		
B. Full Name, Mailing Address and ZIP Code	Purpose of Disbursement	Date (month, day, year)	Amount of Each Disbursement This Period
	Disbursement for: ☐ Primary ☐ General ☐ Other (specify):		
C. Full Name, Mailing Address and ZIP Code	Purpose of Disbursement	Date (month, day, year)	Amount of Each Disbursement This Period
	Disbursement for: ☐ Primary ☐ General ☐ Other (specify):		
D. Full Name, Mailing Address and ZIP Code	Purpose of Disbursement	Date (month, day, year)	Amount of Each Disbursement This Period
	Disbursement for: ☐ Primary ☐ General ☐ Other (specify):		
E. Full Name, Mailing Address and ZIP Code	Purpose of Disbursement	Date (month, day, year)	Amount of Each Disbursement This Period
	Disbursement for: ☐ Primary ☐ General ☐ Other (specify):		
F. Full Name, Mailing Address and ZIP Code	Purpose of Disbursement	Date (month, day, year)	Amount of Each Disbursement This Period
	Disbursement for: ☐ Primary ☐ General ☐ Other (specify):		
G. Full Name, Mailing Address and ZIP Code	Purpose of Disbursement	Date (month, day, year)	Amount of Each Disbursement This Period
	Disbursement for: ☐ Primary ☐ General ☐ Other (specify):		
H. Full Name, Mailing Address and ZIP Code	Purpose of Disbursement	Date (month, day, year)	Amount of Each Disbursement This Period
	Disbursement for: ☐ Primary ☐ General ☐ Other (specify):		
I. Full Name, Mailing Address and ZIP Code	Purpose of Disbursement	Date (month, day, year)	Amount of Each Disbursement This Period
	Disbursement for: ☐ Primary ☐ General ☐ Other (specify):		

SUBTOTAL of Disbursements This Page (optional) . . . .

TOTAL This Period (last page this line number only) . . . .

SCHEDULE C
(Revised 3/80)

Page ____ of ____ for
LINE NUMBER ____
(Use separate schedules
for each numbered line)

LOANS

Name of Committee (in Full)			

A. Full Name, Mailing Address and ZIP Code of Loan Source	Original Amount of Loan	Cumulative Payment To Date	Balance Outstanding at Close of This Period
Election: ☐ Primary ☐ General ☐ Other (specify):			

Terms: Date Incurred _____   Date Due _____   Interest Rate _____%(apr)   ☐ Secured

List All Endorsers or Guarantors (if any) to Item A

1. Full Name, Mailing Address and ZIP Code	Name of Employer
	Occupation
	Amount Guaranteed Outstanding: $
2. Full Name, Mailing Address and ZIP Code	Name of Employer
	Occupation
	Amount Guaranteed Outstanding: $
3. Full Name, Mailing Address and ZIP Code	Name of Employer
	Occupation
	Amount Guaranteed Outstanding: $

B. Full Name, Mailing Address and ZIP Code of Loan Source	Original Amount of Loan	Cumulative Payment To Date	Balance Outstanding at Close of This Period
Election: ☐ Primary ☐ General ☐ Other (specify):			

Terms: Date Incurred_____   Date Due _____   Interest Rate _____%(apr)   ☐ Secured

List All Endorsers or Guarantors (if any) to Item B

1. Full Name, Mailing Address and ZIP Code	Name of Employer
	Occupation
	Amount Guaranteed Outstanding: $
2. Full Name, Mailing Address and ZIP Code	Name of Employer
	Occupation
	Amount Guaranteed Outstanding: $
3. Full Name, Mailing Address and ZIP Code	Name of Employer
	Occupation
	Amount Guaranteed Outstanding: $

SUBTOTALS This Period This Page (optional) . . . .

TOTALS This Period (last page in this line only) . . . .

Carry outstanding balance only to LINE 3, Schedule D, for this line. If no Schedule D, carry forward to appropriate line of Summary.

SCHEDULE C
(Revised 3/80)

LOANS

Page _____ of _____ for
LINE NUMBER _____
(Use separate schedules
for each numbered line)

Name of Committee (in Full)

A. Full Name, Mailing Address and ZIP Code of Loan Source		Original Amount of Loan	Cumulative Payment To Date	Balance Outstanding at Close of This Period
Election: ☐ Primary ☐ General ☐ Other (specify):				
Terms: Date Incurred _____ Date Due _____ Interest Rate _____ %(apr)			☐ Secured	
List All Endorsers or Guarantors (if any) to Item A				
1. Full Name, Mailing Address and ZIP Code	Name of Employer			
	Occupation			
	Amount Guaranteed Outstanding: $			
2. Full Name, Mailing Address and ZIP Code	Name of Employer			
	Occupation			
	Amount Guaranteed Outstanding: $			
3. Full Name, Mailing Address and ZIP Code	Name of Employer			
	Occupation			
	Amount Guaranteed Outstanding: $			
B. Full Name, Mailing Address and ZIP Code of Loan Source		Original Amount of Loan	Cumulative Payment To Date	Balance Outstanding at Close of This Period
Election: ☐ Primary ☐ General ☐ Other (specify):				
Terms: Date Incurred _____ Date Due _____ Interest Rate _____ %(apr)			☐ Secured	
List All Endorsers or Guarantors (if any) to Item B				
1. Full Name, Mailing Address and ZIP Code	Name of Employer			
	Occupation			
	Amount Guaranteed Outstanding: $			
2. Full Name, Mailing Address and ZIP Code	Name of Employer			
	Occupation			
	Amount Guaranteed Outstanding: $			
3. Full Name, Mailing Address and ZIP Code	Name of Employer			
	Occupation			
	Amount Guaranteed Outstanding: $			

SUBTOTALS This Period This Page (optional) . . . .

TOTALS This Period (last page in this line only) . . . .

Carry outstanding balance only to LINE 3, Schedule D, for this line. If no Schedule D, carry forward to appropriate line of Summary.

Page _____ of _____ for
LINE NUMBER _____
(Use separate schedules
for each numbered line)

SCHEDULE D
(Revised 3/80)

DEBTS AND OBLIGATIONS
Excluding Loans

Name of Committee (in Full)	Outstanding Balance Beginning This Period	Amount Incurred This Period	Payment This Period	Outstanding Balance at Close of This Period
A. Full Name, Mailing Address and Zip Code of Debtor or Creditor				
Nature of Debt (Purpose):				
B. Full Name, Mailing Address and Zip Code of Debtor or Creditor				
Nature of Debt (Purpose):				
C. Full Name, Mailing Address and Zip Code of Debtor or Creditor				
Nature of Debt (Purpose):				
D. Full Name, Mailing Address and Zip Code of Debtor or Creditor				
Nature of Debt (Purpose):				
E. Full Name, Mailing Address and Zip Code of Debtor or Creditor				
Nature of Debt (Purpose):				
F. Full Name, Mailing Address and Zip Code of Debtor or Creditor				
Nature of Debt (Purpose):				

1) SUBTOTALS This Period This Page (optional) . . . .

2) TOTAL This Period (last page this line only) . . . .

3) TOTAL OUTSTANDING LOANS from Schedule C (last page only) . . . .

4) ADD 2) and 3) and carry forward to appropriate line of Summary Page (last page only) . . . .

Page _____ of _____ for
LINE NUMBER _____
(Use separate schedules
for each numbered line)

SCHEDULE D
(Revised 3/80)

DEBTS AND OBLIGATIONS
Excluding Loans

Name of Committee (in Full)	Outstanding Balance Beginning This Period	Amount Incurred This Period	Payment This Period	Outstanding Balance at Close of This Period
A. Full Name, Mailing Address and Zip Code of Debtor or Creditor				
Nature of Debt (Purpose):				
B. Full Name, Mailing Address and Zip Code of Debtor or Creditor				
Nature of Debt (Purpose):				
C. Full Name, Mailing Address and Zip Code of Debtor or Creditor				
Nature of Debt (Purpose):				
D. Full Name, Mailing Address and Zip Code of Debtor or Creditor				
Nature of Debt (Purpose):				
E. Full Name, Mailing Address and Zip Code of Debtor or Creditor				
Nature of Debt (Purpose):				
F. Full Name, Mailing Address and Zip Code of Debtor or Creditor				
Nature of Debt (Purpose):				

1) SUBTOTALS This Period This Page (optional) . . . .

2) TOTAL This Period (last page this line only) . . . .

3) TOTAL OUTSTANDING LOANS from Schedule C (last page only). . . . .

4) ADD 2) and 3) and carry forward to appropriate line of Summary Page (last page only) . . . .

SCHEDULE E

ITEMIZED INDEPENDENT EXPENDITURES

(See Reverse Side for Instructions)

Name of Committee (in Full)				I.D. No.

Full Name, Mailing Address & ZIP Code of Each Payee	Purpose of Expenditure	Date (month, day, year)	Amount	Name of Federal Candidate supported or opposed by the expenditure & office sought
				☐ Support ☐ Oppose
				☐ Support ☐ Oppose
				☐ Support ☐ Oppose
				☐ Support ☐ Oppose
				☐ Support ☐ Oppose
				☐ Support ☐ Oppose

(a) **SUBTOTAL** of Itemized Independent Expenditures . . . . $ _____

(b) **SUBTOTAL** of Unitemized Independent Expenditures . . . . $ _____

(c) **TOTAL** Independent Expenditures . . . . $ _____

Under penalty of perjury I certify that the independent expenditures reported herein were not made in cooperation, consultation, concert with, or at the request or suggestion of any candidate or any authorized committee or agent of such candidate or authorized committee. Furthermore, these expenditures did not involve the financing of dissemination, distribution, or republication in whole or in part of any campaign materials prepared by the candidate, his campaign committee, or their agent.

_____   _____
        Signature   Date

Subscribed and sworn to before me this _____ day of

_____, 19_____

My Commission expires

_____

_____   NOTARY PUBLIC

SCHEDULE F

ITEMIZED COORDINATED EXPENDITURES MADE BY POLITICAL PARTY COMMITTEES OR DESIGNATED AGENT(S) ON BEHALF OF CANDIDATES FOR FEDERAL OFFICE (2 U.S.C. §441a(d))

Page ____ of ____ for
LINE NUMBER ____

(To be used only by Political Committees in the General Election)

Name of Political Committee (in Full)				

Has your Committee been designated to make coordinated expenditures by a political party committee? ☐ YES   ☐ NO
If YES, name the designating committee:

Full Name, Mailing Address and ZIP Code of Subordinate Committee

Full Name, Mailing Address and ZIP Code of Each Payee	Name of Federal Candidate Supported, State, District & Office Sought	Purpose of Expenditure	Date (month, day, year)	Amount
	Aggregate General Election Expenditure for this Candidate—$			
Full Name, Mailing Address and ZIP Code of Each Payee	Name of Federal Candidate Supported, State, District & Office Sought	Purpose of Expenditure	Date (month, day, year)	Amount
	Aggregate General Election Expenditure for this Candidate—$			
Full Name, Mailing Address and ZIP Code of Each Payee	Name of Federal Candidate Supported, State, District & Office Sought	Purpose of Expenditure	Date (month, day, year)	Amount
	Aggregate General Election Expenditure for this Candidate—$			
Full Name, Mailing Address and ZIP Code of Each Payee	Name of Federal Candidate Supported, State, District & Office Sought	Purpose of Expenditure	Date (month, day, year)	Amount
	Aggregate General Election Expenditure for this Candidate—$			

SUBTOTAL of Expenditures This Page (optional) . . . .

TOTAL This Period (last page this line number only) . . . .

political action report

Editor: Nathan J. Muller

Volume 3 Number 22 November 30, 1980

SPECIAL FEATURE: Of the four or five key conservative activists most responsible for the phenomenal success of the New Right in recent years, Morton C. Blackwell stands out for his tireless dedication to recruiting and training young people for participation in election campaigns and developing their leadership potential for sustained involvement in the conservative movement at the national, state and local levels. As former Chairman of the Committee for Responsible Youth Politics (CRYP), he has recruited and trained thousands of young men and women over the years, many of whom now hold responsible positions within the conservative movement. Described by Human Events *as the "eyes and ears" of the New Right, Blackwell edited* The New Right Report *before joining the staff of Sen. Gordon Humphrey (R-NH) last year as Policy Director. During the election season, he oversaw the 1980 Youth for Reagan effort and, since the election, has taken on the additional responsibility of Policy Coordinator for the Reagan transition team at the Federal Election Commission. Few people are more qualified than he to discuss youth involvement in politics. The editor of* Political Action Report *met recently with Morton Blackwell to discuss this and other aspects of the Reagan campaign. Excerpts from the discussion follow.*

MORTON C. BLACKWELL:
THE DRIVING FORCE BEHIND ORGANIZED CONSERVATISM

Q: You oversaw the youth effort on behalf of Ronald Reagan; but why bother organizing young people for political purposes when, as a group, they tend not to vote? What do young people have to contribute to politics and campaigning? Anything?

BLACKWELL: Young people do vote in lower numbers than the eligibles of any other age group. But young people often prove that they have a great deal to contribute to the electoral process. Many do vote. They draw their families and friends into the camp of their candidate. They help create a favorable public image for their candidate and help to create a win psychology for him. The advertising experts on Madison Avenue found out long ago that youth involvement sells products, perhaps because youth symbolizes energy and vitality.

It was particularly gratifying and useful for Reagan to clobber Carter and Anderson in campus mock elections in our target states.

Over the long haul, conservatives have a responsibility to encourage youth involvement in campaigns to help them develop their leadership potential. Through campaign work,

POLITICAL ACTION REPORT is a bi-weekly, nonpartisan newsletter providing current information on the political action and education activites of the private sector, including: business and industry, labor and employee organizations, trade and membership associations, political parties and the New Right. It provides concise, up-to-date information and useful reports on the political and educational programs and activities of political action committees at the state and national levels, and is concerned with the practical and concrete applications of political action techniques and methods for improving the responsiveness of government at all levels. Published by Tyke Research Associates, Inc., P. O. Box 2431, Springfield, Virginia 22152; 703/569-6851. All rights reserved. Reproduction in whole or in part without the permission of the publisher is prohibited.

continued from page 1

young people can see that our system does work, that there is a reasonable relationship between effort intelligently expended in a campaign and the election outcome.

Q: Young people today seem to have plenty of reason to organize for political action. After all, the rate of unemployment is highest among their age group. Those who do work are forced to pay into a Social Security program that will be bankrupt before they retire. They cannot afford homes because inflation has priced them out of the market. And, in the case of war, they will be the first to be called. Why then are today's young people largely inactive politically?

BLACKWELL: I have found in over 20 years experience in politics with young people that most students are always apathetic about politics. Voting is an acquired taste, like drinking beer or listening to grand opera. Nobody is born with the habit of voting; it has to be learned. But many young people will work in politics, given a good opportunity to participate. Whenever a candidate does decide to pay attention to young people and intelligently goes about organizing them, he finds it is a good investment of time and effort.

Q: With our public schools dominated by the liberal establishment it is no surprise that young people lean to the left politically. What can possibly convince them to work for a conservative like Ronald Reagan, let alone pitch in for causes the New Right espouses?

BLACKWELL: I think it's a myth that young people naturally lean toward the liberals. Left to their own devices, young people would be more inclined to cram themselves into telephone booths, swallow goldfish or go streaking. There is hardly any such thing as a spontaneous student political activity. Almost without exception it is organized by somebody with a specific purpose in mind.

The usual liberal or left wing campus environment is the result of the left paying more attention to young people, particularly in non-election years. When conservatives pay attention to organizing students for political action they beat the socks off of the liberals on campus, as we did this year.

Q: Every campaign begins with a set of basic assumptions about the opposition. What basic assumptions did the Reagan campaign have about Jimmy Carter?

BLACKWELL: The Reagan campaign began with the correct, basic assumption that Jimmy Carter was vulnerable on just about every issue — the economy, defense and the social issues. The polls showed the economic issues were paramount, so inflation and jobs were the campaign's major themes. That doesn't mean the other issues are less important to Ronald Reagan. But you should go hunting where the ducks are.

Q: What was the general strategy that guided the Reagan campaign for almost two years?

BLACKWELL: As I saw it, the generally followed Reagan strategy was, first, to keep his solid conservative base of support — one which must not be alienated. Second, to communicate key issues effectively to people who were not in that original base. And, third, to cooperate with party-building activities and with conservative groups that were allied to the Reagan campaign. For local Republican activists who lived through the arrogance of the 1972 Nixon presidential campaign, the 1980 Reagan campaign was like a breath of fresh air.

Q: One of the objectives of any organization is to early identify the weak points which may cause problems later on. What were some of the weak points of the Reagan campaign in its initial stages?

continued on page 6

continued from page 4

actually gains in terms of productivity. The Hewlett-Packard Company has made flextime available to its 50,000 employees since 1973. Aside from increasing productivity, flextime has improved morale, and decreased tardiness and sick leave. As a perquisite of membership, flextime also gives employees the flexibility they need in their daily schedules to take part in the political activities they are being encouraged to engage in!

- Shared Values. O. A. Ohmann, former Assistant to the President of Standard Oil of Ohio, made the astute observation that employees are sensitive to spiritual qualities. They want to work for someone who believes in something and in whom they can believe. "Bread alone will not satisfy workers," he said in 1955. "Man is searching for anchors outside himself. . . . and looking for new 'skyhooks' --for an abiding faith around which life's experiences can be integrated and given meaning." Being sensitive to this need, top management can provide employees with a new "skyhook" by encouraging their participation in a Political Resources Development program.

THE ROLE OF TOP MANAGEMENT

Top management not only has a responsibility to provide employees with outlets for personal growth, but a responsibility to humanize the workplace. In so doing, the company benefits from higher productivity, lower rates of absenteeism, and more efficient use of resources.

For that to happen, top management must initiate change and set the parameters for acceptable behavior. Some steps toward achieving this, include:

- Establishing a written code of ethics. No code of ethics by itself is going to transform an organization, but with the example set by senior executives it is an important step in establishing norms that shape attitudes toward the company as well as the political process. At the very least, a code of ethics legitimizes political activity and can be an effective tool for communicating and even encouraging political activity.

- Recognizing that employee political activities, especially in connection with a company-sponsored program, provokes the exercise of individual responsibility, which both motivates and builds confidence among employees.

- Appreciating the contribution of politically active employees toward an environment of honesty and fair play. The trust that emerges in such an environment promotes efficiency, which is necessary for increasing productivity and for improving the overall internal organizational climate.

- Shunning the short-term, opportunistic approach to corporate political involvement commands the respect of employees. A clear and consistent approach in matters of politics and public policy making builds employee commitment to the company, to the point where employees are proud to represent their company to external constituencies and defend it against misguided attacks from anti-business elements.

A sound program of Political Resources Development is a practical alternative to this or that theoretical approach to organizational development (OD) — one that can effect fundamental, value-oriented changes in employee attitudes towards work, the company and the free enterprise system. It's no panacea, but only a start in the right direction.

continued from page 2

BLACKWELL: In the early stages, before the New Hampshire primary, the weak points included overcentralization and taking Gov. Reagan's conservative base too much for granted. In the later stages, the former anti-Reaganites on the post-convention bandwagon had
a serious lack of confidence in Ronald Reagan's ability to hold his own in debate with
Jimmy Carter, a doubt not shared by me and which subsequently proved groundless. Actually, the Reagan campaign was reasonably well run, although it was more of a coalition than
a conventional, centralized campaign organization.

*Q: The media portrayed Ronald Reagan as one prone to contradict himself. In your opinion,
did Reagan demonstrate a lack of consistency on public policy matters?*

BLACKWELL: I think Ronald Reagan seriously believes in the principles he has been enunci-
ating for so many years and that he is in agreement with the principles of the Republican
Party platform on which he ran. To the extent that he is able to do so, I think he will
endeavor to implement those principles as effective public policy.

Every successful politician needs a little leeway on issues, but I think there is little
chance that President-elect Reagan will repeat the Carter shift. Carter ran against the
Washington establishment and then packed his administration with McGovernites.

*Q: Reagan appeared to have delegated much of the details and operational plans to his
managers during the campaign, while concerning himself only with strategic matters. Is
this style of leadership likely to manifest itself in the Oval Office? When it comes
to formulating and implementing public policy objectives, isn't it a mistake to delegate
too much authority?*

BLACKWELL: It is a mistake to delegate too much authority, but I don't think it has
been demonstrated that President-elect Reagan did delegate too much authority. I think
Jimmy Carter would have been a much more successful president if he had surrounded himself with reliable and trustworthy people in whom he had confidence and in whom he could
delegate responsibility. But Carter went so far as personally to schedule the use of the
White House tennis courts.

The delegation of authority is absolutely essential in any executive position and im-
mensely important in the office of President of the United States. The questions are:
To whom does the President delegate authority? And how much does he delegate? Right now
we know relatively few of the people who will be running the new administration, so it
would be premature to make a judgment. But it is my guess that the Reagan administration
will be politically successful. The more the people see of him, the more they will have
confidence in him.

*Q: From your vantage point, did anyone in the Reagan organization have a clear vision
of where the campaign was going, or would it be more accurate to say that Reagan won by
default?*

BLACKWELL: Having planned and overseen the Reagan youth effort, I had a perspective of
the inner workings of the campaign that others did not have. The Reagan campaign was
unlike a normal race for the U.S. House or Senate. In most campaigns there is a campaign
manager who gives orders to everybody else; a highly centralized operation. But in the
Reagan campaign the usual situation of a general issuing orders to colonels who passed
them to majors who gave them to captains did not exist.

In many ways the Reagan campaign was more a coalition rather than an organization. It
was an alliance of "barons" who were working toward the goal of unseating the incumbent.
These barons didn't consider themselves particularly under the orders of one another,
but considered themselves to be in large measure equal to one another. The result was a

continued on page 7

continued from page 6

dispersion of power in the campaign. All being intelligent men and women, they knew they couldn't order each other around. Each felt that he should have a strong say in planning, and some thought they should have veto power over decisions made in the campaign. Under these circumstances, it was often difficult to arrive at a decision. But when it was necessary to make a decision on a matter of real urgency, they were able to pull together. As it turned out, this method of operation worked much better than President Carter's.

Q: To what extent was Reagan able to influence the direction of his own campaign? Or was he largely carried away by unfolding events?

BLACKWELL: Ronald Reagan was the single best asset of the campaign. He clearly came across to the public as a dedicated, sincere, decent and principled person. He was prepared to say what he believed, but was able to state his beliefs in such a way as to communicate effectively with people. The more they heard him, the more comfortable they were with him.

The decisions he made in the campaign, such as whether or not to debate, were influenced by his advisors. As is usual in campaigns, he was often confronted with conflicting advice. But far more often than not, he took the right advice, and his responses to real political situations ought to be reflected in a successful administration.

Q: Jimmy Carter was widely credited with being a very shrewd politician. How, then, could he have so underestimated Ronald Reagan — to the point of portraying him as a racist?

BLACKWELL: I never subscribed to the theory that Jimmy Carter was a shrewd individual. He won the 1976 nomination with a lot of hard work and in the absence of high-quality opposition. But the obvious failures of his administration in almost every policy area successfully undermine any thought that he is a particularly shrewd politician.

As to why he began to attack Gov. Reagan, calling him a racist and a warmonger, I think that's quite consistent with the strategy he adopted in his campaigns for Governor of Georgia. He had a streak of meanness in him, which he showed against President Ford in 1976 and against Sen. Kennedy in this year's primaries. President Carter found out, to his sorrow, that a campaign based on meanness and distortion doesn't work very well against Ronald Reagan.

Q: Did the New Right exert any influence at all either over the strategy or the direction of the Reagan campaign?

BLACKWELL: Input yes, control no. The vast majority of the conservative movement supported the Reagan campaign and, toward the end of it, support was virtually unanimous, although some supported Reagan at arm's length.

One of the important things to realize about the Reagan campaign is that the managers themselves were very sensitive to the conservative movement's priorities. The campaign seldom ventured in directions that were going to be upsetting to the original base of Ronald Reagan's support.

Even the late boarders on the Reagan bandwagon did not push very hard, certainly not successfully, to get the campaign to move away from the conservative position on many issues. For the most part, the campaign stuck to those issues which were the priorities of the 1980 platform and the long-held views of Ronald Reagan himself.

Q: Since Reagan won by a landslide margin, can movement conservatives take much credit for his victory? Has the New Right demonstrated, at least to Reagan's satisfaction, that

continued on page 8

continued from page 7

movement conservatives should be given the opportunity to influence and shape public policy?

BLACKWELL: Let's talk first about the makeup and the extent of that lanslide. This lanslide was very different from the 1972 Nixon landslide. Nixon ran far ahead of the Republican ticket almost everywhere, in large measure because the White House hogged all of the political and financial resources that could be grabbed.

Reagan's victory was a victory of a different sort. Most Reagan leaders held to a determination to run a unified campaign and to maintain at all times the support of both the Republican groups and the conservative movement. As a result, Senator-elect Jeremiah Denton did better in Alabama than President-elect Reagan. Similarly, Senator-elect Bob Kasten in Wisconsin ran ahead of the Reagan campaign. In Georgia, Senator-elect Matt Mattingly carried the state in the face of a Carter victory. This happened in House races as well. In Texas, Jack Fields won over Rep. Bob Eckardt and ran ahead of Ronald Reagan.

Our House and Senate victories, and in some cases, state and local victories, were due to the same factors that were working in the presidential campaign.

What has altered the political structure of the U.S. is the successful building over the last several years of an enormous number of conservative organizations. These groups have added incrementally to the pool of political activists. Taken together, there were enough new activists to affect dramatically the course of many elections. The rising conservative tide lifted all ships.

Unless there is some disaster in the conduct of the Reagan administration, which I certainly do not anticipate, we will see a continuation of this growth before the 1982 elections. Most of these groups have concentrated on developing technological expertise, building up resources, training activists and communicating with their contributors. Now they have a large number of liberal scalps tacked on their barn doors, and they will be eager to get more scalps in 1982. When they go back to their contributors and ask for their assistance, they will make good use of their proven track record to attract more support.

Q: But the question is, what impact will this have on the Reagan administration? Will the Reagan administration recognize these forces?

BLACKWELL: I think they will because these forces are not going to be silent. In 1969, when the Nixon administration came in, there were no independent sources of political power within the Republican Party or within the conservative movement who dared to challenge him. The result was that the Nixon White House was able to gather unto itself virtually unchallenged authority. It was unthinkable for years for anybody in the Republican Party or the conservative movement to speak out against Nixon. As a result of that experience, blind loyalty to the center of power has been rather thoroughly discredited. Loyalty to principle is more acceptable now than in the Nixon years.

Today conservative groups exist independently of each other and independent of the White House as well as of the Republican Party. Many of the newly elected conservative senators and congressmen, as well as those elected in previous years, are not going to stand idly by when they see things moving in a direction that is contrary to what they think is in the best interest of the country. So I think the Reagan administration will frequently be made very much aware of the conservative viewpoint. Conservatives will be out there, feeling with justification that they are largely responsible for this victory. They are in many ways responsible for the 1980 victories across the board. Do you think they are likely to sit back quietly and watch things drift left?

continued on page 9

continued from page 8

Q: Is there the danger that the nation is expecting too much from President-elect Reagan? Haven't our great expectations far outstripped practical realities?

BLACKWELL: I don't think so. There are, I think, three main expectations that most people have of the Reagan administration. First, they believe that the government cannot continue heaping burdens on the people that have the effect of increasing inflation and unemployment. They expect President Ronald Reagan to eliminate policies that are hindering growth and productivity. Second, they believe that U.S. wishful thinking does not impress the Soviets or have a healthy impact on our defense of foreign policy. They expect Reagan to be more realistic in his assessment of the problems confronting the United States internationally and that he will take corrective action. Third, they expect Reagan to take action in the conservative direction on a whole range of social issues. In all these regards, I have no doubt that Reagan will make a good faith effort.

However, there are still too many Democrats in the House and Senate. Republicans have often managed to prevent the passage of harmful legislation by taking advantage of such tactics as the filibuster. My guess is that we will see the Senate's liberal minority take up the use of such tactics. But if the Reagan administration is run effectively, Reagan must communicate this situation to the American people and explain how implementation of his policies is being obstructed. Thus he can help strengthen his majority position. I think he is better qualified than any other politician to take his case to the people, so much so, that contrary to past mid-term elections, we may see substantial further gains for the GOP and for conservatives in general in 1982.

Q: Finally, if Reagan fails for whatever reason to revitalize the economy, will conservatives have to carry the burden of spawning a whole new generation of non-voting cynics?

BLACKWELL: It is true that voting appears to have declined over the years, but I do not think that is the result of a declining economy. The two don't seem to show any direct relationship. Enfranchisement of 18 year olds has lowered the percentage of eligibles voting.

Non-participation in general has largely been the result of the failure of the parties to serve as vehicles by which public policy can be changed.

One problem with our Republican Party is that it has tended to operate on the lowest common denominator basis. That is, party organizations have tried to do nothing that would offend either Sen. Jacob Javits or Sen. Jesse Helms. Operating under these constraints, it is very difficult to do forceful and dynamic things in the area of public policy. Given this situation, it is not difficult to understand why so many people conclude that it doesn't matter whether or not they participate in politics.

If the people think parties stand for nothing, if they cannot discern the differences between parties, then many will decide it is useless to go out and vote.

If the new administration is largely staffed by people who enthusiastically want to implement the policies and platform Ronald Reagan was elected on, then it can be a success politically. It will go a long way toward restoring people's confidence in the system. They voted for change. If they do indeed get change, they will perceive that the system works. But if they don't get change, we are likely to see a continued drop off of political participation.

It is going to be up to the conservative leadership to keep the spotlight on the Congress as well as on the Reagan administration.

FYI: Due to the holiday mail rush, the December issues of Political Action Report may arrive late. We're sorry for the inconvenience, but will strive to be on time again by January 15.

political action report

Editor: Nathan J. Muller

Volume 4   Number 1   January 15, 1981

SPECIAL FEATURE: Practically every one of the business-oriented, conservative can-
didates who ran for Congress in 1980 did so with massive support from the business
community. But identifying and recruiting suitable candidates was still not pursued
systematically, as it was with some of the New Right organizations. One of the busi-
ness groups moving toward a well-defined program of candidate recruitment is the
political arm of the U.S. Chamber of Commerce — the National Chamber Alliance for
Politics. NCAP is already hard at work perfecting its communications link with its
business constituency as well as getting feedback from members regarding potential
candidates for the 1982 congressional elections. For NCAP there is no "off election"
year. Although the November elections could be construed as a major victory for busi-
ness, the battle to restore the free market economy is far from over, says John A.
Kochevar, executive director of NCAP. The editor of Political Action Report *met re-*
cently with Mr. Kochevar to discuss business political strategy and tactics, to as-
sess business' political strength in the wake of the November elections and to find
out how the success or failure of the new administration will impact on the public's
perception of businessmen in general. Excerpts from the discussion follow.

ALSO IN THIS ISSUE	Number of PACs Increased By 500 Over Last Year. Reading & Reference: New Books, Articles, Studies.

JOHN A. KOCHEVAR:
WORKING TO BUILD BUSINESS' POLITICAL MUSCLE

Q: With the general election behind us, what should business PACs be doing now to
prepare for 1982?

KOCHEVAR: Most business PACs will be trying to raise more money. What I would like
to see them do is start working on being more sophisticated in their approach to the
political process. They should, for example, start making plans now to engage in independent expenditures and start doing more in terms of internal communications, which
we still haven't seen a great deal of from the business community.

Q: What kind of activities will NCAP engage in during this off election year, and what
will be the highest priority?

KOCHEVAR: We've already begun to look at the races that we think are going to be opportunities for the business community in 1982. Of course, we will be honing our skills
and be trying to increase our own level of political sophistication. The more success-

continued on page 2

POLITICAL ACTION REPORT is a bi-weekly, nonpartisan newsletter providing current information on the political action and educa-
tion activites of the private sector, including: business and industry, labor and employee organizations, trade and membership associa-
tions, political parties and the New Right. It provides concise, up-to-date information and useful reports on the political and education-
al programs and activities of political action committees at the state and national levels, and is concerned with the practical and con-
crete applications of political action techniques and methods for improving the responsiveness of government at all levels. Published by
Tyke Research Associates, Inc., P. O. Box 2431, Springfield, Virginia 22152; 703/569-6851. All rights reserved. Reproduction in whole
or in part without the permission of the publisher is prohibited.

continued from page 1

ful we become, the more critical the determination of who we select for support or defeat. We will endeavor to refine our communications devices so that we can better help
our business constituents make their decisions.

*Q: Now that there is a Republican administration and a Republican-controlled Senate,
is there any danger of the business community becoming too complacent in the belief
that they have won and there's not much else to do? Or, will the election results
stimulate further political activity on the part of business?*

KOCHEVAR: You raise an interesting question; the vote is still out on that. It fright-
ens me to think that people would believe the battle is over. The Democrats in the Senate had a 58 to 41 margin and they lost it. If the Republicans think they've got the
Senate sewed up for the next four years, they're sorely mistaken. If business thinks
they have won the entire battle because they helped win a slim majority in one house,
they are short-sighted. But I frankly don't see that attitude. If the inquiries to my
office are any indication, there seems to be a very large movement of businessmen who
are just now getting started in the political process. There really seems to be a movement toward more activity, rather than a drift away from it. I'm getting a lot of calls
from people who want to know how to get started.

*Q: But if companies have not yet established employee PACs or instituted programs of
political education, what incentive do they have now to do it?*

KOCHEVAR: They now see that some of their peers around the country have scored major
successes in the political process. The 1980 elections proved beyond a doubt that
business can participate in election campaigns very responsibly and resourcefully.
What we're seeing is a lot of people who previously shied away from political activity or who had other priorities showing a great deal of interest in playing this game.

*Q: Looking at the performance of business PACs in November, can you identify areas of
activity that could stand improvement?*

KOCHEVAR: I think the criteria that business uses for selecting candidates for contributions constantly needs to be reassessed. There is still not enough sophistication in
that whole process. Business has to be more hard-headed and much more strict in the
application of whatever criteria they might have. Beyond that, I would say that things
other political action committees are doing have almost been ignored by business so
far. Business PACs can be so much more effective with in-kind contributions and independent expenditures. We can still learn a lot from our labor friends and from the in-
novations made last year by some of the New Right groups.

*Q: Speaking of labor, the AFL-CIO announced recently plans to form a PAC modeled after
the National Conservative Political Action Committee — one that would act independently of candidates and chip away at the image of targeted incumbents. Why haven't business PACs been as aggressive in election campaigns as some of the New Right groups?
Do they find something inherently repugnant about that kind of activity?*

KOCHEVAR: Business PACs for some reason have really not been in the vanguard of political action; they have not labored to do remarkable and startling new things. The conservative movement has, and have brought down some of the incumbents they have worked
to defeat. But the business community I don't even think ever thought of doing that.
Business is still learning how to play in this game. Of course, they have imposed some
restrictions on themselves which may be remnants of years past when slush funds were
the topic of scandal and federal investigation.

That labor is now setting up a political action committee similar to the ones the conservatives have, I find very interesting. Labor was highly critical of how some of the

continued on page 3

continued from page 2

New Right groups operated in the last election. Ironically, labor will legitimize the tactics they were so critical of when they were employed against their friends in Congress.

But, no, "repugnant" is probably too strong a word. Whether business would ever adopt such methods if they ever thought about it, is hard to say. That kind of activity on the part of business is at least five years away. Right now business is pretty much satisfied with giving money to candidates they want to see elected. That's a good and valuable role, but not necessarily the only one.

Q: More businessmen ran for public office in 1980 than in any previous election year, and many were successful. Does this signal a changed attitude toward government service on the part of businessmen?

KOCHEVAR: Not as much as I would like to see. For most people it is a hardship to seek public office. If you are a successful businessman, it is certainly a hardship to leave your home, family and successful career in the company you built from nothing for the sole purpose of campaigning. At the same time, these are just the kind of people we need more of in Congress. It takes a special kind of person to commit themselves to public life and, quite frankly, the incentives are just not there for most business people.

I'm gratified to see more business people run for office. It comes from the general feeling that what this country needs is more people with business expertise in positions of authority and who are involved in the decision making process. But whether this means that the attitudes of businessmen have changed toward public service I think is too soon to say.

Q: Public opinion, as reflected in the election returns, seems overwhelmingly on the side of business. How can the business community capitalize on rising public esteem and the changed political climate to win public policy victories?

KOCHEVAR: First of all, business in general and the Chamber in particular have been talking about inflation, the high cost of government and overregulation for a lot of years. Today, for the first time that I can remember, the goals and objectives politically as well as legislatively of business meshed with those of the general public. This was certainly a key element in the successful election of 1980 from a business perspective. What business does now is going to be critical in determining how long that trend goes on.

If in fact we try to solve all of the problems that have accumulated over the past 25 to 40 years in the next 6 to 18 months, or even the next four years, we're going to mess up and accentuate those problems, perhaps cause some very serious new problems. If that happens, then I think this benign mood of the public will rapidly dissipate if there is not a reasoned and cautious approach to solving the problems of this country.

Q: Are you saying, then, that esteem for business will rise or fall with Ronald Reagan's fortunes?

KOCHEVAR: To some extent. President Reagan has established certain goals and objectives and priorities which are more in alignment with business than with any other group in society. Whether or not the Reagan administration goes down the road hand-in-hand with business is one question; another question is the *perception* of the American public. I think most people have been led to believe by the media that business and the Reagan administration are one and the same. If the new administration doesn't solve some of the more pressing economic problems, particularly inflation and unemployment, then, yes, business will suffer for it along with the Reagan administration. Both will have been

continued on page 4

continued from page 3

considered non-effective.

Q: In your opinion, is the confidence the business community placed in Ronald Reagan before the election still justified on the basis of his cabinet choices? Or is there now cause for alarm?

KOCHEVAR: I don't believe there is cause for alarm. I tend to think that the business community's confidence is justified. There's a lot of discussion about the various appointments, but what concerns me is the lack of haste in which they were made. I would just as soon see an administration take some time to make the right choices rather than have to clean house after a year or two. But everything I have heard from our constituents indicates a great deal of satisfaction with the cabinet choices. Sure, everybody has their own preferences, but generally speaking there's a good deal of satisfaction.

Q: Aside from the Reagan victory and a GOP Senate, in this changed political climate what opportunities can the business community take advantage of to make public policy gains?

KOCHEVAR: I think the business community has to recognize and understand that now the goals and objectives of the American public and business generally are pretty much going in the same direction. Business ought to be spending some time and making a good effort to communicate with the public to make sure that mood keeps moving along. If in fact the American public regresses to the liberal mode as they were a few years back, business can say whatever it wants, but it won't achieve those political and legislative successes it so urgently needs. It's not only the legislative branch that business has to deal with, it's the people themselves. Business has to communicate and prove the real worth of private enterprise. More and more public policy decisions are going to be made by the American people themselves through the ballot box. They are coming to understand that whatever decisions they make affect them directly and will be in the best interests of the country.

Q: Some Reagan insiders have expressed concern that the conservatives' social agenda may tie up Congress and prevent immediate action on economic matters. Is this a legitimate concern?

KOCHEVAR: I think the new administration is smart enough to realize that there are massive, pressing economic problems in this country that have to be dealt with. Some elements of the conservatives' social agenda are fine and worth pursuing, but they are not going to be accomplished until we have a strong, solid economy. I think even the conservatives are going to recognize that.

Q: Finally, what role will NCAP play in stimulating business political awareness during this off election year?

KOCHEVAR: We don't really believe there is an off election year. We are already beginning to look at the races that business should be concerned about. We'd like to see business get involved more in the recruitment and selection of candidates, and that is the nature of our work in the off election year. We are already working with our business members in trying to identify people who we would like to see run in 1982. We will continue to do seminars to try to increase political awareness and interest in the electoral process. 1980 was only the beginning. There's a lot more business should and can do. We see ourselves as catalysts.

FYI: The Campaign Works Speakers Bureau has available a directory of political consultants who will speak about campaigning and political action at your next meeting. Send inquiries to The Campaign Works, 20 West 9th St., Kansas City, Missouri 64105; or call 816/421-0197.

Democrats May Lose Edge
In Contributions from PACs

Democratic congressional candidates traditionally have received the lion's share of the campaign funds doled out by political action committees (PACs). But this year may be different.

A Congressional Quarterly study of the financial reports of 10 large PACs shows that committees representing businesses have stepped up their giving to Republican candidates. The PACs studied were chosen as representative of the different segments of the PAC community — business, labor and ideological. *(PAC list and contributions, chart, p. 3406)*

In addition, the overall number of business PACs is increasing rapidly while the number of labor units has remained nearly static.

Those changes are causing concern among Democrats, who in the past benefited the most from PAC money because they held the majority in Congress. In the 1978 election, for example, they received $19.7 million from all PACs, compared to $15.3 million for Republicans.

In the Nov. 4 elections, however, the Republicans captured control of the Senate and picked up 33 seats in the House, which could reduce the Democrats' share of PAC contributions. *(Senate results, Weekly Report p. 3300; House results, p. 3317)*

Democratic candidates have held the lead because they had a virtual corner on money given by labor union PACs and also used to be able to count on getting about a third of the campaign contributions made by business groups. *(1978 Weekly Report p. 3260)*

But the trend toward business giving more — and to Republicans — is likely to continue as business grows more aware of its ability to affect the political process through contributions and the number of business PACs increases. Four years ago, there were 303 labor PACs and 450 corporate units.

—By Larry Light with research by Phil Duncan and Tom Watson

This year, unions have 318 PACs, while the number of corporate committees has mushroomed to 1,226.

Labor is unlikely to step up its contributions. "We have just a finite number of unions and we've reached our level," said Ben Albert, a spokesman for the AFL-CIO Committee on Political Education (COPE).

Business, on the other hand, has "developed a great deal of political sophistication, which it lacked in the past," said H. Richard Mayberry, a Washington-based campaign finance attorney who advises businesses on how to operate PACs. "Business PACs are forming in record numbers, and

that's bound to have an effect on the political process.... This year will show that business PACs finally have come of age."

The expansion of business PACs was sparked by the landmark 1974 campaign law revisions (PL 93-443), which placed a $1,000 per-election ceiling on individual campaign contributions in an effort to curb the influence of so-called "fat cats." *(1974 campaign act amendments, Congress and the Nation Vol. IV, p. 991)*

The law also prohibits unions or businesses from using their own funds for political giving. As a result, they have set up PACs funded by voluntary donations solicited from members or

employees. Other PACs have been set up by independent groups of citizens interested in a cause, such as defeating lawmakers who favor abortion. PACs are permitted to give $5,000 to a candidate per election. A primary and a general contest each counts as a separate election.

Spending Estimates

A Federal Election Commission (FEC) summary of campaign finance activity through Labor Day showed that 1,687 PACs had contributed $32.4 million to House and Senate candidates. That nearly equals the $35.1 million that 1,459 PACs gave during the entire 1977-78 election cycle.

The House Democratic Study Group (DSG) estimates that PACs will end up giving $60 million during this election cycle, nearly double the 1977-78 amount.

That compares to $22.6 million spent by PACs on the 1976 congres-

"Business PACs are forming in record numbers, and that's bound to have an effect on the political process.... This year will show that business PACs finally have come of age."

—H. Richard Mayberry, campaign finance attorney

sional elections and $12.5 million for 1974 races, according to Common Cause, the self-styled citizens' lobby.

Of contributions made in the 1979-80 election cycle, FEC data show that through Aug. 31 Democrats had gotten $5.2 million and Republicans $6.6 million from all corporate PACs.

And after Labor Day, when most contributions are made, business PACs began pouring even more of their money into Republican coffers, CQ's study of FEC records shows.

For example, the PAC of the International Paper Co. (Voluntary Contributors for Better Government) gave 60.8 percent of its contributions to Republicans before Labor Day, and 75.2

Contributions of Selected Political Action Committees*

(Jan. 1, 1979, to Oct. 15, 1980)

	Contributions to Congressional Candidates	Share Given to Party Candidates		Share Given to Incumbent/Non-Incumbent Candidates			Success Rate	
		Republican	Democrat	Incumbent	Open	Challenger	Won	Lost
AFL-CIO COPE Political Contributions Committee	$ 748,920	3.4%	96.6%	57.1%	19.4%	23.5%	49.2%	50.8%
Amoco Political Action Committee (Standard Oil of Indiana)	146,750	84.1	15.9	45.7	11.1	43.2	75.7	24.3
American Medical Political Action Committee (American Medical Association)	1,219,410	72.2	27.8	60.2	14.9	24.9	79.4	20.6
Automobile and Truck Dealers Election Action Committee (National Automobile Dealers Association)	932,976	58.5	41.5	71.1	11.2	17.7	81.4	18.6
Business-Industry Political Action Committee	129,620	90.2	9.8	24.2	23.1	52.7	65.3	34.7
Gun Owners of America Political Action Committee	122,526	92.8	7.2	9.2	23.7	67.1	54.0	46.0
National Conservative Political Action Committee	128,169	92.3	7.7	19.6	23.7	56.7	39.1	60.9
Realtors Political Action Committee (National Association of Realtors)	1,226,115	66.7	33.3	68.2	13.4	18.4	80.4	19.6
UAW Voluntary Community Action Program (United Auto Workers)	1,359,676	1.4	98.6	67.1	15.4	17.5	62.3	37.7
Voluntary Contributors for Better Government (International Paper Co.)	147,014	64.1	35.9	74.3	11.6	14.1	85.5	14.5

* Figures do not include independent expenditures.

SOURCE: Compiled from Federal Election Commission summaries and committee reports filed with the FEC.

percent to GOP contenders during September and the first half of October.

The National Automobile Dealers Association PAC showed a similar pattern. It allocated 53.8 percent to Republicans before Labor Day, and 69.6 percent to GOP candidates from Sept. 1 to Oct. 15.

The findings parallel those of a 1978 CQ survey of the same 10 PACs. The biggest difference is that the corporate preference for Republicans is even more pronounced now. *(1978 Weekly Report p. 3260)*

That stronger business support of the GOP is illustrated by the Amoco Political Action Committee, which is sponsored by Standard Oil Co. of Indiana. This PAC had given 84.1 percent of its money to Republicans as of Oct. 15. At roughly the same point in 1978, Amoco PAC had donated 76.8 percent to GOP contenders.

Labor PACs, for their part, likely will continue to favor Democrats.

Typically, the United Auto Workers (UAW) gave only 1.4 percent of its funds to Republicans.

In the 1978 election, labor PACs contributed $10.3 million to candidates, outdoing the $9.8 million of corporate groups.

Preliminary figures by the FEC, however, indicate that the situation has been reversed substantially for the 1980 election. FEC data show that all corporate PACs had contributed $11.8 million as of Aug. 31, compared to

$7.7 million given by labor PACs. Labor giving broke down to $7.2 million for Democrats and $540,017 for Republicans.

The final 1979-80 election cycle tally will not be known until early next year, when the FEC finishes tabulating the financial reports of the 2,660 registered PACs. (Usually, about two-thirds of the registered committees actually give money.)

Contributions to Democrats

To be sure, corporate PACs make certain not to neglect powerful Democrats. As the majority party in both houses during the 96th Congress, Democrats — particularly senior ones — benefited from business giving.

As a result, Amoco PAC gave $5,000 to Democrat Russell B. Long of Louisiana and $500 to Republican Robert Dole of Kansas, who will replace Long as Finance Committee chairman in the 1981 GOP-controlled Senate. Both men are friends of oil companies, but observers expect Dole to get much more from Amoco next time he runs — provided that Republicans retain their Senate majority.

A study released Sept. 30 by the Democratic Study Group concluded that "business PACs ... [give] support to Republican challengers running against Democrats whose seats are not secure, while continuing to buy access to those Democrats who have safe seats and who are generally responsive to business concerns. In other words, help the healthy and shoot the sick."

Contributions' Effect

Although not the only factor in this year's Republican successes at the polls, few doubt that the extra business PAC money had an effect.

Business PACs — with their overwhelming support of Republicans — had a better won-lost record in 1980 than labor committees that went overwhelmingly for Democrats.

Of the candidates backed by the five business PACs studied by CQ, more than 65 percent won. The highest business PAC score was that of the International Paper Co.; 85.5 percent of the candidates it supported were successful. Three other business PACs had success rates ranging from 76 to 81 percent. Business-Industry PAC (BIPAC), which saw 65.3 percent of its candidates win, had the lowest score.

The two union PACs surveyed —

the AFL-CIO's COPE and the UAW's Voluntary Community Action Program — did not do so well. Just over 62 percent of the candidates supported by the UAW were successful. COPE had a 49.2 percent success rate.

Business PAC officials were heartened by the election results, believing that the new Republican Senate will be much more responsive to business viewpoints. "Democrats can't afford to be obstructionist now," said Brad Larson, regional manager of corporate affairs for International Paper Co.

Business

Six PACs sponsored by corporations, trade associations and professional groups were examined by CQ, and their partisan preference was clear. Republicans received more than 60 percent of the contributions made by all six.

The largest were the American Medical Association's PAC (AMPAC), which had given more than $1.2 million through Oct. 15, and the Realtors PAC, affiliated with the National Association of Realtors, which also had contributed about $1.2 million.

Following their practice in the 1978 election, these six PACs moved

into the campaign early with large pre-primary contributions of $1,000 to $5,000 to selected Republicans in 1979. Incumbent Democrats, mostly moderates and conservatives, also got a smattering of early-season help from these groups, although the donations to them generally ran below $1,000.

In May 1979, for example, AMPAC gave its biggest contribution that month ($3,000) to Republican Rep. Henry J. Hyde of Illinois and its smallest ($100) to Democratic Rep. Jerome A. Ambro of New York.

In deciding who gets what, one criterion that business PACs use is how closely a candidate represents their views, although sometimes his connections with people in the organization can override this consideration.

"The decisions are made by our local dealers — they make recommendations to us and we usually follow their recommendations," said Bill Hancock, chairman of the Auto Dealers PAC. "Sometimes, that means we give money to those we don't agree with."

Business PACs are apt to forgive a candidate for a particular vote, as long as he remains what they see as "pro-business." For example, al-

---

How Funds are Distributed

Here are two examples of how political action committees (PACs) give their money. Congressional Quarterly compiled a list of contributions from 10 large PACs in the Illinois and Iowa Senate races.

The Illinois contest involved an open seat, being vacated by a Democrat, that stayed in Democratic hands. In the Iowa match, an incumbent liberal Democrat was defeated by a conservative Republican. The giving for the primary and general election campaigns broke down this way:

Illinois Senate

Alan J. Dixon, Democratic candidate: $7,250 — AFL-CIO COPE; $1,300 — American Medical Assocation PAC; $10,000 — Automobile and Truck Dealers PAC.

David C. O'Neal, Republican candidate: $2,000 — Amoco PAC; $1,000 — Business-Industry PAC; $3,000 — Gun Owners of America PAC; $1,500 — International Paper Co. PAC; $5,900 — National Conservative PAC.

Iowa Senate

John C. Culver, Democratic incumbent: $8,500 — AFL-CIO COPE; $350 — Realtors PAC; $9,200 — United Auto Workers PAC.

Charles E. Grassley, Republican challenger: $10,000 — American Medical Association PAC; $9,150 — Amoco PAC; $5,300 — Automobile and Truck Dealers PAC; $4,618 — Business-Industry PAC; $2,500 — International Paper Co. PAC; $4,756 — Gun Owners of America PAC; $5,000 — National Conservative PAC; $10,000 — Realtors PAC.

---

though the association lobbied for 1979 aid to the ailing Chrysler Corp., a number of lawmakers who voted against the measure (PL 96-185) received money from the auto dealers' PAC anyway, Hancock said. They included Sens. Jake Garn, R-Utah ($3,600), Paul Laxalt, R-Nev. ($5,000), Robert Morgan, D-N.C. ($2,500), and Bob Packwood, R-Ore. ($3,000). Of those, only Morgan lost re-election. *(Chrysler, 1979 Almanac p. 285)*

"Our candidates do not view government as the answer to our problems," said an AMPAC official. "We don't keep voting records."

The official noted, for example, that AMPAC contributed heavily to GOP candidate Richard H. Huff in Arizona, even though his opponent, Democratic Rep. Morris K. Udall, supported the association's position on hospital cost containment.

Udall, who agreed with AMPAC in his 1979 vote to gut the Carter administration's bill to control the rise in hospital bills, got nothing from the physicians' group, while Huff received the maximum, $10,000 ($5,000 for the primary election, $5,000 for the general election). *(Hospital cost containment, 1979 Almanac p. 512)*

By and large, the same names kept cropping up as recipients of business PAC largess. Republican Cleve Benedict, who won an open House seat in West Virginia, is a case in point. He got $6,000 from AMPAC, $3,000 from the Realtors, $1,000 from the auto dealers, $1,000 from Amoco and $2,093 from BIPAC.

Of the six business groups studied, BIPAC contributed the largest share to GOP candidates.

BIPAC's president, Joseph J. Fanelli, said his organization went so solidly for Republicans because, on a race-by-race basis, there was "a clear philosophical difference" between them and their Democratic opponents.

"We searched long and hard for Democrats," said Fanelli. "We have a bipartisan board of three Republicans and three Democrats who make the decisions. They're all chief executive officers of corporations."

Because it does not lobby for legislation, BIPAC felt freer to follow its conservative sentiments than some PACs connected to companies.

Consider Rep. Al Ullman, D-Ore., whose authority over taxes and tariffs as chairman of the House Ways and Means Committee commanded deference in the business community. Ullman received $6,000 from the auto dealers, $4,000 from International Pa-

per Co., $500 from AMPAC and $500 from Amoco — but nothing from BIPAC.

Through Oct. 15, none of the groups that had contributed to Ullman had provided money to his more conservative adversary, Republican Denny Smith, who defeated Ullman Nov. 4. BIPAC donated $1,000 to Smith. The Realtors gave $5,000 to Smith, but also sent Ullman $250.

BIPAC's relatively aggressive stance is illustrated by the proportion

Reuss Retirement Slated

Two weeks after winning a 14th term with 78 percent of the vote, Wisconsin Democrat Henry S. Reuss told the *Milwaukee Sentinel* he would not run again.

Reuss, who underwent heart surgery earlier this year, said his health was not the reason for quitting. He made his decision known Nov. 18, after contemplating retirement, he said, for several years. Although he did not fear being redistricted out of office, Reuss said the fact that his Milwaukee district would be redrawn next year did play a role in the timing of his announcement.

Reuss, 68, is the first member of Congress to officially declare he will not be a candidate in 1982.

Joint Committee Chairmanship

The week before announcing his retirement, Reuss disclosed that he would give up the chairmanship of the House Committee on Banking, Finance and Urban Affairs, which he has headed for six years. Instead, he will become chairman of the Joint Economic Committee (JEC) when the 97th Congress convenes in January.

Though the House-Senate economics panel has no authority to write legislation, Reuss said he thought the JEC chairmanship would offer him the best opportunity to help solve the nation's economic problems.

"The nation and the Democratic Party need a new economic program — oriented toward industrial redevelopment, jobs, reconstruction of cities and transportation networks and toward long-term stable growth without inflation," Reuss said in a statement.

Henry S. Reuss

The JEC chairmanship, which alternates between the House and Senate, currently is held by Sen. Lloyd Bentsen, D-Texas.

Banking Panel Successor

Reuss' departure from the Banking Committee leaves Fernand J. St Germain, D-R.I., as his likely successor. St Germain, currently chairman of the Banking Subcommittee on Financial Institutions, has a reputation as a maverick.

St Germain played a key role in drafting landmark banking deregulation legislation (HR 4986 — PL 96-221), which cleared early in 1980. Major banking issues also will face the committee in the next Congress. *(Weekly Report p. 964)*

of its contributions that went to challengers, 52.7 percent. The other business PACs devoted the bulk of their funds to incumbents.

Labor

The two organized labor PACs studied — the AFL-CIO's COPE and the UAW's Voluntary Community Action Program — followed past patterns and gave most of their money to moderate and liberal Democrats in the

Northeastern and Midwestern states. Only 14.7 percent of the money the UAW gave in Senate races went to Southern candidates. COPE devoted 9.2 percent of its funds to those races.

Among the Democratic Senate incumbents depending on labor money were Birch Bayh of Indiana ($10,000 from the UAW and $9,000 from COPE), Mike Gravel of Alaska ($10,000 from the UAW and $4,500 from COPE) and Gaylord Nelson of Wisconsin ($10,000 from the UAW and $2,500 from COPE). All three lost, Gravel in the primary and the two others in the general election.

Democratic House incumbents supported by labor included James C. Corman of California ($10,000 from the UAW and $8,500 from COPE), John L. Burton of California ($10,000 from the UAW and $1,500 from COPE) and Thomas S. Foley of Washington ($5,000 from the UAW and $4,800 from COPE). Corman met defeat and the other two won.

"There's not much encouragement for us" in the election returns, said COPE's Albert. "Our principal objective was to hold onto embattled senators and congressmen in marginal situations."

COPE had given $748,920 to congressional candidates by Oct. 15, with 96.6 percent of that going to Democrats. The UAW's preferences were similarly lopsided; Democrats got 98.6 percent of its contributions.

The few GOP beneficiaries had pro-labor records. The Republican senators getting the most from the two union PACs were Jacob K. Javits of New York ($5,000 from the UAW and $5,000 from COPE) and Charles McC. Mathias Jr. of Maryland ($10,000 from the UAW and $6,000 from COPE). Mathias was re-elected but Javits lost his primary to a conservative, Alfonse M. D'Amato, who went on to capture the seat.

The current Congress, unlike its predecessor, had no big labor votes, so unions this year did not concentrate on opposing Democrats who disappointed them on key issues.

Two years ago, union PACs said they would punish such faithless friends, but eventually went against only a few. One was Rep. Lamar Gudger, D-N.C., whose primary opponent got COPE funds after Gudger voted against the 1977 common-site picketing bill and the 1978 labor law reform measure. This time, the group simply ignored Gudger, who lost to a Republican, William M. Hendon.

Conservatives

This was a banner year for conservative groups. They quickly took credit for knocking off many of the defeated Democrats. *(Weekly Report p. 3372)*

CQ examined the direct giving records of the National Conservative Political Action Committee (NCPAC) and the Gun Owners of America Campaign Committee, which gave an overwhelming portion of their money to Republicans.

The biggest part of NCPAC's spending, however, was concentrated on independent expenditures — those made without consulting the candidates they favor. Independent spending is not subject to the legal ceilings on direct contributions. Independent committees may spend an unlimited amount to support a candidate as long as they have no contact with the contender. *(Background, Weekly Report p. 1635)*

NCPAC disbursed $1.2 million in independent expenditures to dislodge six Democratic senators, winning in four of those races, and nearly that much to elect Ronald Reagan president. The Gun Owners independently spent almost $25,000 overall against the Democratic senators in three states — Indiana, Iowa and Idaho — and was victorious in all.

In direct contributions, the two ideological groups emphasized getting rid of Democratic House incumbents they believed were too liberal. Challengers got 56.7 percent of NCPAC's donations and 67.1 percent of the Gun Owners'.

But in campaign finance, an attack strategy also entails a high risk of failure. Consequently, NCPAC had a success rate of 39.1 percent, and the

Gun Owners backed victors in 54 percent of the races to which they contributed.

The business PACs studied had much better performances because they supported more incumbents — and the odds favor the re-election of incumbents.

Among the losses the two ideological groups had were Republican House challengers Tom Pauken in Texas ($500 from the Gun Owners and $1,389 from NCPAC), David G. Crane in Indiana ($2,477 from the Gun Owners and $2,000 from NCPAC) and Huff in Arizona ($500 from the Gun Owners and $2,355 from NCPAC).

Pauken ran against Jim Mattox, Crane against David W. Evans and Huff against Udall.

Major successful challengers the conservatives directly backed were Rep. Charles E. Grassley of Iowa for the Senate ($4,756 from the Gun Owners and $5,000 from NCPAC), and for the House, Bobbi Fiedler of California ($10,000 from the Gun Owners) and Smith of Oregon ($2,000 from the Gun Owners and $1,139 from NCPAC). Grassley opposed John C. Culver, Fiedler defeated Corman and Smith ousted Ullman.

Conservative groups tended to direct their money outside the Northeast, where liberal candidates tend to do better. The Gun Owners sent just 11.3 percent of its direct donations to Northeastern candidates. NCPAC gave 20.8 percent of its direct contributions to Northeasterners.

"We went after open seats and vulnerable incumbents, which is a continuation of what we started in 1978," said Bill Saracino, executive director of the firearms group. "Of course, we're pleased with what happened." ∎

New Reapportionment Projection

The 1980 census will give Sun Belt states more new House seats than previously forecast, Census Director Vincent P. Barabba said Nov. 18.

Census estimates had indicated 14 congressional seats would shift from Frost Belt to Sun Belt states after reapportionment based on the census figures. The new projection, however, is that the states of the South and West are certain to gain even more than that.

The count has turned up roughly 4 million more people than

census experts estimated, Barabba said, and most of those 4 million reside in the Sun Belt. He said the unexpected increase may be partly the result of an increase in the count of illegal aliens who were overlooked by the bureau's early demographic estimates.

Speaking to the Senate Governmental Affairs Federal Services Subcommittee, Barabba said the census results would be tabulated in time for delivery to the president on Dec. 31. *(Background, Weekly Report p. 2747)*